Earth's Farthest Bounds

Earth's Farthest Bounds

by BARRY BLACKSTONE

RESOURCE *Publications* • Eugene, Oregon

EARTH'S FARTHEST BOUNDS

Copyright © 2019 Barry Blackstone. All rights reserved. Except for brief quotations in critical publications or reviews, no part of this book may be reproduced in any manner without prior written permission from the publisher. Write: Permissions, Wipf and Stock Publishers, 199 W. 8th Ave., Suite 3, Eugene, OR 97401.

Resource Publications
An Imprint of Wipf and Stock Publishers
199 W. 8th Ave., Suite 3
Eugene, OR 97401

www.wipfandstock.com

PAPERBACK ISBN: 978-1-5326-9880-4
HARDCOVER ISBN: 978-1-5326-9881-1
EBOOK ISBN: 978-1-5326-9882-8

Manufactured in the U.S.A.   OCTOBER 14, 2019

I dedicate this book to the future missionaries, pastors, evangelists, and lay workers of the Indian churches of Kerala, Orissa, Assam, Manipur, Chhattisgarh, and Haryana: the 2016 graduating class of Kerala Baptist Bible College.

Other Books by Barry Blackstone

Though None Go With Me

Rendezvous in Paris

Though One Go With Me

Scotland Journey

The Region Beyond

Enlarge My Coast

From Dan to Beersheba and Beyond

The Uttermost Part

Homestead Homilies

Rover: A Boy's Best Friend

North to Alaska and Back

Another Day in Nazareth

Sermonettes from the Seashore

Contents

Acknowledgment | ix

Prelude—Earth's Farthest Bounds | 1

1. Times of Refreshing | 5
2. Sunrise and Sunset in Doha | 9
3. First Meeting, Prayer Meeting | 13
4. Saturday Sermons and Supplications | 17
5. A Senior Citizen in India Remembering | 21
6. The Tale Continues—The Book that Changed Everything | 25
7. A Return to Venmony | 29
8. Werther's Original Birthday | 33
9. Bacon Sandwiches and Bible Conference | 36
10. The Tale Continues—The Foolishness of Preaching | 40
11. The Kids of the KBBC | 44
12. The Tale Continues—He Leadeth Me Beside the Still Waters. | 48
13. The Cool of the Day | 52
14. When Faith Confronts Abortion | 57
15. Four 50-Year-Old Male Elephants | 61
16. An Elephant Blesses a Home | 65
17. The Tale Continues—Open Doors | 69
18. A Night at the Simons | 73
19. Graduation Address | 77
20. The Rains Came to End Graduation | 81
21. Vision Bible College's First Graduation | 84
22. Off to Tamil Nadu—A Woman on the Way | 88

23 Baptism in a Water Trough | 92
24 What a Blessen | 96
25 In the Shadow of Hinduism | 100
26 Tamil Nadu Extension Program | 104
27 The Story Continues—I Had Fainted Unless | 108
28 North to the Punjab | 112
29 Still, Soft, Slow Songs | 116
30 The Tale Continues—A Good Wife | 120
31 India/Pakistan Border | 124
32 The Tale Continues—In Journeyings Often | 128
33 Punjab Praise | 132
34 Cycle Rickshaw and Auto Rides in Amritsar | 136
35 The Golden Temple of the Sikhs | 140
36 The Trees of the Golden Temple | 143
37 Barry Singh | 147
38 Manohar Singh | 150
39 Magnum Bars in the Punjab | 153
40 Kentucky Fried Chicken Indian Style | 156
41 A Desire without a Date Is Only a Dream | 159
42 Farewell to the Punjab | 163
43 The Tale Continues—A Church of a Lifetime | 166
44 Overnight Train to Agra | 170
45 Taj Mahal—Closed? | 173
46 God's Plan B at the Taj | 177
47 Agra Fort | 180
48 The Tale Continues—Forget Not All His Benefits | 183
49 Visiting a Childhood Friend | 187
50 Snubbing the Sticks—Overnight in Delhi | 191
51 Surprise Side-Trip to Orissa | 195
52 Pushing a New Suzuki | 199
53 India/Pakistan Cricket Match | 203
54 Sion Shramika Baptist Church | 207
55 Guru Caves of Udayagiri | 211
56 The Tale Continues—Lord, I Believe… | 215
57 Eight States in Ten Days | 219
58 Last Day in Kerala | 223

Postlude—The Long, Long Road Home | 227

Acknowledgment

I would not have gotten this book project finished if not for the editing and compiling by my dear sister Sylvia. I would like to thank her for the hours and days she spent reading, rereading and correcting the errors and mistakes in the original script. Thanks again, Sis!

Prelude
Earth's Farthest Bounds

"For these are our instructions from the Lord: "I have appointed you to be a light for the Gentiles, and a means of salvation to *Earth's farthest bounds*."

—ACTS 13:47 *THE NEW ENGLISH BIBLE*, EMPHASIS ADDED

I am before my old Spartan laptop computer, as with the Psalmist, "a ready writer" (Psalm 45:1), to record another wonderful, spiritual adventure I have just experienced. I am writing a short, two-week postscript about another trip to the subcontinent of India. This was my fifth trip to that fabled land in ten years, and in some respects, the Good Lord, my travel guide and companion, left the best for last. It is my heart's desire and my upmost wish that this wasn't my final excursion into India, but if it was, it is well worth recording.

The verse that highlights this prelude was discovered long before I made this spiritual journey to Kerala, six other Indian states, and the district of Delhi. In keeping with my nearly fifty-year desire to take the Gospel to *The Uttermost Parts,* the title of my last India book published by Wipf and Stock Publishers, I determined after reading the New English Bible version of Paul's statement that if I ever got back to India I had found the title of my next mission book. Now I begin adding chapters under this title, and as you will see, it is certainly a fitting title and theme for this short-term mission's trip to India.

The purpose for this trip began during my last trip in 2012 when I spent three weeks teaching at Kerala Baptist Bible College (KBBC) in the little village of Edayappara, India. Among my students that year were eight future graduates of the 2016 graduation class of KBBC. I was asked by the president of the college to be the graduation speaker. This was my third invitation to be commencement speaker at KBBC since my first address in 2007. I returned in 2010 as well, but, to my surprise, I would eventually be graduation speaker for three Indian graduations on consecutive days in the second week of March 2016.

However, it was what happened after those graduations that underlines and highlights the title of this memoir. In 2010, after graduation exercises at Kerala Baptist Bible College, my host Shibu Simon, his brother Shaju, and another friend Joy Thomas took me on a weeklong mission trip to the Indian state of Andrah Pardesh. This adventure was related in a book I called *Enlarge My Coast* also published by Wipf and Stock Publishers. This 2010 mission trip into the desert interior of central India reminded me of my first short-term mission's trip in 1972 to the Gibson Desert Aborigines of Western Australia. This journey I recorded in a book I called *The Region Beyond* also published by Wipf and Stock Publisher. Our journey deep into the hinterland of India reignited my passion for unreached people groups in the uttermost places on this planet. When I returned in 2012 to teach at the college, after my lessons were done, Shibu Simon and Joy Thomas, the man who directs the Orissa Outreach Mission for the Associated Missions of India, a ministry of the Independent Gospel Baptist Churches of India, took me on my second India mission's trip. But this time, we went to the tribal people of central Orissa State on the northeastern coast of India. I traveled by plane and train and car into the remote village of Dangul to meet face to face, on their own turf, a persecuted Christian group that only four years before had been driven out, burnt out, cast out of their villages by hostile Hindus. Before I left for India on this trip, Shibu told me that I would be taking another Indian mission's trip, but this time we would be traveling to the northwest corner of India and to the State of Punjab. My mission spirit surged with excitement, but in my wildest imagination, I couldn't have dreamt of what awaited me in "earth's farthest bounds" in northwest India and beyond.

There is something different about a spiritual path when that path leads you to a distant, unfamiliar corner of God's earth. Not an open highway, but a road that is noisy and crowded and congested to the point you wonder if you will ever pass through. Granted, the roadways are paved, but they might just as well have been a dirt path or a pasture lane for the speed that you could travel. For those that are wondering of what I speak, I am talking about 150 miles that takes seven hours and sometimes more. These paths invite you onward and sometimes upward to faraway places that you never thought you would visit let alone minister in. These unheard of places have strange sounding names like Kanythar and Chandigarh, Mohali and Khasa, and Amritsar and Shramika. But now I can trace my path on a map to these places and many more, a path that was filled with wonderful sights and sites, marvelous people and places. Have you ever noticed that God's ways in the Bible are often called paths? When writing of finding wisdom, Solomon says, "Her ways are ways of pleasantness, and all her paths are peace." (Proverbs 3:17) I can honestly say that in my total of 137 days in India in my five trips every road I have traveled has been a peaceful path. Granted, I traveled through some dangerous places, but I have only found peaceful paths in India. Solomon also wrote, "But the path of the just is as a shining light, that shineth more and more unto the perfect day." (Proverbs 4:18) I believe the perfect day that is coming is "the day of the Lord", and the paths leading to that day have taken me through numerous byways and highways in India with shining paths. I have yet to have a dark day in India!

India has also been a reminder of two of my life's verses, instilled in me at a very young age by my mother: "Trust in the Lord with all thine heart; and lean not unto thine own understanding. In all thy ways acknowledge him, and he shall direct thy paths." (Proverbs 3:5-6) I believe that every step, every way, every road, and every place I have gone in India, this trip or the other four, have been God-ordained steps. "The steps of a good man are ordered by the Lord . . ." (Psalm 37:23) It is sheer joy when you are walking in God's paths. David writes, "Make me to go in the path of Thy commandments; for therein do I delight." (Psalm 119:35) My India trails have been just that, pure delight. There were those that feared for me on this trip because of the current state of terrorism in the world, and, as you will see, I did go to some dangerous areas, but I was as safe as if I was in my bed in Maine because I was following a God-ordained commandment to go. That very command is printed at the beginning of this opening chapter. "Teach me thy ways, O Lord, and lead me in a plain path, because of mine enemies." (Psalm 27:11) Shibu loves to keep me in the dark about our travels because he loves surprises, and I would experience numerous surprises on this trip. Despite the uncertainty of exactly where I was going, I was confident that it was my Saviour that was directing my comings and goings, not Shibu.

At the end of this amazing trail, I would rediscover the meaning of David's verse in Psalm 16:11. "Thou wilt shew me the path of life: in Thy presence is fulness of joy; at Thy right hand there are pleasures for evermore."

Oh what joys and pleasures I enjoyed on this trip because I was always in the presence of my Lord! You can't go wrong when you allow Jesus to be your travel agent. So come along with me, and I will share with you the spectacular sites I experienced and the marvelous memories that will last forever more—the marvelous memories that can be experienced in "earth's farthest bounds".

1

Times of Refreshing

One of my favorite spiritual choruses goes like this. "Times of refreshing, here in Thy presence, not greater blessing than being with You. My soul is restored, my mind is renewed, there is not greater joy Lord than being with You." (Harris and Nystrom) One of the first joys of going to "earth's farthest bounds" is the time spent getting there. Don't get me wrong. I am not a fan of delays in airports—waiting for the next flight, waiting that can take hours. I am no fan of long flights that last half a day or more. I am no fan of airport food, airport noise, or airport seats. If you have traveled at any length, you know the boredom, the weariness, the jetlag, and the frustration that often accompanies foreign travel. On this trip, I passed the 100,000 mile-mark just in my five trips to India. Yet over the years, I have come to enjoy these interludes before you get to your destination because of one simple truth—I never travel alone. I have learned to treasure the "Jesus and me" moments of these trips. I would hit India on a dead run, and my twenty days in country would be filled with many events and appointments and even more travel. On this trip, Shibu and I would travel nearly four thousand miles in country in just ten days, but for the nearly two days it took to me to get from Ellsworth, Maine to Edayappara, India and the two days that it took me to get from Edayappara to Ellsworth, there were plenty of "Jesus and me" moments: wonderful times of refreshing in His presence, now seasons of refreshing just recalling those times.

I introduce this India adventure by sharing the wonderful truth of the peacefulness and pleasantness that comes when you allow the Almighty to "direct thy path". I ended those thoughts with the concept from Psalm 16:11—"in Thy presence is fulness of joy." When I left my Maine coast town of Ellsworth on March 2, 2016, my trip had started. Most wait to get to their destination before they see the beginning of their trip, but I have learned from the beginning moment the Lord is there every step of the way. Sometimes the journey to get somewhere can be as joyful as actually getting there. So, after my dear wife Coleen, who had many troubles with this trip because of the current state of affairs, (the infamous bombing in Brussels would take place during my trip to India) dropped me off at the Bangor Airport, I was on my own, just "Jesus and me", but the fellowship that finally got me through the nine thousand miles to my India home was wonderful.

I have never had any fear of traveling because of the wonderful promises my Saviour gave to His fellow disciples and me just before He left for Heaven. Promises like the following: ". . . Lo, I am with you always, even unto the end of the world (earth's farthest bounds!)" (Matthew 28:20) Then, what about, "I will never leave thee nor forsake thee." (Hebrews 13:5) I have never once thought that God doesn't get on the plane with me. As I took an American flight from Bangor to Philadelphia, I knew the Lord was with me. As I waited for that flight and as I waited for my Qatar flight in Philadelphia, I felt the Lord with me. We talked, I read His Word and He talked to me and I prayed and I talked to Him, just as if He sat in the airplane seat beside me, just as He sat in the airport seat before me. I can't even imagine traveling without the knowledge that He is near, both a companion and a guide, and yes, in this world, a bodyguard! People speak of the hardships of travel, the difficulties of travel, the delays of travel, and the change of schedules in travel, the mechanical troubles, and, I will be honest, I have at times been frustrated, but once I think of Who is really in charge and in control of it all, I relax and enjoy the ride. On my last trip to India I was delayed in my return to the States by Hurricane Sandy. I saw it as the Lord giving me two more days with people I love to be with.

So as I got off American Airlines Flight #4637 at Gate C31 and walked to Gate A16 for my Qatar Flight #728 to Doha, I walked with the Lord. As I waited four and a half hours for that flight, I waited with the Lord. We must come to the realization that if we are in Christ than He is always with us no matter here or there. It would take us eleven and a half hours to fly to Doha, Qatar, and every mile of our flight path the Lord was directing the flight. One of the things I have enjoyed doing while traveling is keeping track of where I am in the world. I haven't traveled in many of the lands I have flown over, but I like to think I have visited them even at 38,000 feet. Interestingly, our flight path to Doha took us back over the very states I flew over to get to Philadelphia: Hartford, Connecticut, Boston, Massachusetts, up the coast of Maine and just south of my city of Ellsworth, then over Nova Scotia and Newfoundland before heading out over the North Atlantic. Sometimes we fail to see our God as a global God. The Psalmist talks about "whatsoever passeth through the paths of the sea." (Psalm 8:8), but now we know of the paths of the sky. The Psalmist's conclusion: "O Lord our Lord, how excellent is Thy name in all the earth." (Psalm 8:9) So whether over the Atlantic or the country of Spain, our first land mass, or back over the water as we flew across the Mediterranean Sea just south of the boot of Italy before crossing into Egyptian airspace, the Lord is to be praise because His name is still praised by some in all these places. I know for sure there was at least one passenger on Qatar Flight #728 that was praising the name of the Lord all the way!

Eventually we crossed the Red Sea just south of the Gulf of Aqaba. Every time I get near to Eilat, I remember the marvelous trip Marnie and I took to Israel in 2010. Once we hit the coastline of Saudi Arabia, we headed due east across the Arabian Peninsula to the capital of Qatar and the massive, brand new Hamad International Airport. Seeing the huge terminals of this new airport built on the shores of the Persian Gulf was a new experience for me. I had flown Qatar Airlines on one of my earlier trip to India, but had flown into the old Qatar airport. This new state-of-the-art airport was built on land extended out into a bay so you fly in over water until you touch down. It is impressive with the skyline of Doha in the background. This wealthy state knows how to show-off, and their new airport is no exception. A two-floor terminal leads to five wings (A, B, C, D, E), the hub of Qatar's world-class airline; in my opinion, Qatar Airlines is the best I have ever flown with.

Disembarking with me was my Lord and Saviour. I know this Muslim country doesn't have anything to do with Jesus, but little did they know He was passing through with a preacher from Maine. For the next fourteen hours, yes, you read it right, fourteen hours we would walk the terminal floors waiting our flight to India. In all my travels to date, I have never spent so much time waiting. I would keep records of my waiting times and before the trip was over, I would wait forty-eight hours in airports for my next flight. It often reminds me of another departing flight (II Timothy 4:6) I am waiting for. That flight will take me on a direct path to glory and in the presence of the One I have loved for nearly sixty years now (II Corinthians 5:8). But though I am going to Him doesn't mean He isn't waiting with me. I am convinced that is what the Hebrew prophet Jeremiah was writing about when he wrote, "Thus saith the Lord, Stand ye in the ways, and see, and ask for the old paths, where is the good way, and walk therein . . ." (Jeremiah 6:16) The old paths are the paths in which we walk with the Lord. It is the old ways that the pilgrims once trod. It is time that we walk in the belief of the continual presence of the Lord in our lives whether in Philadelphia, USA or Doha, Qatar. Let us not be like those who answered Jeremiah with "We will not walk therein." (Jeremiah 6:16)

2

Sunrise and Sunset in Doha

I flew into Doha, Qatar as the sun was rising in the east, and before I boarded another Qatar flight for Kochi, India the sun would set in the west. As I flew from Philadelphia to Doha, I also lost eight hours, so my body was already experiencing the time change and my day was already backwards. Normally I would be sleeping, but now my mind and bodily functions were all mixed up. It was time to adjust to my sunsets being sunrises and my sunrises being sunsets in a brand-new, state-of-the-art, modern airport.

Over the next fourteen hours, I would walk several miles exploring the new Hamad International Airport. I begin reading a selection of books I brought along for times like this. In my carry-on, I brought two books written by my favorite author Vance Havner: *Pleasant Path* written in 1945 and his autobiography called *That I May Know Him* written in 1948. They would be a joy throughout my travels as I finished both of them before I arrived back in America. I also had a lot of time to meditate and ponder, and one of the things I recalled was a first for me in all the airports I have traveled through since my first flight in 1972. (Before I returned to Maine, I would travel through my 44th airport in Bangalore, Karnataka.) But in that entire time, I had never heard my name over the loud speaker. But while I was waiting in the Philadelphia International Terminal, I heard "Barry Blackstone from Maine, please see the attendant at the Qatar Desk at Gate 16." Because it had never happened before, I wondered what was up. I had left Maine with my father not well, my wife very nervous about the trip, and a 95-year-old church member wanting to go to heaven. I had only left my wife about five hours before, so what could be wrong? As it turned out, they only wanted to issue me a new boarding pass because I had gotten my first boarding pass from the American Airlines clerk in Bangor. It is strange the things we recall and think about when we're waiting between sunrise and sunset in a strange airport abroad.

I had plenty of time for lunch in Doha, so I stopped at the Burger King in the food court for what I believed would be my last meal of the trip. As I had been telling anyone that would listen, I don't go to India for the cuisine. I despise spicy foods, and India has some of the hottest foods I have ever eaten. I am an All-American boy when it comes to food: hamburgers, hot dogs, French fries, pizza, steak and potatoes with just a little salt, a little pepper, and some butter and that is it. Most call it bland, but it is just right for me. So a Burger King Burger was just what the doctor ordered for this country boy staying a day in Doha. It wasn't the best burger I'd eaten, the fries were a bit cold, and the Coke a bit watery, but a taste of home was worth the ten dollars I had to spend.

After lunch, I found a quiet place to read my Bible. For this trip I had brought along my Grandmother Blackstone's old Scofield King James Bible I had gotten when I inherited her home in 2009. I had been waiting an occasion to reread it, and what better time than on a trip to India. I have been rereading the Bible since I first finished reading the Bible in the early 1960s. One of the first books I read after I learned to read was the Bible. I was taught by my parents to systematically read the Bible through. It mattered not how much you read a day, but that you read every day and you will finish the greatest literary work of all time in a short time. Since I finished my first reading in 1962, I have been keeping track of how many Bibles and New Testaments I have read. Currently I am reading seven Bibles. I have a New Testament in my back pocket that I read when I have to wait somewhere; I have a Bible by my chair that I sometimes read in the evenings when the television programs are boring; I have a Bible in the bathroom (where Grammy Glenna's Bible stays when not on a trip to India) that I read in the morning and at other times when I have to stop by that room in the house; I have two Bibles by my bed that I read every night (two different version for comparison), and I have two Bibles in my office that I am reading: one is my study Bible that I prepare sermons from and the other is my newest translation, the English Standard Version. I am trying to read as many of the versions that I can—my 22nd to date! I believe that we are not to just read the Bible once and set it on a shelf like we do other books. The Bible it not any ordinary book; it is God's Word to us, and we will never fully hear His Words unless we reread it again and again. The New Testament that went to India with me and back was my 66th reading of the New Testament. I finished it during this trip. I have finished reading the entire Bible over 30 times and, as you have noted, I am in the various stages of reading it six more times. Downtime, delay time, Doha time is a great time to pick up an old Bible and read it again.

As I wandered and walked and watched the sunset on my second day on trip number five to India, I was reminded of this verse from the Psalmist: "The mighty God, even the Lord, hath spoken, and called the earth from the rising of the sun unto the going down thereof." (Psalm 50:1) No matter where we are in the world, no matter the location on the earth, the Lord God speaks. That has been one of the great joys of travel for me. No matter where I am, the Lord speaks to me. One of the other things I did during my first fourteen hours in Doha, and repeat on my return trip, was to put a couple of messages together: "Because of Unbelief" based in Romans 11:20 and "A Sudden Departure" based on Psalm 78:36-37. Before the trip was over, I would put together twenty-six new messages. Some I would share in India, and the others I would share with the flock of the Emmanuel Baptist Church when I returned; whether a day in Maine or a day in Doha, the Lord is speaking at all times. The question is "Are we listening?" Despite the busy, noisy airport, I heard my Lord from the rising of the sun unto the going down of the same. Oh, that we would recognize that daytime is a great time to listen for the Lord's messages. Of course, you can hear Him in the nighttime in airports as well!

The Psalmist also wrote, "From the rising of the sun unto the going down of the same the Lord's name is to be praised." (Psalm 113:3) I really began to praise the Lord when after a long hike down Terminal B I discovered the Men's Quiet Room. One of the greatest features of the new airport was resting rooms. In these rooms were long chairs that you could literally lay out on, a first in any airport for me. My only regret was that I discovered the room in my 12th hour in Doha. But I was able to get a bit of a nap before boarding my next flight—"the Lord's name be praised!" To me one of the greatest blessings of the Lord to is rest and sleep. I also like the Psalmist's proclamation, ". . . for so He giveth His beloved sleep." (Psalm 127:2) When you're traveling great distances, proper rest is essential for you to arrive at your destination fit to enjoy your trip. I have always been someone that demands a good rest at night so I can function the next day. These quiet rooms were blessings the Lord had for me periodically on my journey. I never thought I would find my first in Doha. I knew that at the Simon House I had such a place waiting, and when I arrived the next day I took advantage of it and crashed for five hours before I was off to my first meeting, but to find a place in Doha was for me a God-given gift. I have always had trouble sleeping on planes, so to find this quiet room in the vast expanse of Hamad I was blessed. It was another sunrise to sunset praise of God.

3

First Meeting, Prayer Meeting

My in-country adventure began at 2:30 AM early on the morning of March 4, 2016 when I landed at the Kochi International Airport in Kerala. My first little fright took place when the baggage carousel stopped, and my check-in bag was nowhere in sight! Because of various times I have traveled into India, I remembered after my mini-panic attack that sometimes because of the huge volume of bags and packages there are attendants in the airport that take bags off the carousel and place them in a corner of the baggage claim terminal so that more luggage can to put on the carousel. Sure enough, as I scanned the luggage in that area of the room, I saw my green bag. God not only sees that His passenger arrives safe and sound He even takes care of his bag. What a God we serve! After retrieving my bag, immigration and customs was as simple as previous times with less than an hour to get through all three. After that, I exited the main terminal into the hot, humid air of tropical Kerala, quite a difference between the temperatures of Maine in the teens with spitting snow, just two days before. Because non-passengers can't enter India airports, I knew my India friends would be somewhere outside the terminal. Always before I had spotted Shibu or Shaju as I exited, but this time the crowd was huge, and I saw no friendly face! It was then I had my second little fright as I scanned the crowd for a familiar smile.

The increased expansion of the Kochi Airport, a brand new, first of its kind international terminal that will be powered entirely by solar energy, has resulted in more passengers, which results in more people waiting for disembarking passengers or embarking passengers. I waded through the throng beyond the walkway and the driveway that runs parallel to the main terminal and still no Shibu. I was nearly to the parking area before Shibu's shining face emerged from the dim lights of the Kerala night. My second mini-panic attack was over, and I knew for the rest of my days in India I wouldn't be outside the sight of this dear friend. It was then I realized that Shibu wasn't alone. To my surprise, Binu, the young man who had been my driver during my first two trips to India but who was now an engineer working in Kuwait was there. He and his new wife Raymol were home on vacation, so he decided to surprise an old friend and pick him up in Kochi at 3:00 in the morning! His face appeared in the line of brown faces waiting for their passenger to arrive. Then a third familiar face appeared as a black car drove up. A young man I had gotten to know on previous trips, just a teenager then, was now one of Shibu's primary drivers; his nephew Sin-gin! We put my luggage into the back of Shibu's car, and we were off on a slow, winding three-hour drive to the Simon's home in Edayappara.

Shibu and I talked most of the way home that is until two hours into the journey Sin-gin got tired and Shibu had to take over. The familiar road hadn't changed much since my last trip nearly three and a half years before. Despite the early morning, the traffic was constant and crazy, and for just a few seconds my third fright of the morning happened as a bus barely missed us on a sharp corner. However, my third mini-panic attack passed quickly as I remembered that this was not abnormal on an Indian roadway. In the thousands of miles I have now travelled in a car on Indian highways, I have witnessed numerous close calls, but no accidents yet. This trip would not be an exception to this India rule. I am as safe in the hands of God on a plane, in a car, Maine or Kerala, and as before, we arrived safely in Shibu's yard just before seven in the morning. Julie, Shibu's wife, was waiting for us wanting to fix me breakfast, but I graciously refused her offer preferring to go to bed. I was quickly upstairs and off to sleep. It was well after noon when I awoke in what felt like an oven!

Besides the heat, another typical India reality came to light, no power. I had seen this in India before, but on this trip I experienced it every day I was in Kerala. It seems the typical January through March wasn't very typical this year. Normally, the weather is a bit cooler with a bit more rain than other times of the year, but this year the weather had stayed hot and humid with little rain, so the State was in a drought and facing an extended heat-wave taxing the electrical grid. I found it hotter and more humid that I had remembered. The good news was that the Simon's had a battery backup in their home, so we could at least use the ceiling fans. But after a few days, I wondered if that wasn't making me hotter. I soon discovered the only period of the day it wasn't unbearable was between 2AM and 7AM. The sun sets in the sky just after six in the evening, but it takes nearly eight hours of darkness to cool things down. Sleep is difficult, but I was so exhausted after my Maine to India travels that I didn't notice it much until I awoke, a bit refreshed and ready to start my fifth India mission. It was over toast and bananas that I learned my first service in India in 2016 would be a Friday night prayer meeting at the James house.

The Kangazha Baptist Church had moved their Sunday Morning Prayer Meeting to Friday Night because they found the time less hurried. On this particular Friday, it was the James' family's turn to host the service. Located only about a mile from the Simon house, we parked the car beside the lane and walked about one hundred yards along a rocky path until we came to a typical Kerala home of brick walls and a tin roof. Before the meeting was through, nearly fifty people gathered with most having to sit out in the courtyard. I preached my first message on "The Work of Christ"—His work, my work, and our work based on Colossians 1:28-29. Afterward they had a simple luncheon, typical of most India meetings. How they like to fellowship and feast! I ran into some old friends like the Jacob John family, the local Auto-Taxi driver. We would meet again and he would take me on one of my best adventures in Kerala in just a few days. As I watched the people visit after the prayer meeting, and despite the fact I couldn't understand a word they were saying, I was impressed with the importance these people still have for the prayer meeting!

The prayer meeting, Wednesday, Sunday, or Friday, is nearly dead in Maine. We are one of a few churches in Ellsworth that still have a weekly prayer meeting. The Emmanuel Baptist Church Prayer Meeting still exists because of a core of ten individuals that are determined that it will not die. I have tried for years to promote the prayer meeting as a ministry, not a service. Even if, unlike India, we only share prayer requests and pray. There is no singing, no preaching, just praying. I am reminded of the cottage prayer meeting described in Acts 12 when Peter was in jail. It says, ". . . prayer was made without ceasing of the church unto God for him." (Acts 12:5) This prayer meeting was also in a house, not the James house, but Mary's house (Acts 12:12). No matter the week, no matter the State (Maine or Kerala), there is someone that needs our prayers, and we as the church of God ought to be praying. It was refreshing to start my 2016 India ministry in a prayer meeting, in a believer's house, surrounded by scores of neighbors and friends supplicating and interceding for the Peter of their world (Philippians 4:6). There is nobody beyond the realm of prayer (I Timothy 2:12). We could use our Friday nights for nothing better than to take an hour to prayer. "Sweet hour of prayer, sweet hour of prayer, that calls me from a world of care, and bids me at my Father's throne make all my wants and wishes know; in seasons of distress and grief my soul has often found relief..."

4

Saturday Sermons and Supplications

On every trip to India, I have arrived either on a Thursday or Friday so that I could be in Kerala before the weekend. This is my primary time of ministering in the churches of the IGBC. My first weekends in Kerala have always been like a bright morning after a dark night. The jetlag that sets in when you travel nearly halfway around the world makes your days become nights and your nights become days. My fifth arrival in my adopted country was no exception. Friday night was a gathering of the Kangazha Church to pray. Saturday would be another day of prayer, but this time it would be the kids of Kerala that would lead the sweet hour of prayer. The old hymn comes to mind. "Sweet hour of prayer, sweet hour of prayer, Thy wings shall my petition bear. To Him whose truth and faithfulness engage the waiting soul to bless; and since He bids me seek His face, believe His Word and trust His grace. I'll cast on Him my every care, and wait for thee, sweet hour of prayer." I would have two such hours on my first two days in Edayappara. What a start to any short-term mission trip abroad!

I was awake by 5:00 AM but rested in bed until 7:00 AM to get full advantage of the cooler air lightly blowing into my room. I knew shortly after the sun came up the hot, hazy, humid air would quickly enter my room through the double windows in the corner of the Simon's prophet's chamber. During Saturday breakfast, Shibu told me that I would have a quiet day before starting on a daily schedule that would be full until I got back on a plane for Maine. The only appointment of the day was an invitation to an hour prayer meeting at the Kangazha Church with the youth of the church.

It seems that March 5, 2016 was a day of prayer for the young people of the association. From 8:00 AM to 6:00 PM, the various youth groups of the Kerala churches would take an hour to pray for the needs of their individual churches and the collective needs of the Kerala churches. Our time was between 4:00 and 5:00 that afternoon. It was an invitation I immediately accepted!

After breakfast I returned to my room and tried to find some relief from the oppressive heat and the overwhelming humidity that had descended on my second full day in India. To take my mind off the heat, I put together four sermons over the next few hours: 1—"Superficial Dedication" based on Psalm 78:36-37, a message on one of the problems of modern Christianity, the lack of dedication on behalf of the average Christian. I used five of Jesus' parables in which He deals with this dilemma in the Church. 2—"Earthquakes: God's Favorite Environmental Tool" based on Isaiah 29:6, a message on the Biblical references to God's use of an earthquake to highlight and underline a specific message. I used five Scriptural tremors to illustrate God's determination to warn man in an environmental way. 3—"God's Pinch of Salt" based on Matthew 5:13, a sermon on the qualities of salt that ought to be found in the Christian. I used seven characteristics of salt to emphasize the reason Jesus called us to be 'the salt of the earth'. 4—"Spiritual Smog" based on Ephesians 4:14, a message on the moral, political, and the spiritual smog that is blinding the eyes of many people today. Smog is always a man-made problem and never a God-made problem. By the time I finished these sermons, it was time for a nap!

By mid-afternoon I was up, a bit revived, and ready for an hour of prayer with the children of Kangazha. Shibu and his family, including his two children Joshua (Jos) and Abigail (Abby) and wife Julie took me by car to the church. A car ride, even a short car ride, was a pleasant event on this trip because it was the only time the attributes of an air-conditioner could be enjoyed. I have yet to be in an Indian home with an air-conditioner, but nearly every Indian car has one. So car travel is one of the few ways to beat the Indian heat! We arrived in the courtyard of the church almost too soon, but I also couldn't wait to see some of the young people I had gotten to know over the years. In 2012, I left kids and found them young adults in 2016. That is what kids will do to you!

Besides Joshua and Abigail, there was Jeffin and Jason, and, of course, the orphanage kids. I was sad to see them because I knew this would probably be the last I would ever see them. Since I had been to India, the situation with Mercy Children Home had worsened with the political situation in Kerala. The state government had started to inflict unbelievable regulations on the home simply to make it harder for Hindu children to be brought up in a Christian environment. They would rather have them on the streets than provided for in a Christian home! The second Sunday after I returned to Maine, the Kerala government forced the boys of Mercy to leave, forcing the IGBC to decide whether they would have a boys' home or a girls' home, but not both. They had had a boys' and girls' home for nearly thirty years. The mission decided that with the college girls also living at the home it would be the best to go with a girls' home, but also because girls are treated as second-class citizens compared to boys. The good news is that the boys found homes within the Kangazha church that would care for them until they found a place to go. It was a joy to see so many children at the church and with one of the young men leading the gathering. Of course, they had a song or two and a bit of scripture, but no sermon even from a preacher from Maine. I was pleased. We spent the bulk of the time praying, and I got to pray after I received a small piece of paper on which were written these ten requests: 1) prayer for the IGBC (Independent Gospel Baptist Churches) and the AM (Associated Mission) workers; 2) prayer that churches will be started in all the districts of Kerala; 3) prayer for Rev. T. S. Joseph (one of the pastors and professors, the uncle of Shibu, and a good friend of mine) and his health needs; 4) prayer for Joshua and Abby and their spiritual growth and studies; 5) prayer for the graduation at KBBC; 6) prayer for Pastor Blackstone's health; 7) prayer for Bethany School; 8) prayer for Mercy Christian Children's Home; 9) prayer for the youth group at Kangazha; and 10) prayer for Josekutty. I found out later this was a young man in the church who had been paralyzed in a logging accident.

 We then split up into groups of three and interceded for the rest of the time. After the season of prayer, I was able to visit with those who had come. I finally got to meet Binu's bride Raymol and was excited to receive another prayer request. It was Binu and Raymol's desire to have a baby. I was told they had already lost three, and Raymol was having a hard time carrying a baby. I told them I would pray. I would just add that before I left India I found out that they are pregnant again, so we pray until the child is born! I also walked over to the college, my first chance since I had arrived in Kerala. I immediately recognized a couple of the boys getting the dining hall ready for supper. I was excited to learn that eight of the twenty graduates were students that I had had in 2012; it was going to be a wonderful week of activities for that reason alone. We got back to the Simon's house after dark, and I continued to pray into the evening for the requests I had heard and for the up and coming days ahead. I knew the trip had been immersed in prayer, and I had plenty of people at home praying, but it was also refreshing to know I was in the midst of prayer warriors both young and old. This trip could not go wrong because prayer supported it: "Praying always with all prayer and supplication in the Spirit, and watching thereunto with all perseverance and supplication for all saints. And for me, that utterance may be given me, that I may open my mouth boldly, to make known the mystery of the Gospel." (Ephesians 6:18-19) That was my prayer as well.

5

A Senior Citizen in India Remembering

I woke to another hot, hazy, and humid day in India with temperatures well into 100 degrees shortly after the sun had come up over the Kerala hills. My first Sunday in India was also my 65th birthday. This was not my first birthday in India; I celebrated my 59th birthday in India in 2010 with an Indian cake of 59 candles. What a fire! This one would be different as I passed the threshold into old age, or so says the modern standard for age classification in America. Before I left for India I had signed up for Medicare, and though I have decided not to retire as of yet, I knew that I had come to India an older man than the younger man that first crossed the coastline into Southern India in 2006. Was that one of the reasons I was feeling the heat more this time than at other times? As I got up early that morning, I began to ponder what had gotten me to where I was on the morning of my 65th birthday. It was certainly a long way from the small northern Maine city of Caribou to the small southern Kerala village of Edayappara.

Over the years I have attempted a few chapters of an autobiography but have never been able to put it together in book form. I doubt that I ever will, but if one reads the books that I have written over the years one will get a sense of the life the good Lord has given me. As the Psalmist says, "We spend our years as a tale that is told." (Psalm 90:9) It is pieces of that tale I would like to share in this book as I had plenty of time to ponder my life in the downtimes surrounding my 65th birthday. I decided to write this story down.

"In the granite hills of Maine's Aroostook County, between the towns of Wade and Woodland, there lies a family farm that sits on one of those hills. From the top of the hill a commanding view stretches out in all four directions. To this day I have yet to find a hill with a more glorious vista than the hill of my youth. To the north, the woods and fields mark the extent of the homestead in that direction. To the west, the land falls into the Salmon Brook Valley with stands of maple and fir, pine and spruce lining the shores of the small winding brook that descends from Salmon Lake to the Aroostook River, nearly seven miles as the crow flies. To the south, the landscape is a series of rolling hills, but on a clear day you can see all the way to Mars Hill, not the one in Greece. To the east, the hills rise higher than the Perham hills, so the view is blocked except for the fields and forest between here and there. On a dark night the lights of Caribou can be seen, and it was in a small hospital in that town that I was born on March 6, 1951. I came into the world on the heels of a blizzard that prevented my father from making the thirteen-mile trip from our home in north Perham. Over the years, the hills of my hometown have stood like faithful sentinels over my life. As I write these lines, I will be returning tomorrow to those hills to visit my aging parents (both in their 90s now). How many trips have I left? To a little country lad who played among the maples that circled his humble farmhouse at the foot of one of those hills, the towns beyond were never an attraction for me. I was never drawn to Washburn though I attended high school there because Perham Elementary only went to the eighth grade. I was never drawn back to Caribou though I was born there because my little hamlet of Perham had no hospital, no clinic, and no doctor. I was never drawn to Presque Isle even though my mother's parents lived there and we visited often, mostly on Friday nights, but the twinkling lights that spoke of man's achievements, of progress and civilization never appealed to me. Perhaps that is why the rural villages of Kerala have such a draw on me, they are like home. My hometown was called Perham named after the governor of the State of Maine at the time of it incorporation in the 1860s. My family had homesteaded in Perham long before it was called Perham, so my roots in this place are very deep. My great-great-great grandfather was the first to build a framed house in Perham. I have a cousin who still lives in that house, though not for long. The time of the Blackstones in Perham is about over as the Amish from Pennsylvania are moving in as I write this. By the time I finish this story, the farm might not have a Blackstone left. So my great-great grandfather, my great grandfather and my grandfather all farmed the land growing mostly potatoes, but also raising cows and selling milk. They tapped the trees for maple syrup, sold firewood, planted apple trees, and by the time my father took over the homestead in the fifth generation, it was a fully functioning family enterprise. My dad had just returned from the Second World War, had married my schoolteacher mother, and had my sister Sylvia before I showed up. The home that I was born into had no lace or lavishness to it. There were no rugs, no fancy furnishings, and hardly any modern conveniences. But in that home and around that house were all the blessed things that make for a proper upbringing. It was a plain home in a healthy environment with the best drinking water in the world. We ate three square meals a day, food that stuck to your ribs. There were pastureland and forestland to ramble through and springs and brooks to wade through. On the front porch we could hear the crickets in the summer, the frogs in the fall, and sounds of numerous birds talking about their flight south in the fall. Twice a day it was milking time, and from the earliest of ages, I was taught the benefits of work, the joys of labor, and the rewards of a job. Father was the master of the home, the authority of the house, and mother didn't seem to mind that. He was in favor of what an old preacher called "the posterior application of superior force when necessary", but rarely was it necessary in our house. I only remember one time it was applied. Dad always stood a head and a shoulder above every other man that I ever meet and still does despite old age, bad health, and a feeble mind. He was as faithful to the Perham Baptist Church as he was to the Blackstone Homestead, and on top of that he had a great helpmate in mother, my first love. Mother was and still is practical and faithful. She knew her place, her station, her orbit and she stayed in it, but that didn't make her speechless. I was blessed, in my opinion, to have had the greatest parents in the world and on this my 65th birthday I still have them. One of my last acts before I flew out to India was to visit them again. How many 65-year-olds have the privilege of saying they still have their parents with them? It was into this old-fashioned house and home I was raised. I was the second arrival, but not the last. My parents would have two more sons and one more daughter, but they would wait over a decade to start their second family. So I had a chance to grow up in a leisurely era, the first days of the mechanical age on the Blackstone Homestead. I just missed the horse-and-buggy days with the last horse leaving the farm just a few years before I was born. My horse was a John Deere, and my buggy was a 1947 International pickup. My early years were around milking Holsteins, raising pigs for bacon, feeding chickens and gathering their eggs, picking potatoes, and enjoying Saturday night beans and brown bread. I was raised with my dog Rover, and I never smelled my first cigarette until I was a teenager. I have yet to drink a bottle of beer because cigarettes and beer were not found on the farm. There were plenty of woods to walk in, plenty of grass to lie on, plenty of fresh air to breathe, and plenty of Godly examples to follow and emulate. I learned early to hunt, to milk, to pray, and to read God's Word. How often have I seen India as a going back in time?"

6

The Tale Continues
The Book that Changed Everything

"The memories that linger most clearly are those remembrances that have to do with the book of my fathers. My grandfather and father got saved during the great Perham revival of the early 1940s, so by the time I arrived on the Perham scene, faith was a huge part of the farm; more important than mammals and mammon. Despite the demands of the farm, faith had become a priority to the Perham Blackstones. Sunday was for worship even though it had to be done around milking time. Prayer before every meal and family time around the Bible were important as well. I knew most of the Bible stories before I could read them because they were told to me at home and at the Perham Baptist Church year after year after year until I could read them for myself. My parents told me I was in church the next Sunday after my birth, and I have missed few since—Maine or India. As I reminisce this first Sunday in India, I will soon leave for a Sunday morning service at the Venmony Baptist Church. Chief among the books in our home was the Grand Old Book, Holy Writ, aided by a Bible picture book or two. The stories of old came alive to me one by one by one. Early in my development, I learned the names of Paul and Peter, Joseph and Joseph, David and Daniel along with my sister Sylvia, Clayton, my first cousin born just a few weeks after me, and Morris, my first best friend and a neighbor. From my earliest memory I recall the story of Cain and Abel and learned which are the good way and the bad way. I have always believed in Noah and the Flood, and never questioned Creation even when they were questioned later in my schooling. My favorite stories were the stories of Jesus and, though I didn't accept Him as my Saviour until the age of seven (1958), I believe I can honestly say I loved Him from the beginning because of His stories and what He did for me on Calvary. That is why at an early age I placed my hope and trust in the carpenter from Galilee. I have, for all these years, never sought another faith or religion to follow; my trips to India have not been about knowing more about Hinduism or Islam to make a switch. When I set my course on the instructions of the Bible, I have never faltered or failed to stay true to what the Bible teaches. I certainly haven't been perfect and have broken many of the commandments as we all do, but I have never had a waking moment or a wandering eye in search of another Christ, another course, another Church. I am so thankful that I was raised in a generation when the television didn't come along until I had been well-established in the faith. The programs we listened to on the radio were clean and clearly pro-God verses the anti-God that floods the airwaves today. I was not brought up on Hollywood and the movies and the silly comics of fantasy, but my nurture and nourishment was in and by the Word of God. I know this is boring to the now generation and the depths of boredom to the modern youngster who has to go to church, but I loved those times from the start. Perhaps it was because I didn't know anything different. There was joy to see my aunts and uncles at church on Sunday; to see the grocer, my schoolteacher, my grandparents, my cousins, and the neighbors up the road all there on Sunday morning to worship in the only church in town. Feasting on the trash of a 21st century diet of cartoon fluff and video peanut butter that sticks to the roof of your mouth but never satisfies the soul, many boys or girls know nothing of the Bible. When they hear the stories of the Word, they hear them as fairy tales, fantasy, and make-believe. Of course there are a myriad of adults supporting this belief. I only heard action-packed, amazing adventures, and I believed every one, and I still do six decades later. David and Goliath, Jonah and the Fish, the destruction of Sodom and Gomorrah, Jesus walking on the water, the crossing of the Red Sea, Jesus' resurrection have, for all my life, been a part of the story of my life, and they remain valid and vital to this day! My parents believed in Solomon's precept. "Train up a child in the way he should go: and when he is old, he will not depart from it." (Proverbs 22:6) The Word of God trained me when I was a child, and now that I am old I am not departing from the Word of God. To this day, I can return to the church building of my youth and find the spot that was my conversion place. It was from that church I grew in grace and in the knowledge and understanding of my Lord and Saviour Jesus Christ. (II Peter 3:18) I am so grateful the Lord brought me to Himself when I was a child, so I have had a lifetime of service to the One that did so much for me! For it was from that moment to this that I have had the Lord on my side, and I have been protected from all the ills of this world and the evils of this earth. It was also from that place that I preached my first sermon in the spring of 1966. My ventures into public speaking began the year our BYF Youth Group (Baptist Youth Fellowship) was asked by our pastor Relland Clark to lead an evening church service at the end of our youth year that ran from September to May. I was fifteen when Pastor Clark asked me to share the sermon. I was speechless and tried at first to give every excuse why I was not the right youngster to do that part of the service. I had been reading scripture and praying and leading the music for a few years doing my part to share, but to preach the sermon was out of the question or was it? Eventually Pastor Clark talked me into it by saying, "Just share what the Lord shows you from the Bible." That precept has been my guiding principle to this day, fifty years later. I started preparing and through the Spirit I was directed to John 15:14 and on eleven 8 ½ by 11 inch lined pages, I put together a message I called "Commandments Christians Regularly Break". When it came time for me to speak, I walked to the pulpit, put my pages on the podium, never once raised my eyes to the congregation, and read every line. I left the platform that night thinking that was my last sermon. But during the week, my Uncle Read, my grandfather's brother and partner on the family farm, heard I had preached that Sunday. He told me if I could preach at the Baptist church in Perham then I could preach at the Advent church in Wade, the town between Perham and Washburn. Read would eventually pastor the Advent Christian Church in Wade for forty plus years, but in the spring of 1966, he wanted his nephew to preach for him. So the next Sunday night, I preached my second sermon called "Walking with God" based on the life of Enoch and Noah. Again I thought that would be it, but I was just getting started! The sermon I will preach at Venmony this morning in India would draw me very close to the 15,000-sermon mark. The best way I have been able to explain what took place in my life in 1966 was the experience that Samuel had as described in I Samuel 3 when he heard the voice of the Lord. At first, he didn't understand it was the Lord, and I too wondered often if I was hearing from God, but through my late teens, I began to understand that I like Samuel had messages to deliver. In the sometimes and in the somewheres of life, the unmistakable Voice of the Almighty was heard in my heart, and I knew I must share what I found in His written Word. So, from my earliest days a black covered book with two bold words printed on the front have changed my life. I can honestly say that the Holy Bible has been the guide book of my life, the instruction book of my life, and the purpose of my life. I know not how many hours I have spent reading, studying, pondering this Book, but Shibu has just called me. I am off once again to share this Book with a group of believers in the small hamlet of Venmony, Kerala, India!"

7

A Return to Venmony

My daydreaming was over for the moment as Shibu and I got into his car for our thirty-mile, Sunday ride to Venmony. I knew I would have time to revisit my past and the unchanging purpose of God for my life. However, for the moment, I was returning to a place I hadn't seen in six years, but my path and that place were now a decade old.

Many years ago I came to the conclusion that the one-chapter books of the Bible were well worth a slow and deliberate look. One commentator has called them, "the choicest gifts wrapped in the smallest packages." Philemon is one of those books. This first Sunday in India, I was intrigued with the ninth verse and the phrase "Paul the aged" because I was celebrating my sixty-fifth birthday. I must admit I was feeling a bit aged in the heat and humidity of Kerala 2016!

You know the story of Onesimus the slave who had stolen from his master Philemon. In the providence and purpose of God, Onesimus met Paul in a prison cell in Rome and was converted to Christ. Paul saw this connection between Onesimus and Philemon and God's plan for their lives when he wrote in verse fifteen, "For perhaps he therefore departed for a season, that thou shouldest receive him forever!" Though no prison cell and no prisoners are involved in my relationship with Venmony, the providential plan of God certainly can be seen in the outcome of the story. I have no theory or interpretation of God's plan to offer. I am also not venturing into some theological discussion on the permissive will of God versus the perfect will of God as can be applied to my first visit to Venmony. I am simply going to tell you what happened to me at Venmony and let you be the judge.

In 2006, I traveled to Kerala for the first time. Before my 40-day trip was over, I had the privilege of visiting over a dozen of the churches of the Independent Gospel Baptist Churches of Kerala. I loved every minute with the congregations and their pastors, but when I entered the village of Venmony, something was different. I immediately made a connection to Pastor Regi Mathi and his small band of believers in this hostile, Hindu hamlet. I remembered my church planting days in Pembroke, New Hampshire, and I could relate! Within a short time, the Holy Spirit suggested to me that I should do something very special for them. You might think this not unusual for a pastor, but for me this was very unusual because of what the Spirit was suggesting. I have never considered myself a visionary. I have been a simple country preacher and pastor for most of my life. At best I have been a caretaker of other people's work and have never been challenged with anything that could be seen as utopian. Yet there I was with this burden on my heart and a plan in my head. After a service in the house the church was renting and using as a sanctuary and a parsonage, Shibu, Regi, and I went over to a small piece of land on the other side of town that had just been purchased after fifteen years of hoping for this land to be a church building plot. It was ideal for the purpose, but the prospect of a building being built in the near future was slim at best. If it had taken the local asembly fifteen years to raise the money for the land, how long would it take them to raise the money for the building? Was my coming to Venmony an accident, fate, or was the purpose of God being fulfilled? As Shibu and I drove back from Venmony after that first visit, I pondered in my heart what I was to do.

I still can't explain it nor do I suggest that I fully understand it, but before I left India that first time I shared with Shibu what the Lord had placed on my heart for the work at Venmony. I was determined to return to the States and raise the money necessary for a new church sanctuary at Venmony. Not only a church sanctuary, but also for a parsonage as well! Again, I am not telling you that I know the mind of God. All I am telling you is that this kind of vision for another ministry hadn't happened to me before. I returned home to my church work in Ellsworth, Maine and started to tell the church family about the need in Venmony. Within a short time the church family got on board with my vision. We began to take special offerings for the goal of building a sanctuary and a parsonage for our brothers and sisters in Christ at Venmony. Before the year was over, I not only had been asked to be graduation speaker at Kerala Baptist Bible College for the class of 2007, but my church people had raised the projected cost of the buildings, over half a million rupees, nearly $13,000 (eventually $18,000)!

When my daughter and I traveled to India in 2007, one of our stops was at Venmony where we surprised the congregation and the pastor with a check that would allow them to build their church building and the added bonus of a new parsonage on the side. The joy was heavenly, and I felt that God had used this simple pastor from Maine to do something special for a struggling congregation in Kerala.

The joy was multiplied when three years later in 2010 I was able to return to Venmony for the dedication with a deacon from Emmanuel Baptist Church, Russ Coffin. Three years is not an especially long time to build something in India especially when you consider the obstacles and barriers that were put up by the Hindu town council that didn't want the first Baptist church built in their village of Venmony. I can still feel the ecstasy I felt the moment I was allowed to put the key in the lock and open the church door for the first time. I was the first to walk into the sanctuary and to literally see a vision in brick (the walls) and tin (the roof) and concrete (the floor) coming to life. It was beyond description. The crowd was immense as the churches of the association got together to celebrate the new sanctuary and parsonage. So here I was as I returned to Venmony with this flood of memories in my mind. As we drove up to the church, a new wall had been built around the entire property and a new front gate. Behind the cinderblock hedge was the sanctuary and parsonage just as I had left them six years before. The pastor, Pastor Binu, was new and there were a few new faces in the congregation, but my vision for Venmony was still there, a reminder of the purpose of God for a Pastor from Maine!

Perhaps as you read this chapter, you too can testify to the truth of this Indian tale. You may have seen a work of the Holy Spirit in your life. I think now of the decade that has passed and how this aged pastor was able to return to one of his greatest spiritual accomplishments in the category of helping the brethren. Remember, I never set out to explain what God did at Venmony. I write this only to highlight and underline God's unfailing purpose and undeniable providence. Will God ever do another work through the brethren and me at Venmony again? I don't know. All I know is that it hadn't happened before Venmony, and it hasn't happened since Venmony. Oh, the Lord has certainly touched my heart with other projects that resulted in other forms of gifts for the work in India, but nothing that is tangible, nothing that can be literally revisited as I did on that morning in March 2016. That morning I preached a message based on a favorite song, "He Giveth More Grace". The Scripture was James 4:6, but the message was found in the lyrics: "When we have exhausted our store of endurance, when our strength has failed ere the day is half done, when we reached the end of our hoarded resources, our Father's full giving is only begun." I left

Venmony, perhaps for the last time, with the full knowledge that I had been a part of a providential purpose of the Almighty God. I had not only seen the project in my mind and heart before anybody else, but I had the privilege and honor of seeing it through to its completion as Barry the aged!

8

Werther's Original Birthday

Shibu and I got back from our Venmony ministry around two in the afternoon. On the way, he had stopped at a pastry shop and bought me a birthday cake. Julie had lunch waiting for us, and we celebrated my sixty-fifth birthday around the Simon table. I wasn't with my immediate family, but my India family was a great substitute. After lunch I had a chance to catch a nap and plan for my version of an Indian birthday tradition that night at the evening church service at Kerala Baptist Bible College chapel.

I still remember the first time it happened to me in India. I was visiting one of the churches of the Association when a little girl came up to me and gave me a piece of candy. One of my habits ever since I visited India was to take plenty of hard candy to pass out to the kids I met. The first time I found it strange that this little girl was giving me candy. It hadn't happened before. I graciously took the candy to be polite, but I wondered about it. After the service was over I asked Shibu why the little girl had given me the candy. He asked, "Did you notice that she was giving candy to others besides you?" After he asked, I did remember that was the case; she wasn't just giving candy to me. It was then Shibu explained that in Kerala there was a custom that on your birthday you give a piece of candy to honor your own birthday. Before I left for India I remembered that tradition, and I was determined to practice that tradition myself on my sixty-fifth birthday. Part of the weight of my luggage for India was a few pounds of hard candy. But this was no ordinary candy but my favorite candy—Werther's Originals. I have always loved the buttery/toffee flavor, and I had discovered on other trips to India so do the Indians! That morning in Venmony I had passed out a piece of Werther's Originals to each person at Church. As I headed out to the college, my pockets were filled to do the same there.

Shibu and I reached the courtyard of the college around seven, but he was only dropping me off. He had a meeting to attend, so I was on my own. As I walked through the new lobby area of the school and ascended the four flights of stairs to the chapel located on the top floor of the academic building, I handed out "the original" to everyone I met. Even before I climbed the stairs, I had walked over to the residential building to meet my old friend Sabu Andrews, the college dean. He invited me into his apartment, and I was able to visit with his wife and son and daughter. How they had grown in three years! He served me an orange drink as I handout out my Werther's. Nobody seemed surprised by the American handing out candy, each accepting my offering graciously and wishing me a happy birthday. The news had gone before me. The great thing about KBBC is that everybody that ministers there or goes there has to speak English, so all my greeting were in English not Malayalam. As a matter of fact, the message I would speak that night, "Why Should We Be Watching?" based on I Thessalonians 5:1-7, was the only message I was able to share without an interpreter. It was a joy to listen to their birthday greetings in my native tongue and to celebrate my birthday in an Indian way with these Indians.

As I sat and listened to their singing and praying and Bible reading, I was transported back to my Bible college days and this story recalls that part of my life:

"My formal Bible training took place between 1969 and 1973 when I traveled from my home state of Maine to Greenville, South Carolina. For four years, I was called a preacher-boy as I studied the Word of God at Bob Jones University. My connection to this school was through my mother's side of the family. When my Grandfather Barton was ready to send his oldest child, my Aunt Joyce, to Bible School he decided on Bob Jones College then located in Tennessee. The president Bob Jones, Sr. had come to Maine on an evangelistic tour, and Grandfather Barton liked him. Eventually all six of grandfather's children would graduate from Bob Jones, included his next to the oldest child my mother Phyllis. Bob Jones University was certainly much larger that Kerala Baptist Bible College, but the focus was the same— the Word of God as the sole authority for all that is life itself. I would earn a Bachelors of Art in Bible with a minor in History. I would monitor a floor of boys for the last year and a half of my education as well as lead an extension work to Athens, Georgia for the last three years of my training. I even took a mission's trip to Australia between my junior and senior years and would leave the school as only the second group of students to go out from the school to establish independent Baptist Churches in areas around the country. My missionfield would be Southern New Hampshire. My formal, spiritual education was regular and very Southern Baptist, but I never lost my independent Maine nature nor did I align myself with the often contradictory practices with my southern brethren. I was still very old-fashioned and, though I was tempted to stay for graduate work after four years, I was longing just to get at it. I was only twenty-two, but I didn't want more education I wanted more service. I have discovered over the years that some aspiring servants of Christ simply stay too long in the halls of academia. Yes, I am saying, in my opinion, you can get too much formal education. I have come to believe that we need to see the pattern of training found in the Bible. Granted, Paul was formally educated at the feet of Gamaliel (Acts 22:3), but when it came to the Lord's work, Paul was sent to the deserts of Arabia (Galatians 1:17). So for me, the departure from Bob Jones University in 1973 was no accident. Some think you can't study and learn without a college or a professor, but you can if you open your heart to the best teacher of all, the Holy Spirit (I John 2:27). Don't get me wrong. I am not suggesting a formal education is unnecessary or unimportant. If I were saying that, why have I taken five trips to India to help educate the next generation of Indian pastor, professors, and missionaries? It is a part of God's purpose of spiritual education, but it isn't all of it. I tell people to this day that I got a fine education at Bob Jones University, but if I had to do it over again, I would have gone to a Bible School where the study of the Bible is the sole purpose, like Kerala Baptist Bible College. I wish I had gone there or to a place like that in the States or in Canada, such as New Brunswick Bible Institute. I got a well-rounded education no doubt, but I think of the wasted hours of English, math, philosophy, etc. I think of the great courses in Biblical history or Church History or pure Bible I could have taken instead of those academic subjects. Over the last forty-three years since I left Bob Jones University, these are the subjects and topics I have studied."

    I was brought back to reality as I was introduced as the conference and graduation speaker for the coming week. I shared my thoughts without interruption or translation over the next forty-five minutes. It was nice to be back speaking at KBBC. I liked my college experience to say the least, but since 2006 I have enjoyed more teaching and preaching at a Bible college. I shook hands with a lot of the students and thanked them for allowing me to be a part of graduation 2016, and I received a few more birthday greetings. I left the chapel and waiting for me by the residential hall was Lalu, a member of the Venmony church and now a pastor himself, who took me back in his brand new 4-wheel auto, another new experience. I couldn't have asked for a better sixty-fifth birthday. What an original!

9

Bacon Sandwiches and Bible Conference

Monday began a five daylong set of activities at KBBC. It was graduation week. I was up at six enjoying again the only time of the day I wasn't going to be sweating. I had come to Kerala with a stack of 4x6 cards, my method for summarizing my sermons, but I hadn't yet decided exactly in what order I would preach them. That first morning of conference I was led to begin the week of messages by highlighting the life of Elijah. Eventually, I would decide on this order for the four-day conference: Monday-Elijah-I Kings 17-19, practical lessons of supplication, Tuesday-Eliezer-Genesis 24, practical lessons of stewardship, Wednesday-Enoch-Genesis 5, practical lessons of the signs of the times), and Thursday-Ethan-Psalm 89, practical lessons of the songs of persecution. These would be my morning sessions with the students and the Kerala pastors that showed up for the conference. In the evening I would be sharing with a broader audience of local people and folks from the churches as well as the students and professors and their families from KBBC. The messages for those three evenings would be: Monday night -"Please Don't Disturb" based on Hosea 10:12; Tuesday night -"The Four-Fold Focus of the Believer" based on Jude 20-21; and Wednesday night -"God's Pinch of Salt" based on Matthew 5:13. I would speak thirteen times in four days; what a joy!

I descended the stairs of the Simon house that first morning to find a wonderful treat for breakfast. My normal eating schedule while in India was just two meals a day, mostly breakfast and supper, because of the extreme temperatures. I am not a hot weather eater, even in Maine. I have found that I didn't need a lot of food in India, just a lot of water! Over the years I have eaten in the Simon's home more than any other place in India. My primary cook has been Julie, though every once in a while Shibu has cooked for me. On this first day of Bible Conference, Julie prepared for me a new treat—Indian bacon. I love bacon, any kind of bacon: Canadian bacon, fresh bacon, etc. But I had never had Indian bacon before. My most favorite way to eat bacon, though I like it with just about anything or anyway, is to make a sandwich with it. When you combine Julie's toast and her bacon, I discovered perhaps the best bacon sandwich I have ever had, ever! Unlike American bacon, Indian bacon is thick, meaty, and very salty. Unfortunately, I love salt, too! Before I would leave India, I would get this special treat one more time.

After breakfast I was able to finally e-mail my family that I had arrived in India safe and sound. It had been nearly six days since I left Maine, but either the power had been off or the Internet had been out. I also got my first e-mails from home to tell me that my only grandson Judah, the new apple of my eye born on August 18, 2015, had his first two teeth. Two bottom teeth that, according to his mother and my daughter Marnie, were nothing short of sharp daggers. Fingers beware! I heard my wife was suffering with a broken tooth, but all the dentist was able to do was file it down because there was not enough time to pull it before her flight to California that day. While I spent twenty days in India, my wife was going to spend ten days visiting the grandson. After getting and sending a series of e-mails, I was off to the first session of the 2016 KBBC Bible Conference that included two sessions in the morning and one session in the afternoon. The afternoon session would be different than my previous conferences. It was a question and answer session with the students asking the questions and hopefully me giving the answers!

During the first three hours of the conference with a ten-minute break between sessions, I highlighted 1) God's Prayer, 2) God's Provision, 3) God's Power, and 4) God's Presence in the life of Elijah as described in I Kings 17-19. I still am amazed what Indian people will put up with to hear God's Word proclaimed. The first two sessions of conference took place between 9:30 and 12:30. We were meeting in the chapel of KBBC which is located on the fourth floor of the academic building. The structure has a tin roof so you can image just how hot it must have gotten in that upper room by noontime. With only a few ceiling fans and a few floor fans, the heat was intense. I was drinking liters of water just to get through, yet the students and staff listened in the stifling heat to my expounding of the Scriptures in the life of Elijah. Then it was time for a lunch break. I simply returned to the Simon house for a break and a lie down. By two in the afternoon, I was back to the sweat-box for a series of questions asked by the students. These were the questions they asked and I answered in the hour-long session:

1. Why do we get scared during times of persecution or suffering if God is present all the times in our lives?
2. Why doesn't God bless His children equally in their Christian lives?
3. Can you explain about the wages of sin in the life of Elijah and why he didn't die?
4. Can you please explain why a woman cannot be a pastor?

I will leave you to ponder how I might have answered these questions. The one that came up the most was the woman pastor question with a number of follow-up questions. It seems this issue has finally arrived in India with the Church, depending on the State, split over the issue. With eleven different states represented at KBBC, the issue will not go away soon, despite an answer from a pastor from the State of Maine.

Once again I returned to the Simon house for supper and preparation for my first evening message. Because of the increase of attendees, the evening sessions would be held outside in the courtyard of the college. With the setting of the sun around 6:30 and the service beginning at 7:30 it was a bit cooler, but only a bit! That night there was plenty of singing and special music by the students and others, including a young man from the Heavenly Singers, the gospel-singing group of the organization, who sang each of the three nights. Shibu translated for me that first night. The point I made of that sermon is that we have too many Christians asleep at the wheel, and most don't want to be disturbed. It was wonderful to be back in the midst of Kerala Christians. As the first day came to a close, I relished in the joy of walking through the crowd after the service and seeing old friends, old pastors, and older young people. I was especially delighted to see again the vice-president of the group K. J. Thomas. I also saw my old friend T. S. Joseph and was sad to see his declining heath. Since I last saw him, his kidneys had failed, and he was on dialysis. I knew that this was probably be the last time I would see him this side of eternity. I ran into Binu and Raymol and learned of their latest pregnancy. I saw Pastor Regi and his family and Pastor Robin and his family. I also saw many faces I recognized, but their names failed me. Their jovial handshakes and broad smiles told me they were glad to see me again even though the language barrier was still there.

Such would be the pattern for the next two and a half days as I ministered to old friends and new friends, old students and new students, old professors and pastors and new professors and pastors at the Annual Graduation Week Bible Conference. By 9:15 PM I was back in my little room filled to overflowing that the Good Lord had granted me the privilege of being back among my brothers and sisters of Kerala again!

10

The Tale Continues
The Foolishness of Preaching

From March 7-10, 2016, I averaged three sermons a day as I proclaimed God's Word to the students within Kerala Baptist Bible College and the citizens outside the college. I had plenty of opportunity to remember what got me to this place:

"I had been brought to Christ at the early age of seven, and I began to read and study shortly after my conversion. By the age of fifteen, I was preaching and sharing the things I was learning, but I was also struggling with my calling to preach. After my first two sermons in 1966, I began to rebel against God's call. I still remember the moment the Holy Spirit tugged on my heartstrings and started playing the music of the message. The tragedy of that moment in 1967 was I grieved Him (Ephesians 4:30) and quenched Him (I Thessalonians 5:19) at the same time. Not only did I transgress against His calling, but I quenched His leading for the next three years in the area of preaching. I was asked, but I said "No!" Oh, I put up appearances on the outside pretending to be a model teenage Christian, but in the inside I was rebellious and wicked in my thoughts and secret sins. After my first sermons, I wouldn't preach again for nearly four years. It was through that time I threw up to God my excuse for not preaching His Word. Falling back on the excuse of Moses (Exodus 4:10), my excuse was I didn't have the skill in public speaking. The Good Lord in all of His graciousness showed me that He had gifted me in an unusual way. It was the year of my calling (1967) and the year of my junior year at Washburn District High

School. At the end of each junior year, the tradition was a celebration called Junior Exhibition. It was a pre-celebration for what would happen at the end of our senior year. At the heart of this celebration of accomplishment was a speaking contest. If God couldn't show me in the pulpit I could speak in public, He would use another means. That means was a beloved teacher, Tim Humphrey. Most of us have a teacher we just loved to study for, and Tim Humphrey was such a teacher for me. I was blessed by having Tim for a teacher twice in my life. He came to Perham Elementary School straight out of college and was my seventh grade English teacher. Single at the time, Mr. Humphrey took an interest in his students and would even socialize with us outside of school. I still remember when he took a few of my classmates and me bowling for the first time! When I left Perham for high school in Washburn, it wasn't long before Mr. Humphrey followed to eventually become my junior and senior year English teacher. In the spring of 1968, he approached me about participating in the Junior Ex Speaking Contest. I agreed if he would tutor and mentor me. He agreed, and we prepared. Little did I realize what the Lord was doing behind the scenes as I practiced in our brand-new basketball gymnasium for the big night! The first thing we realized was that I had a voice that needed no microphone, for the volume of my voice could fill the place, any space. It is a strength I have to this day. I can still see through my mind's eye Mr. Humphrey at the far corner of the gym telling me that he could hear me clearly. He taught me to project my voice, soften my voice, raise my voice, and inflect my voice according to the story I was telling. My speech that year was on the world-famous accomplishment of Sir Edmund Hillary and his Sherpa guide, when on May 29, 1953 they conquered the highest mountain in the world, Mount Everest. And to my surprise, but not to Mr. Humphrey or my Pastor, I won the contest against nine of my classmates. As I held the trophy I heard that still small voice saying, "See!" I ignored it, but I heard it just like I did the night my pastor Relland Clark was preaching. I heard that same voice tell me that my life would be in the profession of preaching. I fought on against the call, but all along the way the power of the Spirit was breaking down my will. It finally came to a head in 1970 when I was half-way through my freshman year at Bob Jones University. I was struggling in my spirit, homesick for my home, and drifting in my faith. I got permission to retreat to the prayer room at the end of the hall in my dorm on a dark night in January shortly after I had returned from Christmas break. I wrestled with my assurance of salvation. I battled with my besetting sin. I questioned my academic major, which was history at the time. I brought up every issue I could think of, but no amount of confession or repentance would bring peace to my soul and mind. Eventually that still small voice was heard in my heart again, and all it said was, "I want you to preach!" I finally yielded to the reality and from that day onward and, to this day in India, I haven't resisted or refrained from preaching the Word of God anywhere and to anyone as opportunities came. I determined then and there to ". . . be ready always to give an answer to every man . . ." (I Peter 3:15) In the 1950s, I staked everything on a preacher from Nazareth for my salvation. In the 1960s, I listened to a preacher from Perham and delivered my first sermon. In the 1970s, I yielded to God's truth that ". . . it pleased God by the foolishness of preaching to save them that believe." (I Corinthians 1:21), and I began my service for Him. Within weeks I had joined an extension ministry of preacher boys from Bob Jones University that went every Sunday to Athens, Georgia to share the faith in jails and nursing homes. Eventually I was asked to share the Word, and it was during one of those early spring messages in 1970 that Mary Huff, a lady from one of those nursing homes, got saved. I was hooked, and I knew that I had found my calling. After that day, I have never and I mean never rejected an opportunity to preach. As Paul exhorted Timothy to "Preach the Word; be instant in season, out of season; reprove, rebuke, exhort with all longsuffering and doctrine." (II Timothy 4:2) I took my calling seriously. I haven't diverted from these five tenets given to me by an old-fashioned preacher: "Sin is black, hell is hot, judgment is certain, eternity is long, and salvation is free!" Over the years, I would preach three and a half years to the residents of Georgia in the nursing home of Athens Avenue Boarding Home, Banks Jackson Commerce Nursing Home, Hill Haven Nursing Home, and Cider Hill Nursing Home. Besides the nursing homes, I preached the gospel in the Athens' City Jail, the Athens' County Jail, and the Georgia State Prison. I have had the privilege to preach in Maine, New Hampshire, South Carolina, Georgia, and Alaska. I have preached in four countries: United States, Canada, Australia, and India, and before this India trip is over, I will have preached in five states of India: Kerala, Andhra Pardesh, Tamil Nadu, Orissa, and Punjab. I can honestly say that each time I have stood before an audience to share a portion of God's Holy Word I have received a spiritual thrill. Despite the years, I never get tired of preaching. If anything, I am energized even in the humid climate of Kerala. Sometimes, during my trips to Georgia, I would preach seven times on a Sunday—something I covet to this day but have never been able to duplicate. To this day, while most preachers share one message a week, I am disappointed if I don't share the Word at least seven times! By the time I leave India this time, I will have delivered my 281st sermon in 137 days over five years in which I have seen 64 individuals come to the Lord. This is one of the most condensed periods of preaching in my fifty years of preaching. It is only bettered by my 512 sermons in 122 days over a 21-year period at Hampton Bible Camp in New

Brunswick, Canada in which I saw 287 kids come to the Lord. The Good Lord has proven to me that it is through the foolishness of preaching people will get saved! All praise to Him!

11

The Kids of the KBBC

Besides my speaking engagements, I had the privilege of sitting in on two testimonial meetings during graduation week at KBBC. On Tuesday afternoon and Wednesday afternoon, the 2016 graduation class shared how they got saved, how they came to KBBC, and what the Lord was leading them to do after graduation. Because there were twenty in that class, one of the largest for the college, the group was split into two groups of ten. I would like for you to meet the kids of the KBBC. The only way I can introduce them to you is through their personal testimonies:

1. Bhagirathi Kanhar from the State of Orissa. This young man was at KBBC in 2012, my last year teaching at the college. He was a spiritual son of Joy Thomas, the state director of the Orissa Outreach of the Kerala Churches. Kanhar came from a Hindu family, but through the encouragement of Joy he came to KBBC where he got saved during his freshman year. He will be returning to Orissa.

2. Bilifang Borgoyary from the State of Assam. He is another young man who was at KBBC when I was there in 2012. Bilifang came from a Christian home. His father is a pastor in Assam. Saved at a young age, he desired to find Christian training at KBBC through the influence of others who had come to KBBC in the past. He too would be returning to Assam to help his father in the work of Christ.

3. Gaiphiuguang Gonmei from the State of Manipur. Gonmei was new to me, but his testimony was one like mine. He came from a Christian

home and was brought to Christ through the influence of the assistant pastor of his church who also encouraged him to attend KBBC. He would be returning to Manipur to serve God.

4. Jajang Haokip from the State of Manipur. Despite being brought up in a Christian home, Jajang rebelled as a teenager and played the prodigal for many years until his pig pen became a prison cell. Converted in jail, he became a policeman before he felt a need for further Christian education. He came to KBBC through information provided by his pastor and will be returning to Manipur to serve God.

5. Kanil Basumatary of the State of Assam. Another student of my 2012 class, Kanil was raised in a Hindu family, but his mother had to give him up. It was through a near-death experience that he got saved and dedicated his life to serve the God who saved him. He was returning to Assam to pastor in the hill country.

6. Kawijanbou Chawang of the State of Manipur. Another 2012 student, Chawang was raised in a Christian family and saved at an early age. He served the Lord early and came to KBBC through the advice of others who had attended before. Chawang would eventually stay at KBBC for six years graduating with a Master's Degree. He will be returning to Manipur to be an evangelist among the tribes.

7. Kudiyam Dhanesh of the State of Chhattisgarh. During a period of sickness in a hospital, Dhanesh's uncle visited him and led him to Christ. Being very poor he didn't have a Bible but sought its knowledge. Encouraged to study the Bible, he found his way to KBBC and would be returning to his home state to teach the Bible, the book he had known about but never had his own copy.

8. M. David of the State of Manipur. The valedictorian of the class, David was raised in a Christian home and saved at an early age. Six years before attending KBBC he was already involved in teaching Sunday school and Daily Vacation Bible School. He came to KBBC for further training to return to do the same.

9. Madhu Bala of the State of Haryana. A friend led her to the Lord and her grandparents sent her to KBBC. She would be the first graduate of KBBC from her state. Haryana was another state I was able to travel through by train on this trip!

10. Manaiwangliu of the State of Manipur. This young lady attended Sunday school and Daily Vacation Bible School in her hometown and

was eventually led to Christ by a missionary using I Corinthians 1:27. She would return to serve.

11. Modan Narzary of the State of Assam. He was brought up in a Christian family and through an illness he came to Christ. The highlight of his KBBC experience was his baptism just two months before at the Annual Convention of the IGBC.

12. Nejimon M S of the State of Manipur. This young man came to KBBC unsaved, and it was through the witnessing of Sabo Andrews, the college dean, he came to Christ on June 10, 2014. He spoke of having no wings before that day, but now he has wings and he can fly. He would be returning to his home state to preach.

13. Nerswn Basumatary of the State of Assam. Born into a Christian family and saved in 2008, Nerswn came to KBBC to study for the pastorate. It is his desire to return to Assam and be just that.

14. Porgen Narzary of the State of Assam. Born into a big family and saved at an early age, he was sent to KBBC by an uncle in 2012. Porgen was one of the young men I remembered from my 2012 trip. He will be returning to Assam to teach Bible.

15. Presenjit Basumatary of the State of Assam. He was brought up in a Christian family but wasn't saved until he came to KBBC in 2010. He spoke of a terrible temper that God took from him. He was also among my KBBC students in 2012.

16. Rekha of the State of Manipur. A very shy young lady from a Christian family and an early faith, but it was her years at KBBC that brought her out of her shell and her desire is to return to Manipur to serve the local church in her village.

17. Saka Murmu of the State of Assam. Saka came to KBBC without knowing English and being called by another name! Saka had no Bible and no faith, but was saved in 2014!

18. Saroj Kumar Digal of the State of Orissa. He was born into a Hindu family and involved in the 2008 persecution of Christians, but was turned around by Joy Thomas and sent to KBBC where he got saved in 2012. He was another one of my students. He will be returning with Kanhar to help Joy Thomas spread the Gospel to the persecutors.

19. Thakur Murmu of the State of Assam lost his parents at a young age, was brought up by Christians, and sent to KBBC where he got saved and was baptized in 2014.

20. Sophy K. Paul of the State of Kerala. I left Sophy for last because of my ten-year relationship with this daughter of a Kerala pastor. I first met Sophy in 2006 when I visited her father's church in Southern Kerala. The next year I met her again when I returned with my daughter for graduation little realizing I would be her college graduation speaker in 2016. She was also a part of the junior class in 2012. She stayed after her undergraduate degree was finished in 2014 and would be graduating with her Master's in missions. Her testimony included a reference to the students from the north, as being black as they do have darker skin than the Indians in the south and her growth in being able to deal with strangers, like me!

(Postscript: Sophy is now the college librarian at KBBC and is helping other achieve their goals as they study God's Word and train for their life's ministry at her old college!)

As I listened to these testimonies, I started to relive the testimony that got me to Kerala!

12

The Tale Continues
He Leadeth Me Beside the Still Waters.

"As I look back on the path the Lord has led me through the years, I now see a very clear pattern of my paths. They were always by still waters (Psalm 23:2)—the peaceful days on the Blackstone homestead of my youth (1951-1969) with friendly farmers, long strolls along country lanes, hours meditating in the back forty, happy Sundays at the Perham Baptist Church, and the harmony of our family home on the High Meadow Road and the productive years at Brokenshire Hall on the campus of Bob Jones University in Greenville, South Carolina (1969-1973) during my college days. Though I had been reading the Bible for most of my life, it was by these still waters I learned the love of studying the Word of God. It was there I started marking my Bible with my thoughts and began a systematic study of the teaching of Christ through the Gospels. It was there I learned to pray for missions at the evening Prayer Band. It was in the room in the academic building designated for Australia (countries were prayed for in alphabetic order) I got a burden for that land. I would eventually travel to this land for a summer and learn that I wasn't a missionary to a foreign land but a missionary to my homeland. It was during the adventurous days at the Warbunton Hostel of the United Aborigines Mission in the Gibson Desert of Western Australia (1972) that I got a missionary's heart, both foreign and domestic. It was there I heard clearly the message God gave to Ezekiel, but meant for me—And He said unto me, Son of man, go, get thee unto the house of Israel (New England), and speak with my words unto them. For thou art not sent to a people of a strange speech (the Aborigines) and a hard language, but to the house of Israel (my own people); not to many people of a strange speech and of an hard language, whose words thou canst not understand. Surely, had I sent thee to them, they would have hearkened unto thee, but the house of Israel (English-speaking people) will not hearken unto thee; for they will not hearken unto me: for all the house of Israel are impudent and hardhearted." (Ezekiel 3:4-7) My first mission to New England would prove this prophecy true in my own life! I left Greenville for Catamount Hill where Coleen and I had our first home in southern New Hampshire in the tiny village of Pembroke (1973-1978). It was here I learned just how hard the hearts of men had become in New England. My wife and I struggled and sacrificed for five years with little response or reward. It was there we learned the meaning of Margret Clarkson's hymn based in John 20:21. You will recognize the words that can be sung to John Peterson's classic tune 'Toronto'. "So send I you to labor unrewarded, to serve unpaid, unloved, unsought, unknown, to bear rebuke, to suffer scorn and suffering, so send I you to toil for me alone. So send I you to bind the bruised and broken, over wandering souls to work, to weep, to wake, to bear the burdens of a world a weary, so send I you to suffer for My sake. So send I you to loneliness and longing, with heart a hungering for the loved and known, forsaking home and kindred, friend and dear one, so send I you to know My love alone. So send I you to leave your life's ambition, to die to dear desire, self-will resign, to labor long, and love where men revile you, so send I you, to lose your life in Mine. So send I you to hearts made hard by hatred, to eyes made blind because they will not see, to spend, though it be blood, to spend and spare not, so send I you, to taste of Calvary. As the Father hath sent Me, so send I you." Despite the harsh teaching and difficult instruction, there were plenty of still waters that kept us going and, though we wondered and doubted, we never gave up on our commission. We discovered after leaving the Pembroke Bible Fellowship that our pastoral education wasn't over. The turbulent years at Smith Hole, better known as the Calvary Baptist Church of Westfield, Maine (1979-1986), my wife and I believe these were our wilderness years which included a rejection of our home church to be their pastor even though we were sure the Lord was leading in that direction. It was through those years the Good Lord literally gave me still waters in a small trout pond less than two miles from the parsonage. It was the hours spend on those still waters that got me through the most difficult years in my pastorate. Beaten and bruised and battered, we were led to a small island (Moose) off the coast of Maine to recover (1986-1991). From the bluff of Shacksford Head, I was able to watch the tide ebb and flow, the seagulls fly, the seals at play, and breathe the salty air that brings restoration with every breath. The congregation of the Washington Street Baptist Church was just as refreshing as the sea breeze. It was in Eastport that I learned the therapeutic value of writing, a weekly practice I have engaged in since 1988. It was here I wrote my first memory, my first devotional, and had my first writing published in the national magazine *Country Extra*. I would eventually have a monthly article in the local paper, *Quoddy Tides*. Blessed is the preacher that gets called to the still waters of the Atlantic Ocean and a section called Passamaquoddy Bay! It was here I learned it is important to spend some days in Cherith (I Kings 17:5) before you rush off to Carmel (I Kings 18:20)! I remember my days on a rough and rugged coastline where I loved to walk Greenlaw (a parishioner) Beach, hike up Shacksford Bluff, and watch the tide coming in and out along the jetty in Eastport Harbor. My five years in that quiet and quaint coastal village prepared for me for a twenty-nine year plus ministry in a city. These years (1991-2019) were spent in the coastal city of Ellsworth in the downeast county of Hancock. I came to a church in transition with a collection of people trying to unite because of failures in other churches. As I told a friend shortly after I arrived at Emmanuel Baptist Church, it was as if the people had one foot under the pew and the other in the aisle. I found a people shell-shocked over church scandals and years of legalism, yet in the midst were a people that I would learn to love beyond any other. In the dedication of the book I wrote on my years at Emmanuel, I remarked, "I came to Emmanuel a reluctant replacement for the pastor that had left, and then I stayed twenty-nine years, why? Because I found a church of a lifetime!" I was hesitant to move my family from the caring, close church in Eastport to the busy believers of Emmanuel. I felt I was called to a country work, not a city work. My family was eager, but I was wary. My lot to this point had been to country folks, rural pastorates, out-of-the-way places not a crossroad city like Ellsworth. It was then the Lord spoke to me through a poem written by another pastor by the name of George McDonald:

> I said, "Let me walk in the fields."
> He said, "No walk in the town."
> I said, "There are no flowers there."
> He said, "No flowers but a crown."
> I said, "But the skies are black. There is nothing but noise and din!"
> And He wept as He sent me back. "There is more," He said, "There is sin!"
> I said, "But the air is thick, and fogs are veiling the sun."
> He answered, "Yet souls are sick and souls in darkness undone."

I said, "I shall miss the light, and friends will miss me, they say."

He answered, "Choose tonight, if I am to be missed or they?"

I pleaded for time to be given.

He said, "Is it hard to decide? It will not seem hard in Heaven to have followed the steps of your Guide!"

I cast one look at the fields, and then set my face to the town.

He said, "My child do you yield? Will you leave the flowers for the crown?"

Then into His hand went mine, and into my heart came He, and I walked in the light divine, the path I had feared to see."

A river runs through Ellsworth to a bay!

13

The Cool of the Day

It was only when I experienced a Kerala in the cool of the day (Genesis 3:8) did I understand the great significance of Adam and Eve's strolls with the Almighty.

Graduation week at Kerala Baptist Bible College was passing quickly with my Bible teaching in the days and my Bible preaching in the evenings. I was enjoying seeing old friends and making new ones as each session and each service ended. I am not much of a people person, but as my wife says, "I can play a crowd with the best of them!" To me, my best times are my alone times and, despite the busy schedule I still had plenty of alone time that first week in India. The best of times were in the cool of the day!

Graduation activities keep me busy from 9 AM to 9 PM, but the rest of the time was my own. I tell my flock that one of the reasons I love to go to Kerala is for these times; times in which I have no responsibilities whether family or church. These are the times when I walk with God and talk with God, my *In the Garden* times, if you know the message of the hymn with the same title. I have already share with you my *Jesus and me* times coming to India, but I had plenty of Jesus and me times in India, my in the cool of the day!

By Wednesday night, the bulk of the teaching and preaching were over. Thursday would see a change of schedule and a lessening of activities. I had now been in India six days. I had discovered the best way to get a good night's rest was to shower before bed, another way to cool down. The cool of the day in Edayappara in 2016 was between the hours of two and seven in the morning. By Wednesday night, I was resting comfortably and waking refreshed around six. For years I have come awake with these words on my heart, "Oh, Lord my Lord, how excellent is Thy name in all the earth!" When this psalm floats through my thoughts, I begin another day with the Lord. I know that for Adam and Eve their walk with God was probably in the evening, but morning, noon, or night it makes no different for God is ready to fellowship at any time. I believe John wrote of this cool of the day relationship when he said in his first epistle, "... and truly our fellowship is with the Father, and with His Son Jesus Christ." (I John 1:3) We don't know what Adam and Eve and God talked about. We don't know in what form God revealed Himself, but we do know that this was a daily occurrence.

For me, one of the great things that came out of a-cool-of-the-day encounter is the messages the Good Lord gives to me. Between Monday and Friday, I was inspired to put together twelve sermons:

1. What Jesus Did For Me When He Came To Bethlehem—Galatians 4:4?
    a. How many fathers have given their sons for me? John 3:16
    b. How many gods have poured out their hearts for me? John 12:7
    c. How many lords have abandoned their homes for me? John 3:13
    d. How many kings have given up their thrones for me? Matthew 2:1
    e. How many great men have become little men for me? Mark 10:42-45
    f. How many wealthy people have become poor for me? II Corinthians 8:9
    g. How many lambs have given their life's blood for me? I Peter 1:19
2. The Model Servant—Genesis 24:2
    a. A servant does not go unsent. Genesis 24:9
    b. A servant goes where he is sent. Genesis 24:4, 10
    c. A servant does nothing else than what he is told. Genesis 24:11
    d. A servant is prayerful and thankful. Genesis 24:12-14
    e. A servant is wise in winning. Genesis 24:17-18, 21
    f. A servant speaks not of himself but of his master. Genesis

24:22, 34-36
- g. A servant presents a true message and requires an answer. Genesis 24:49

3. What the Bible Means To Me—II Timothy 3:16
    a. Its contents II Peter 1:21
    b. Its concepts Matthew 5:17-18
    c. Its commands Revelation 1:3
    d. Its containers Psalm 119:105
    e. Its conflicts Ephesians 6:17
    f. Its Christ John 14:3
    g. Its course-Joshua 1:8

4. The Last Word Numbers 23:10
    a. Jacob's last words Hebrews 11:21
    b. Joseph's last words Hebrews 11:22
    c. Moses' last words Deuteronomy 33
    d. David's last words I Kings 2:1
    e. Zechariah's last words II Chronicles 24:20-22
    f. Stephen's last word Acts 7:60
    g. John's last words Revelation 22:20-21
    h. Paul's last words II Timothy 4:6-7
    i. John the Baptist's last words John 3:30
    j. Jesus' last words John 19:30

5. What Does The Lord Require Of Us? Deuteronomy 10:12-13
    a. To fear
    b. To walk
    c. To love
    d. To serve
    e. To keep

6. Learning to Lose Matthew 16:25
    a. John the Baptist was a loser. He lost his head. John 3:30
    b. Paul the Apostle was a loser. He lost everything. Philippians 3:7-8
    c. Jesus the Christ was a loser. He lost His life. Philippians 2:8

7. God's Storehouses Job 38:22
    a. Oil-II Kings 4:1-7
    b. Manna-Exodus 16
    c. Wine-John 2:1-11
    d. Loaves and fishes-John 6:9
    e. Fish-Luke 5:5-7 and John 21:6, 11
8. What Time Is It? -Psalm 119:126
    a. What time is it? It is time for God's Word to reign supreme-Psalm 119:126
    b. What time is it? It is time we seek the Lord again-Hosea 10:12
    c. What time is it? It is time for self-judgment in the church-I Peter 4:17
    d. What time is it? It is time to wake up and not sleep-Romans 13:11-4
    e. What time is it? It is time to be serious for the time is short-I Corinthians 7:29
9. Star-Breathing God-Psalm 33:6
    a. The singing stars-Job 38:7
    b. The size of stars-I Corinthians 15:41
    c. The sign in the stars-Psalm 147:4
10. Afluenza: The Weight of Wealth-Deuteronomy 8:17-18
    a. The source of wealth-Deuteronomy 8:17-18
    b. The seduction of wealth-I Timothy 6:9-10
    c. The service of wealth-I Timothy 6:17-19
11. Excuses-Luke 14:18
    a. It has always been that way-Ecclesiastes 1:9
    b. It is here to stay-I Corinthian 7:31
    c. It is just as bad elsewhere-Titus 1:15
    d. It could be worse-II Timothy 3:13
    e. It can't be changed-II Timothy 2:26
12. The Creed of Caesarea-Matthew 16:13-28
    a. Confession-Matthew 16:13-16
    b. Christ-Matthew 16:16

    c. Church-Matthew 16:17-18
    d. Cross-Matthew 16:21-26
    e. Coming-Matthew 16:27-28

I hope these outlines will provoke you into a bit of Biblical cooling in the Word. Some of these messages I would share in India and the rest I would take home to share with my flock in Ellsworth. That is another thing I have learned in the cool of the day. What happens there, what is heard there, what is learned there is not to stay there, but it is to be shared. I have thought if Adam and Eve had shared more about what they learned in the cool of the day, and that being God's warning about the tree of the knowledge of good and evil (Genesis 2:17), they might have been together on the day of Satan's great temptation and supported each other to say NO! Instead they lost their cool rendezvous.

It was also during those seasons in the cool of the day that I spent supplicating and interceding for my loved ones back home. My dear wife's broken tooth and her trip to California was on my mind. Interestingly, when Coleen got to California our grandson cut his first two teeth! Our church family and their needs are always on my mind as well. Just because a pastor is away doesn't mean he can't pray in the cool of the day for his family and flock. It would be through these refreshing temperatures and cool breezes that I would have my most precious, intimate moments with my Lord and Saviour. Whether in Edayappara or Ellsworth, there are still times for refreshing, if we will only take advantage of them. Granted, even I have found these times easier to find in India than America because in America there are so many more distractions. Without television, Internet, cellphone, pastoral responsibilities, and husband responsibilities, I am rarely disturbed in India; in America I am rarely, not disturbed!

14

When Faith Confronts Abortion

My seventh day in India started out with two great naps. I called them naps because a good night's sleep was hard to come by given the extreme heat and humidity, even when the sun went down! I was awake by 5:30 AM on that Thursday morning, but I lay in bed praying and thinking of my last two sessions at the KBBC Bible Conference. I was also contemplating asking Shibu if he would allow me to hire Jacob John, the local auto (taxi) driver, for an excursion to see if I could find the elephants that were rumored to be at the Kangazha Temple. I heard there were as many as five, a rare number to be together. I had the afternoon off with only the graduate supper at the Simons planned for that evening. I also wanted to travel over to see my good friend Johnson Matthews at the Agape Mission. I knew that Shibu was under the weather. He had been taken to the hospital the evening before to get some IV fluids. He hadn't felt well for two days, and the graduate supper was in jeopardy. I was praying about our mission's trip on Monday to the Punjab. I knew it was in God's hands so I cast my cares (I Peter 5:7) and prayed and planned on finishing my first week in India.

I went down for breakfast about eight to discover Shibu was still not feeling better. His stomach had bothered him all night, and Julie was thinking about taking him back to the local clinic. During breakfast Julie and I had a chance to talk and, to my surprise, I heard two stories about the Simon children I had never heard before. Remember, I had been friends with the Simons for thirteen years now. I had been to their home for four extended stays, and they had been to my home in Maine once, and Coleen and I had visited with them in Pennsylvania once. It wasn't that we knew little of them, but there are always pieces of anyone's history we sometimes miss. So it was nice to add a few more pieces to the Simon puzzle that morning around the breakfast table with Julie.

The first surprise was to discover that Joshua had been born on my grandson's birthday, August 18, or should I say my grandson Judah had been born on Joshua's birthday! Julie had gotten pregnant with Joshua while Shibu was studying the Bible in the States. It was during the early pregnancy tests the doctor informed the Simons their baby had Downs Syndrome. They encouraged Julie and Shibu to abort the child. Despite being pressured by the medical profession, this young couple decided to resist all attempts of persuasion towards an abortion. I never had to face that challenge with our children, but Julie talked about the constant suggestion because she was in the medical profession. Julie was a cardiologist's nurse in their days in Dallas, Texas. Throughout the pregnancy, she was hounded and harassed by colleagues and doctors trying to persuade her that an abortion was far better than a Downs Syndrome baby. But their faith stood firm against the onslaught trusting that Downs Syndrome or not they would love the baby the Good Lord was giving them. When Joshua was born, he was a healthy normal child in every way. The young man he is becoming flies in the face of those who think they know better than God with all their fancy instruments and tests. If Joshua's story wasn't amazing enough, Julie went on to tell me about her second pregnancy.

(Postscript: Joshua is now in his first year at Word of Life Institute in New York studying to serve his Lord in whatever ministry He would call him into-isn't the Lord good?)

A few years after Joshua's birth Julie found she was pregnant again. They were still in the States as Shibu finished up his Master's degree at Dallas Theological Seminary. Once again, as the early tests were being run on the fetus, the technicians discovered what they thought was a fatal birth defect in the baby's heart. After doing a series of tests, they concluded that Abigail had just a three-chambered heart. If she survived in the womb, she would not survive long outside the womb. Once again it was the medical professional's opinion that Abigail ought to be aborted. Thinking they had passed the test the first time, how many are required to pass the test twice? Again the weeks and months passed with everybody trying to convince Shibu and Julie that she needed an abortion. They had been lucky the first time, but the evidence was clear? Yet for a second straight nine-month period, my two dear friends resisted all arguments, suggestions, debates and discussions on the decision and put their faith and hope in their God. Julie didn't suggest that it was a walk in the park, but she told me they never once thought of aborting Abigail, three-chambered heart or not. When Abigail was born she was a healthy, normal little girl. The doctors could find no trouble at all with her heart. Today she is a lovely young lady and, like her brother, without any physical defects at all. For a second time the so-called professionals were wrong. It caused me to think how many perfectly healthy children may have been aborted over the years based on the "what-ifs" of medicine. I am not talking about those who abort their children simply because they don't want them, or hadn't planned on them, or just considered them an inconvenience. I am talking about the babies that were diagnosed with a birth defect, and the experts thought they were not worthy of life.

I have, for most of my life, had a ministry or two with the disabled. There are those who through some birth defect have been a burden for someone for most of their lives, if not all their lives. To this day, one of my best ministries is at Birchwood Living Center, a home for the chronically handicapped. Some of the residents at this home can't speak, have barely aged mentally, can't walk, and are seemingly without understanding at all. It has been during my nearly thirty years in this home that I have come to understand through the staff and eventually through the scriptures the meaning of why. God told Moses this, "Who hath made man's mouth or who maketh the dumb, or deaf, or seeing, or the blind? HAVE NOT I THE LORD?" (Exodus 4:11) I am glad that my dear Indian children, Joshua and Abigail, were born healthy, but even if they had not they would have still been the children of God. Is there more work and more caring for such children? Certainly, but what I have found in my years in this field is the fact there are people on this planet that are willing to give that extra care, that extra work, that extra love. I believe Julie and Shibu could have and would have if called on to do so.

I know our nation has been debating this issue for most of my life and that millions of babies around the world, including India, have been aborted. I also know that no argument by me will ever change the minds of those who describe this issue of abortion as women's rights. Isn't that a nicer sounding phrase than the murder of the unborn? What I want to emphasize in this chapter is the simple fact that Biblically speaking the answer to this debate is very clear. God is very clear when life starts and that is at conception (Psalm 51:5). God knows in the womb what we will be (Jeremiah 1:5) and, despite the latest technology, the improved instruments, and the fancy tests, God is still the only one that can really know what is in the womb. Oh, has man gotten better? Surely he has for I saw my grandson in the womb of my daughter long before he was born, and his face and features were pretty clear. But there is one aspect mankind hasn't yet accepted. God gives a child, as God wants that child to be. Many today don't like God's choices, but it is God's choice. "Lo, children are a heritage of the Lord: and the fruit of the womb is His reward." (Psalm 127:3) Whether Joshua or Judah, whether Texas or California, whether Indian parents or American/Mexican parents, whether born on the same date, both born boys, and both born in faith. Next time there is a question, choose faith over abortion! Trust God!

15

Four 50-Year-Old Male Elephants

Before I left breakfast and headed for the final two sessions of the KBBC Bible Conference, I got permission from Shibu for an afternoon adventure. Shibu promised he would call Jacob John for an auto ride to see the temple elephants in Kangazha and Johnson Matthews for a ride to see the completion of his new orphanage/church building in Kumpanthanam. Little did I know what the Good Lord had in store for me!

I finished the Bible Conference with two messages about persecution a little after noon. The theme had been an added thought after hearing the graduates' testimonies over the last two afternoons. India is becoming a very hostile land again, especially against Christianity. I did not know the opposition these young people would be facing as they returned to their home states, so I decided to encourage them by talking about the songs of the psalmists, like Ethan in Psalm 89. My prayer is they will trust in the Word of God when the persecution gets personal and physical. There are those in the Indian government that claimed after the 2008 persecution it would never get physical again, but I am not so sure and neither are my Indian Christian friends. But the Christian Church in India is strong and even more committed to the cause of Christ. I have no doubt when the fires of persecution are lit the Church will endure and expand just like it has in past persecutions.

As I left the chapel for the courtyard below, the students and staff wanted to talk more about elephants than a future persecution. It seems that an annual Hindu festival was going on in Kangazha Temple about four miles from the campus. The conversation revolved around the news that huge bull elephants had been trucked in from other temples to add to the festivities. I told them I was heading out in a couple of hours to check out the rumors, but I hoped what they were saying was true. One professor was sure I would see five, but five or any male Indian elephants would be a treat for me. Over my years in India, I had, to that point, seen forty-three elephants. I had already seen two elephants on this trip: one big male on the back of a truck on the way from Kochi to Edayappara during my trip from the airport on my first day and one on the back of a truck as Shibu and I drove to Venmony on my first Sunday in Kerala. I only got a glimpse, but I wondered now if perhaps the big male elephant was heading for the Kangazha Temple. Over my ten-year experience with Indian elephants, most of them had been female. I have enjoyed every encounter, especially the two baby elephants I got to see and touch in 2007. However, I love the bulls the best. I think I just like the look of the white, ivory tusks against their thick, rough, grayish hide. I have sat on the back of two elephants, both female, and rough is a good adjective! The elephant is still the biggest living land mammal in the world. I like their size, and the males have the size over the female. I was hoping that all the published news reports were correct. Little did I know!

One of the students I walked with to the dining hall was a young man from the Punjab. A. J. John was the son of Pastor V. J. John from the capital of the Punjab. He taught me how to pronounce Chandigarh, the name of the capital, and he hoped we might be able to get together when I traveled there. Unfortunately, we didn't connect. Despite my desire to visit the Punjab, my focus that day was on the possibility of seeing five bull elephants. I returned to Shibu's for a short nap and, by the middle of the afternoon Shibu, who was feeling better, drove me to the Kangazha Church to meet with my bodyguards for the afternoon. Shibu knows my fascination with the Indian elephant and my total lack of fear! He wanted to make sure I would come back in one piece because if I didn't he would never hear the end of it from my wife. To my surprise, there were four men waiting for me by Jacob John's four-wheel auto: Lalu, one of the pastors, and two young men from the Kangazha Church. We all piled into the hot-yellow colored auto and headed out of town.

What I first learned about this new driving machine was just how under-powered it really was. I was told it still had the same gasoline engine as the old three-wheeled autos. On the straight and smooth it performed nicely, but you take it up a slight grade in the road and you can feel the strain on the engine. A couple of times on our way to the temple I thought we might have to get out and push. Five grown men were just too much for the little auto that could! The trip took us about ten minutes as we weaved around animals, people, and other vehicles along the rural road to the Kangazha Temple. I had traveled that same road scored of times, but I couldn't remember a more exciting ride for what I thought I might see when we got to our determined destination.

As we passed the small pond just before the temple complex, my eye began to search the wooded area by the pond. I had seen elephants there in years passed, and I knew that was where they would likely be to beat the hot sun and rising temperatures on this typical, tropical Kerala afternoon. I was not disappointed. Between the rubber trees were three massive bulls. Not five, but three, but I was not disappointed. Each elephant was by far the biggest I had seen to date. Each was chained to a tree having an afternoon snack of banana leaves, a favorite I am told. Jacob John stopped the auto by the highway beside the grove of trees, and I immediately headed for the first elephant. I was quickly cut off at the pass by Lalu who warned me of the danger. Because of previous encounters, I wanted to go up to the elephants and touch them, but my four bodyguards curbed my impulses. I had to be content with viewing them from about twenty-five feet. They did allow me to walk around the grove and get pictures of these marvelous creatures. Each had a set of ivory tusks that had been cut off a bit so they were more flat than pointed. The big bull in the back had one tusk that was partially broken off. I got my picture with one of the handlers, an old man who had cared for his elephant for all of his life, not an uncommon thing. It was through Lalu's conversation with him that I learned all three elephants were at least fifty-years-old. Up until this time, the oldest elephant I had seen was only thirty-seven years old. She was a female elephant in a rescue sanctuary I saw in 2007.

For the next half hour, I wandered around the three bulls taking pictures and getting my photograph taken with them. Each time I tried to get a bit closer, I was discouraged. I know Indians are terrified of elephants and I know why, but it was frustrating for me to be so close to one of God's greatest creations and not be able to touch one. I felt I was safe because each bull was chained and trained, but I respected my guardians' wishes and kept my distance. I had to be content just being in their presence and watching their remarkable trunks picking up their lunch and depositing it in their huge mouths. I observed their massive feet as they chafed against the restraints desiring to be free. Of all the elephants I have seen in India, only one of them has been a wild elephant. Most have been working elephants, or temple elephants, or zoo elephants. As I write this chapter, the Barnum and Bailey Circus is using their elephants in a last show. The animal rights people have finally gotten their desire. What might be true in the United States will never be true in India! As we drove back to the college, I was thrilled to think I had seen three massive bulls together, despite their captivity. Within a mile of the three males, we came across a fourth bull, but unlike his brothers, he was walking freely in the middle of the road decked out in his finest religious garb leading a parade of priests. But, where was this male elephant going?

16

An Elephant Blesses a Home

I couldn't believe my eyes! I had seen pictures of Indian bull elephants parading around at festival time, but up to forty-seventh encounters, I had only seen undressed elephants, working elephants with little more than a rope around their necks. I quickly asked Jacob John to pull the auto beside the road, and, to my surprise, he agreed. I got out and started taking pictures and even had my picture taken with the temple elephant walking beside me. If anything, this bull was bigger than his brothers in the grove! Or did he look that much larger because of the huge shield on the top of his head and the massive breastplate that covered his face and most of his trunk? There was a priest on his back and a set of Hindu priests walking around him. Some were playing flutes, while others were beating drums, and still others were marching in step with the elephant's wide stride carrying flowers. Where were they going? What were they doing?

After the procession passed us, we got back in the auto and drove ahead to get another glimpse of this elephant and his attendants. We eventually stopped where a side lane made a street into a residential area just outside of town. I was spellbound as I watched the elephant take a right turn down the street. It was then I began to beg my companions to let me follow the procession to see where they were going. Once again, to my surprise, they agreed! Were they interested in knowing for themselves what was happening? I think they knew, but they were willing to allow the American to see for himself. But, how close would they allow the inquisitive American to get?

The slight downhill lane passed a couple of homes set behind high walls. I immediately recognized that we were in the nicer side of town. Each home had an ornate gate that opened onto a paved courtyard. As I reached the bottom of the small hill, I watched as the temple elephant walked up a slight incline, through an open iron gate, and stopped in the middle of a patio area surrounded by many flowers and flowering shrubs. The area seemed small compared to the massive bull with all his paraphernalia. I watched as the elephant knelt down, and the priest got off his high back taking the golden, ornate shield with him. I would estimate the bull stood nine to ten feet high. It was then I lost sight of the priest, for my attention was strictly on what the elephant would do next. Within a few minutes, the elephant turned around and faced the small crowd that had gathered outside the gated area. He stood there for a few more minutes before his handler touched his legs, and the massive bull, I would estimate he weighed nearly three tons, walked out of the courtyard and headed down the street for a few feet before making a 180 degree turn. Now this magnificent creature was standing and staring straight at me, just feet away!

As I surveyed the impressive animal, his long trunk that hung all the way to the street first amazed me. It must have been six feet long! Then I noticed the fancy breastplate hanging in front of his face. It was wide at the top and narrower at the bottom. It had a series of circle-shaped rises all over the gold-colored face with different colored tassels all the way around it. Because of its covering, you couldn't see the large bump that is characteristic in the foreheads of large bulls, but I knew he must have one after seeing his brother up close in the grove by the Kangazha Temple. I also noticed that three of his four huge feet had chains around them, but they were not attached to anything. I assumed they would be used to chain him up at night. His handler was standing by him, but the elephant seemed to sense that he was to stand and wait for the ceremony to end. It was then I had a wonderful idea, but would my friends allow me to do it?

I turned to Lalu and asked him if he would talk to the elephant handler and ask him if I could go up to the bull and touch him. To my shock he agreed to ask, and to my surprise the elephant handler motioned me to come forward. Without hesitation I strolled boldly towards the massive creature standing at least a yard taller than me. As I approached, the elephant swung his head away from me. They had brought some banana leaves for him to eat, and another man had just brought a couple of melons they would feed him later. At first, I just stood beside the monster, but within a few minutes I was reaching my hand out to him. He responded by swinging his massive head back towards me. I grab his right tusk with my left hand and the ivory felt slippery on the palm of my hand. I took my right hand and placed it on the side of the elephant's face just below his huge right eye. The large pupil seemed to focus on my face. I knew most of the people around me watching thought I must be worshipping the elephant as a god. But, I was having an intimate moment of worship with the God of the elephant.

Our time together lasted about ten minutes. It was another thrilling experience with India's supreme creature. I would see two more elephants before my travels in India were over: a good-sized female begging at a roadside stand as we passed through a small village in Tamil Nadu and another female walking beside the highway carrying a trunk full of branches as we traveled to Kochi to catch our flight to Delhi. I didn't know if I will ever see my fiftieth Indian elephant in India, but I hope I will. In an old logbook, I have recorded each of my elephant encounters with the date, the place, and the kind of elephant. Beside the page, I have pasted a few of my favorite pictures of these elephants. I have also compiled what I call *My Elephant Tales* book, a collection of all the photographs I have taken of my elephant encounters as well as some favorite postcards of elephants I have bought in my India trips. If I find a postcard that reminds me of one of my Indian elephant experiences, I buy it for the memory. Of the three birthdays I have spent in India (#56, #59, and #65), I have seen an elephant on two of the three. What a birthday gift! I have now been able to witness just about every age, every gender, and every size of elephant. For those that might be wondering on the age of this elephant, the handler told Lalu he was also in the 50-year-old range. I learned that this was not unusual for an Indian elephant whose life expectancy was between forty and sixty years of age—with a few living even longer!

As I headed up to the top of the hill where Jacob John's auto was parked, I must admit I did glance back a couple of times to look at the god of the Kangazha Temple. I learned from the boys that this elephant had come to the home on the lane to bless it. While I was focused on the bull, the priest was sprinkling holy water, scattering fresh flowers, and chanting blessings for a year of success and security for the inhabitants of the house. As the family members of that home were receiving a blessing from the priest, I was receiving a blessing from my Lord and Saviour Jesus Christ. I believe that nothing happens by circumstance or happenstance, so my encounter with the ceremonial-laden, decoratively covered elephant was a blessing for me. Can't you just imagine when the Mighty Creator spoke this creature into existence? This heavy-bodied animal with large, floppy ears, four thick round legs with a head to match and a nose that could be used as a hand or an arm, a nose for feeding and a trunk for drinking and spraying, a tail long and thin with a tuft of hair on the end, with two overgrown front teeth called tusks and nearly hairless hide? Not totally hairless, though. I remember my second ride on an elephant was bareback, and the short rough hairs were actually quite uncomfortable to sit on! What was in the mind of Adam when God first brought this creature to him, and he called it elephant? (Genesis 2:20)

17

The Tale Continues
Open Doors

After several hours visiting the local male elephants, a thrill beyond imagination, I was off to visit my dear friend Johnson Matthews and the Agape Mission about seven miles from Edayappara. I wanted to see the progress made on his new combined church building and orphanage, to visit with his dear wife Lynda, and to see how the boys had grown. In Kerala now, you either have a boys' orphanage or a girls' orphanage. You can't have both. This would be my third visit in five trips. Johnson and Lynda have always run a boys' orphanage since I knew them.

Johnson picked me up at the Simon house on that Thursday afternoon. On our way we passed the Kangazha Temple, and, sure enough, I got another glimpse of two of the elephants, but this time they were bathing beside the road. Their handlers had a huge hose and were washing them using water being pumped from an old quarry that had filled with water during the rainy season. I asked Johnson to stop so I could get a few more photographs of my newest Kangazha friends. The rest of the way to Johnson's mission I told him of my experience with the temple elephant blessing the home. But as we neared his place of ministry, our conversation switched to a more serious subject—reaching the unreached people groups of mountainous Kerala with the Gospel of Jesus Christ!

When I visited Johnson Matthews in 2012, we had a wonderful talk about his desire to expand his work. Johnson was already very active in local evangelism and jail ministries in addition to the church plant and the orphanage. He wanted to minister to the unreached people groups like the Mannan and Oorari people of the mountains of Kerala, residents of the wooded hills and deep forested valleys of eastern Kerala State less than 60 miles away from his house. I had traveled into those regions three times in my visits to experience the spectacular scenery and wonderful wildlife, but I never realized I was that close to primitive tribes still living in the Stone Age, superstitious and unreached with the Gospel. I wanted to hear how the work was progressing or if it even got started. Johnson had started a Bible Institute with some local residents in the areas of concern, training them and teaching them how to evangelize, but in 2012 he wanted to get more involved in actually reaching out himself.

After a quick walk around the new facility (almost completed), a visit with the boys on top of the roof of the new building where some finishing touches were being completed on a new section of roof covering the new kitchen area, and a tour of the new garden plot created to help produce food for feeding the orphans, we had a chance to talk about unreached people groups and the open doors that were developing among three groups: the Mannan (about 5000 in number), the Malapandaram (about 3000 in number), and the Oorari people (about 5000 in number). My love of this ministry started in 1972 when I had a wonderful experience ministering among a similar group of Aboriginal people in the Western Desert of Australia. It was what motivated our support in 1997 when we, as a church, started sponsoring a similar outreach program with the IGBC and Associated Missions in the hill country of central Orissa State. The more we talked, the more flashbacks I had of my past and the open doors the Lord had created for me. Johnson was experiencing the challenge of John to the church at Philadelphia when he wrote, "I know thy works: behold, I have set before thee an open door, and no man can shut it . . ." (Revelation 3:8) Again I recalled this piece of my personal story:

"Once I set my face toward the pastorate, I can see clearly the tale the Lord had written for my life. How wonderfully God has kept His open door promise in my own experience. I have never failed to find an open door to share the Gospel of Jesus Christ whether in a local church setting or the twenty nursing home ministries I have had in nearly fifty years (1970-2020). Then there are the fifty-one Christian camps I have had the honor to share the Gospel with young people. I am thinking through my life, have I ever had one closed door? Then there have been the open doors in India! Once I gave my life in service for Jesus, I realized that He had given me something I love to do. I am not like the little boy who said, "This medicine must be good for me, it tastes so bad!" The ministry for me hasn't been bad tasting medicine. It has been a sweet savor in my mouth every day, and it is getting sweeter and sweeter as the days go by. Oh, I like most have tried a few doors that remained shut to me, but as one learns to lean on Him and realize He will only take you to doors you can open then it becomes easier as the days go by. It is a wonderful experience as you watch the Lord go before and what is so hard in our strength is so easy in His. What we cannot accomplish on our own is so easily accomplished by Him through us. As my early pastorates faded in the rear-view mirror (and that is a proper analogy because sometimes now I even question the five years in Pembroke, the eight years in Westfield, and the five years in Eastport, it seems that Ellsworth has been my whole life), I could see the passing of time as God's open doors, one after another, with the open doors eventually closing behind me. I see now how the Lord protected me from doing a good thing in a bad way. I have watched as many pastors have turned to the modern ministry of program, propaganda, and paraphernalia. Many have switched to entertainment over evangelism, but God has kept those doors closed for me. I still recall the rut I was in in 2005. I was nearing my thirty-second year in the pastorate and fifteenth year at Emmanuel, twice as long as any other pastorate. I was getting bored, dull, and then the Lord opened a way for me to go to India for forty days. It was for me like Moses' forty days on the Mount. I came back to Emmanuel a new man, a different pastor. Ask anyone of my parishioners! I came back with a new outlook, a new vision, a new attitude, and a new open door. My Bible study took on a new focus. My preaching took on a new dimension. My ministry took on a new urgency, and my life was as if I had just started into a new pastorate. I was renewed, restored, rejuvenated, recalled, and as the old preacher once said, "I had not resigned, but re-signed!" It was because of my new friends in India (like Johnson Matthews, my first translator in 2006) and their enthusiastic, zealous, passion for the cause of Christ that I experienced how ministry, prayer, and preaching ought to be again. It is delightful to experience that no matter where you go—the country of Canada next door or the subcontinent of India thousands of miles away. There are always some who gather to hear about the old-fashioned way in an old-fashioned way! It is refreshing to know that in some places on this planet people are gathering in numbers to hear the Word of God preached and taught. It is refreshing to know that in some places on this earth there are young people desiring to serve the Lord no matter the cost. It is refreshing to know the old-time religion is still alive and well pressing on in that old-fashioned way. All I needed in 2005 was a 2006 trip to Kerala and an open door back to the old-fashioned way. Mrs. C. D. Martin put it best when she wrote, 'They call me old-fashioned because I believe that the Bible is God's holy Word, that Jesus, who lived among men long ago, is divine and the Christ of God. Old-fashioned, because I believe and accept only what has been spoken from heaven; old-fashioned because at the cross I was saved, at the cross-had my sins forgiven. Old-fashioned, because I am bound to do right, to walk in the straight narrow way; because I have given my whole life to God, old-fashioned, because I pray. Old-fashioned, because I am looking above to Jesus, my glorified Lord; because I believe He is coming again, fulfilling His holy Word. My sin was old-fashioned, my guilt was old-fashioned, God's love was old-fashioned, I know; and the way I was saved was the old-fashioned way, through the blood that makes whiter than snow." That was the first open door I walked through in 1958 and every door since has been a glorious trip through the house of my Lord and Saviour."

I was so excited to be in the presence of another man that couldn't wait to walk through a door back in time to reach a people group with the Gospel and to see, in turn, these people walk through the redemptive door of salvation. I returned two hours later rejoicing in the Lord and determined to financially help my friend walk through God's open door, which I have ever since!

18

A Night at the Simons

I got back to Shibu's house just in time to help entertain the twenty graduates the Simons' had invited for supper and a final time of fellowship before graduation the next day. I sat on the front porch greeting graduates as their brown, smiling faces emerged from the darkness. My eight students from 2012 were the most familiar, but the newer graduates like David, the top student of the class, was now recognizable. It was a joyous group as they gathered in the living room, the porch, and the dining area knowing this night was the cumulating of four or six years of their lives. This was the celebratory supper that put the cheery on the top of the sundae. The next day they would eat the cake!

In the past, the night before graduation had been set aside to entertain the staff of KBBC and to thank them for a year of dedication and hard work. I had been honored to attend two of these functions, but this was my first graduation party. As I watched and listened to the groups of twos and threes chattering, I was reminded of my input in their lives and the final honor of speaking to them at their final commencement service. One of the boys had brought along his guitar, and they began to sing praise songs while Julie, Abigail, Joshua, and Shibu got the meal ready. It would be a typical Kerala meal with rice, the flat bread, and a variety of curries to put on top. Shibu called for a prayer, and the meal began. I helped serve making sure everybody had enough water as I walked among the happy eaters filling their glasses. Joshua and Abigail went around after each graduate had filled their plates with ample piles of rice topped with some very spicy, hot curries.

I still marvel just how much an Indian eats. Young or old, the plates are full and seconds are commonplace. Joshua and Abigail kept the plates full until the hand went up signaling enough. Dessert was a series of sweet cakes bought from a local vendor.

After finishing their meal and washing their hands, the graduates gathered in the foyer for an informal meeting. Shibu shared a few words about the goal the college had when a new student came, and he wanted the group to share their experiences at KBBC. Each graduate was given some time to share what their college years meant to them and how KBBC had impacted their lives. I sat next to Shibu as I listened to the testimonies and the excitement of twenty young witnesses. As I have learned over the years, witnesses (Acts 1:8) can be a noun and a verb—we are to be witnesses! By our lives and by our lips we are to show the world Christ, and I am confident that the Lord has twenty wonderful, young soldiers to do just that into the far corners of India.

It was just after nine that the graduates left the Simon house, the girls returning to the orphanage where they stay and the boys to the residential hall where they stay. I climbed the stairs to my room and settled in for a very uncomfortable night struggling to find rest. It wasn't because of my responsibility at graduation, but the heat! If anything the temperature and the humidity had only increased in the week I had been in India. It was the worst I had ever experienced, or at least that is how I felt that night. Because sleep eluded me, I had a chance to meditate and ponder a bit. These were my thoughts on a night at the Simons, and this was the question. Why do I keep desiring to go back to India?

I do not desire to go back to India because of the cuisine! The food in India has never been appealing to me. I know that Indian food is becoming the rage all over the world. We even have a new Indian restaurant in our little coastal city of Ellsworth to cater to all the tourists that pass through our town heading for the national park of Acadia. The locals have developed a taste for spicy food. I meet people all the time who find out I have been to India, and their first remark is about how I must like the food. I don't!

I do not desire to go back to India because of the climate! I am a cold or cool weather kind of guy. My roots in the northern hemisphere of northern Maine created that liking. If the temperature never got above 70 for the rest of my life, I would be very content. When I go to India I endure the heat. I endure the humidity, and I endure the hot temperature. All three were at extreme levels on this trip. Most desire hot over cold, but I think I can say I have never been really cold in India!

I do not desire to go back to India because of the culture! I am no expert nor have I experienced many cultures around the world, but I have a few like the arrogant Parisians, the snobbish Israelis, the proud Scots, the hospitable Palestinians, the stoic Brits, the friendly Canadians, and the independent Australians. In India I have found diversity depending on where I have traveled. I love my Christian friends, and they have been wonderful to me, but sometimes their ways of doing things still puzzles me.

I do not desire to go back to India because of the country! Granted, the nation of India is making great strides in the world, but the country of India that I have gotten to see is a third world country at best. The gap between the rich and the poor is as wide as the distance from Jupiter to Mars. It is a nation of trash, of dirty, abandoned children, and where animals have more rights than people. Its current government is anti-Christian, and the only thing that is keeping it from a national persecution on Christendom is the black eye it would bring to its economy because, like the rest of the world, the god of gold—and how they love their gold in India—is now even more important than any of the Hindu gods!

I do not desire to go back to India because of the church! You might be surprised by this one, but as I pondered late into the night and early into the morning as sleep escaped me in the heat, the Church of India is in some respect better off than the Church of America. Before I would return to the United States, I would have visited my sixty-third local assembly. I was humbled by each one: their pastor, their people, and their places, from simple straw-roof rooms to larger concrete sanctuaries, but mostly the homes of the people themselves. The people have been hospitable and kind, but I go back not for them either!

After much thought, and not the first time my mind has wondered on this topic, I came to the ultimate conclusion of why I still desire to go back to India, as is still my desire. It is in India that I have had the closest encounters with the Christ. I never realized it at first because I was caught up in the excitement of the spiritual adventure that comes from leaving your comfort zone and venturing out into a different place. Yes, even a dangerous place. It took me a few trips before I realized what a sense of freedom comes with just Jesus and me, with no responsibilities but ministry responsibilities like preaching and teaching and praying, a freedom between such times to meditate and ponder without the modern distractions that I face in America. I do not come to this place by loving the food, the weather, the culture, the country, or even the Church or the Christians. Is not that why Jesus kept asking Peter, "Lovest thou Me more than these?" (John 21:15-17) Until our desire is to love Him more, to know Him better, to spend more time with Him, any other desire will be baseless at best. Until our desire gets back to the basic desire and that being time with Christ, an intimate relationship with Jesus, until He becomes the beginning and the ending and the middle, how can we really go? Whether on the homefront or the foreign field it matters not. I struggle more in America than I do in India because of added distractions, but whether here or there it should matter not—Christ first!

19

Graduation Address

Between gaps of meditation, I was able to get a bit of sleep on graduation eve. If the heat was that intense during the dark hours what would the daylight hours be like, especially in a cap and gown in the out-of-doors with no air conditioner in sight? During our breakfast of pancakes and honey, Shibu prepared me for after graduation and the ten-day marathon that would begin when we left for my second graduation address in two days. A third would follow the next morning, but that is for another chapter and another time.

Graduation rehearsal took place between 11:00 and 12:00, a foretaste of the furnace we had stepped into for graduation 2016. The graduation was to take place under a metal canopy that was only heating up with each passing hour. Though the direct sun was off us, the heat building up under the canopy was like an oven being heated seven times hotter than ever before—Daniel 3:19. By 3:00, we were decked out in our academic finery having our pictures taken in Annamma's front yard. It was a joy to see the graduates' faces and to proudly stand beside each of them for a keepsake photograph. By 4:00, we had gathered in the courtyard at the college to line up with the professors and the graduates that would march that day. The procession under the afternoon sun only added to the sweating and dripping as the line wound its way up the Main Street of Edayappara that runs in front of the college, Shagu's house, the Kangazha Church, Bethany Christian Middle School, and Mercy Christian Home. We took a right turn into the courtyard of the Kangazha Church were family and friends of the graduates were waiting for us. We stepped through the crowd in unison with the music being played. If not for the color of the skin, the graduation looked and felt much like any American graduation at a small Bible college.

Then came the opening prayer by the Reverend P. C. Mathai, a retired pastor from the IGBC, followed by the congregational hymn "To God be the Glory". Then, Professor Biju Devasia, a wonderful teacher I had met for the first time in 2012, gave another prayer. The Scripture reading was Joshua 1:1-8 led by Professor Shibu Chacko and Romans 13:11-14 led by Professor T. P. Georgekutty. Professor Joji Matthew delivered the official welcome followed by the academic report by Professor Sabu C. Andrews. The national hymn, "Naniyode Njan Sthuthi Padidum", was sung followed by M. David's valedictorian speech. A special song by the college choir was next followed by the presentation of the degrees to the graduates: three diplomas in theology, thirteen bachelors of theology, one master of mission ology, and three masters of divinity. Reverend T. Sackson Simon offered a special prayer of dedication, and the IGBC Kangazha Choir sang a special song. I was next on the official program.

My address came from the graduation verses Shibu had sent me nearly eight months before—"For surely there is an end; and thine expectation shall not be cut off. Hear thou, my son, and be wise, and guide thine heart in the way." (Proverbs 23:18-19) They were great graduation verses because an end was certainly upon them and expectations were before them. Now it was time to "hear thou, my son." I have always seen younger people I have led to the Lord or young people I have mentored as my spiritual sons and daughters. The KBBC kids before me were no exception. One of the graduates, Sophy Paul, was a pastor's daughter. I had been a part of her life for ten years. I first met her in 2006 when I had a service at her Dad's church on my way out of India. In 2007, when I returned with my daughter Marnie, we stopped to visit the Paul family. In 2010, Russ Coffin and I visited the Paul home on one of our first days in India and the year Sophy started her spiritual education at KBBC. In 2012, she was in the Junior Class, and I got to know her even better. It was as if my own daughter was graduating from college.

On that afternoon, my words to the graduates were to be wise. Words I hoped would "guide (their) thine heart in the way" came from Paul's challenge in I Corinthians 14:3: "But he that prophesieth speaketh unto men to edification, and exhortation, and comfort." I would develop these thoughts around the title, "What the World Needs is a Prophet" and the theme of the New Testament ministry of prophesy.

1. The Ministry of Edification—a strengthening ministry—the work of the teacher. People need to be built up in the Lord (Ephesians 4:11-14), and the teacher is one of the gifted agents God has given to the Church to strengthen the saints through instruction by the Word—"teaching them to observe all things . . ." (Matthew 28:20), with a promise that His Word will not return void (Isaiah 55:11). I sent the graduates forth into a ministry of edification, a strengthening service of teaching.

2. The Ministry of Exhortation—a stirring ministry—the work of the evangelist. Though God did gift some to be evangelists (Ephesians 4:11) that doesn't mean that every member of the Body of Christ isn't supposed to be involved in the work of an evangelist (II Timothy 4:5). People need to be challenged with the Gospel. I like to call this a stirring. "And there is none that calleth upon Thy name that stirreth up him to take hold of Thee . . ." (Isaiah 64:7) Such is the nature of man. He will not, on his own, seek God or stir his spirit towards God, as we know from Romans 3:10-12. "As it is written, there is none righteous, no, not one: There is none that understandeth, there is none that seeketh after God. They are all gone out of the way, they are together become unprofitable; there is none that doeth good, no, not one." An exhorter awakens, arouses, and alarms the individual, so that the individual will be stirred to salvation. I sent the graduates forth that day into a ministry of exhortation, a stirring service of evangelism.

3. The Ministry of Encouragement—a soothing ministry—the work of the pastor. Paul uses the word comfort (I Thessalonians 5:14), but for me the best concept of comfort is the soothing ministry of encouragement (Joshua 1:6, 7, 9). There are a lot of troubled people, and sometimes everybody needs to act like a pastor, or a shepherd to anoint a person with the soothing oil (Psalm 23:5) of kindness and comfort. Some words from an old hymn I love go like this—"Jesus the name that charms our fears, and bids our sorrows cease. Tis music to the sinner's ear, tis life and health and peace." I sent the graduates forth that day into a ministry of encouragement, a soothing service of pastoring.

What we often forget is that the word prophet isn't just a foreteller, but a forth-teller as well! What we need are a few more prophets who are willing to go forth and teach, evangelize, and pastor to a world that needs the service of all three. My final challenge to the graduates that hot afternoon was to take up the ministry of strengthening, stirring, and soothing in the village or town they settle in. My prayer was that they would take seriously Paul's instruction of edification, exhortation, and encouragement.

When I finished, the graduation class got up on stage and sang together for the last time. Julie Simon presented a gift to each graduates from the school and family. My wife Coleen who loves to make cards, created a special graduation card for each graduate. This was a KBBC first and a first for my wife. Reverend T. S. Joseph closed in prayer and Reverend K. J. Thomas gave the benediction. And the Lord's gift? A cooling rain!

20

The Rains Came to End Graduation

After a week of terrible heat and suffocating humidity, the heavens opened after the final graduation prayer with a monsoon kind of downpour and with it a cooling and refreshing breeze. Focused on the proceedings, I never noticed the sky darkening. Remember we were under the canopy of the front porch of the Kangazha church, and the congregation was under a roof of corrugated steel. The air grew still and cooler. My first recognition that something had changed was the first clap of thunder, almost an Amen to the ceremony! We were so far under cover we didn't see the first lightning flash. God's sending a late afternoon rain was a proper exclamation point to the wonderful graduation we all had shared. As I watched the rain descend like a waterfall, I was reminded again of my love of rainy days.

I have experienced many rainy days in my life, and I have enjoyed most of them. Despite the rain, God's grace has taken me through every rainy day and brought me safely through each one. I am always amazed at the mellowness of God's goodness in the extreme heat of my life. As the years pass and the accumulating days of my life pile up, I often like to look back on the road I have traveled and the paths I have trod and the guiding hand of God on my life. When I needed rain, rain came at just the right moment. Indians have a unique way of helping groups of people through the rain. Six young men would take a tarp and put it over their heads. A group of people would get under the tarp and the young men and the group would walk together. The tarp would act like a gigantic umbrella! As the guests at the graduation worked their way over to the dining hall for a graduation banquet, I lingered with those who wanted to enjoy the sound of the rain on the canopy, the damp air flowing under the canopy, and the thunder and lightning show happening over the canopy. Besides, we had plenty to share in the fulfillment of the group of twenty that had just graduated.

One by one I traced my rainy days, and I discovered they were as John wrote to the Church at Philadelphia—like ". . . an open door, and no man can shut it . . ." (Revelation 3:8) I can now clearly see each rainy day was for a purpose and part of the plan of God—". . . that all things do work for good . . ." (Romans 8:28), even rainy days. My best rainy days have been fishing, fish bite better in the rain, but like that Kerala rain I was fishing for something else. I can now see God's pattern of hot days and rainy days, a period of extreme stress followed by a seasonal shower of refreshment. I fear I have not always acknowledged His hand (Proverbs 3:5-6), but I believe I have never doubted that He has directed my paths, even the wet ones! For often the wet days are the best days. Chastisement brings with it an understanding of a fault that needs to be corrected. A discipline has resulted in a mistake being forgiven. Rainy days help us reflect on the sunny days by showing the contrast and the carefully scripted plan of God that brings us in and out of the rain. We can't grow cold or careless if we daily see the rain as a plotted and planned part of God's guiding hand. When the clouds appear and the lightning flashes and the thunder echoes through our brains, remember God wants to reveal something to us. It is His way of speaking sometimes (Psalm 19:1-2). On that late Friday afternoon in the courtyard of the Kangazha Church, I was listening.

So what was God saying? As I watched the crowd slowly drift over to the dining hall, I lingered longer because I knew there wouldn't be much there for me to eat. Besides I was feasting on a meat that few see. Jesus feasted on similar meat at Jacob's well when He said to His disciples: "I have meat to eat that ye know not of." (John 4:32) My meal of meat was filled with spareribs of joy, a couple of steaks of rejoicing, and some tenderloins of happiness. To be a little part of sending twenty young believers off into the fruitful missionfield of India is worth a few hot and humid days. Do you remember the context of Jesus' famous meat comment? "Say not ye, There are yet four months, and then cometh harvest? Behold, I say unto you, Lift up your eyes, and look on the fields; for they are white already to harvest. And he that reapeth receiveth wages, and gathereth fruit unto life eternal: that both he that soweth and he that reapeth may rejoice together. And herein is the saying true, One soweth, and another reapeth. I sent you to reap that whereon ye bestowed no labour: other men laboureth, and ye entered into their labours." (John 4:35-38) I had a lady in my last church that gave me the perfect explanation of Jesus statement when she called this, "Plucking Someone Else's Fruit"!

To say I have reaped where I haven't planted would be an understatement. To say I have sown where I have never reaped is equally an understatement. I have experienced both sides of Jesus statement, and I was doing it again on a rainy day in Kerala. I had sowed into the lives of these twenty graduates in 2012 when I labored at Kerala Baptist Bible College for three weeks putting the letters of Paul into the hearts and minds of these young people. I forevermore have "entered into their labor". I will not know until the great day of reward (II Corinthians 5:10) what I actually will be rewarded for, but I have sown and these twenty will reap. As the rain continued to pitter-patter on the steel above my head, I imagined the multiplication in missions that I was a part of. I have come to believe the best way to leave any ministry behind is to plant yourself in the lives of those who will outlive you. This is the only way you will ever produce what Jesus called "that your fruit should remain" (John 15:16)! As I visited with the families of the graduates, my mind was off in the deep, dark corners of India where these young missionaries would soon reside. By now you know it was my earliest desire to ministry in one of those deep, dark corners of the uttermost parts of the world (Acts 1:8). It never happened for me, but for a few fleeting days on a few short term missions' trips to Australia and India, a piece of me is there still in the lives of a handful of young missionaries.

As the water dripped from the edge of the canopy and the rain found its way into the tiny opening of the roof, I dodged the moisture by moving from place to place. I would soon have to leave the sanctuary for the dining hall to be at least polite and eat with the graduates and their guests. In my final thoughts, I brought to mind the classic lines from an old church hymn. "He leadeth me, O blessed thought! O words with heavenly comfort fraught! Whatever I do (speak at a graduation ceremony), wherever I be (under a canopy on a rainy afternoon in India), still, it's God's hand that leadeth me." He had led me to India for a purpose and that purpose was to sow seeds of evangelism into the hearts of a group of young, passionate Indians. It is also important on this kind of rainy day to make plans for another kind of rainy day that may happen, the day when you hear that it hasn't gone well for the young people you have placed your hopes in. We just had a situation happen to a young lady that was once a part of my church; a young lady with a missionary heart married a young man with a missionary heart. They eventually had four children and decided the Lord was calling them to Bangladesh. They were there barely a year in the capital city when a terrorist attack just blocks from where they lived happened. They are home again pondering what to do with the rainiest period of their lives. It is what you do with the rainy days of your life that will define you as a Christian.

21

Vision Bible College's First Graduation

One of the big surprises on my 2016 trip to India was the number of graduation speeches I would give. I came with one and would deliver three. The first was known, my graduation address to the class of 2016 of Kerala Baptist Bible College. I hadn't been in India long when Shibu asked if I had a second sermon for graduates. I wasn't shocked by his question for, if I had learned anything in my four trips to Kerala, it was to be prepared for anything. Many events in India are at the spur-of-the-moment, so I told Shibu I could come up with one, but why? It seems that Shibu's youngest sister Sheila's husband Munsee had started a small Bible school two years before. The first graduation was taking place the day after KBBC's graduation. When I woke on my second Saturday in India, I was heading for my second graduation exercise in two days. It was a first.

The rain after Friday graduation had cooled the air a lot, and my night's rest was the best so far. I woke at my normal time, just before sunrise, and pondered my message for the Vision Bible College graduates. I had decided I would adapt a message I had put together on "Our Exhortation, Jesus's Example" from Philippians 3:14 –"pressing towards the mark for the high calling in Christ Jesus." I would challenge the graduates to follow Christ's pattern in five areas:

1. When Jesus was here on earth He kept His eye on *the goal not the going*—Hebrews 12:2.

2. When Jesus was here on earth He kept His eyes on *the prize not the process*—Philippians 2:5-9.
3. When Jesus was here on earth He kept His eye on *the treasure not the trial*—Matthew 6:19-21.
4. When Jesus was on earth He kept His eye on *the joy not the journey*—Hebrews 12:2 and
5. When Jesus was here on earth he kept His eye on *the Cross not the criticism*—Luke 9:51, 53, 13:22, 17:11, 18:31, 19:11, 28.

   I would challenge them to follow that example in the pilgrimage they had left on their journey. I was excited to have another chance to exhort another group of Christians as they impacted their towns and communities. It also gave me a chance to visit with a man and his family I had gotten to know on my first visit to Kerala.

   I liked Munsee from the first time I was introduced to him. His English was good, so we had wonderful conversations together. By profession he was a school teacher and by his faith a Brethren. One of the first things I learned about Indian Christianity was the lack of hostility between the denominations. When Christian Indian parents are looking for a bride or groom for their child they don't always look just to their preferred denomination. So Sheila was married to Christian Brother! My first meeting with Munsee was the day he came to the Simon house to take his wife and newly born daughter Libby home. It is a custom in Kerala for the new mother and new child to stay in the home of the parents for a month before going home. (I wouldn't have enjoyed that custom!) Munsee had arrived at the Simon home with his parents and a few other relatives to claim his wife and daughter. They had hired a taxi (an event that only happens on important occasions) to take them all home together. I found Munsee a humble man and very dedicated to his family of four. Lydia came along a few years later. The other thing I picked up quite early in my relationship with Munsee was his love for the Bible. He was a school teacher by trade, but a lay preacher by passion. I didn't know it until I got to India in 2016 that he had turned that passion into a small Bible college to teach the laymen and women of his denomination the Word of God. When he heard I was coming for the KBBC graduation, he asked Shibu if I might be the keynote speaker for their first graduation; for me it was an honor!

   As I got ready for my second graduation in two days, I also packed for what would be happening after the Vision Graduation. Right after the benediction, we would be leaving for the State of Tamil Nadu (the state with Kerala that shares the southern tip of India) and my third graduation in three days. We were off to the Tamil Nadu Extension graduation of the KBBC project of teaching the pastors and laymen and women of the Tamil Nadu churches. It would be a seven-hour trip by car into a region of Tamil Nadu I hadn't yet visited. I was looking forward to meeting the individuals my Uncle Paul's trust money had underwritten. The entire Simon family was going with us. It would be an adventure again filled with many surprises. I was also warned by Shibu to get my rest because we would be returning right after graduation to Kerala and would have little rest before we got on a plane in Kochi for the Punjab. A "wild whirlwind" is a good description to explain my second weekend in India.

We arrived at the Munsee house around one in the afternoon. The graduation exercise was going to take place in the front yard of the Munsee house. The place was decked out in all kinds of signs, and the entire yard was covered both sides and top with a series of cloth panels. I learned immediately the Brethren were richer than the Baptists! The program started around 2:00 and lasted for a couple of hours. Each of the twenty-three graduates had on a cap and gown, and we had a formal procession from the next-door neighbor's yard into Munsee's yard. By the time we got under the shade, the afternoon had turned unbearably hot! They had made a little stage for the guest speakers, and the graduates were seated to the left of us. The formal program went something like this before I gave the charge: Professor O. J. John opened in prayer followed by the Scripture reading of Joshua 1:1-8 by Professor Joshi Abraham and Romans 13:11-14 read by Professor Biju Thankachen. Sounds familiar, doesn't it? It was the same as KBBC. Jacob Sam had the welcome and introduction with Baby John giving the valedictorian speech. The Vision Choir, a group of six girls including Munsee's two daughters, sang about five songs throughout the program including leading the congregation in "Onward Christian Soldiers". Jacob John (not the taxi driver from Edayappara) presented the graduates, and Shibu and the chief executive officer of the Brethren of India conferred the degrees. Professor Shibu gave the pledge, C. Chacho gave the prayer, and then I shared the charge. Munsee introduced me, and as so often happens, I was introduced as Marnie's father. Most in Kerala, including Munsee and Shelia, know my daughter better than they know me. This was my first visit to their home in the town of Thadiyur, despite the fact it is only twelve miles from the Simon's house. After my address, there were six more speakers: Aby Itty Avira, the administrative officer of the Thiruvalla hospital, Rev. Dr. Vadakkemuriyil Idiculla Philip, former chaplain from Ludhyana, Punjab—once I found out he was from the Punjab, I talked to him after the service about my up and coming trip, and I found I would be meeting his son in the Punjab,—Evangelist Abraham Thomas, chaplain of the Thiruvalla hospital, Jayan Pulickel,

President of the Ezhumattoor GramaPanchayat, Thomas Jacob, ward member of the Ezhumattoor GramaPanchayat, and Lalu John, district notary of the government of India. Matthew Jacob gave a note of thanks, K. A. John gave the closing prayer, and C. J. Chacko gave the benediction.

We stayed just long enough to get a few pictures taken with the graduates, Munsee and his family, and then a quick bite to eat before getting in the Simon's car for Tamil Nadu. It was a relief to get my cap and gown off in the oppressive heat, but the fellowship was good. Two graduations down and one to go, perhaps, the best one of the three!

22

Off to Tamil Nadu
A Woman on the Way

Shibu warned me that we wouldn't be able to stay very long at the Vision Bible College graduation because of the amount of time it would take to reach our next destination in the neighboring state of Tamil Nadu.

It was late afternoon when we once again piled into Shibu's car with Ronnie behind the wheel. Only Abigail was missing from our original group as she would stay behind and spend the weekend with her two cousins. There were only Shibu, Julie, Jos, our driver, and me to travel on. Once again I was in the front seat beside Ronnie as we made our way towards the hills that separate the State of Kerala and the State of Tamil Nadu. I had been to Tamil Nadu three times before, but I would venture deeper into that state than I had ever been before. Tamil Nadu and Kerala share the tip of India with Tamil Nadu occupying three quarters of the space. These two states are as different as night and day. Kerala is the mountainous and hilly part while Tamil Nadu is flat and spacious. At its heart is the fertile Kaveri Valley, a land of rice fields upon rice fields upon rice fields. The trip through the mountains was similar to the treks I had taken through the Western Ghats before: plenty of winding roads, sharp corners, tree-lined roads, and lots of traffic. India knows nothing of by-passes, so despite the steady progress outside of the towns and the cities, our progress came to a halt numerous times to get through the bottleneck each village created. Our goal was the city of Erunelveli and a resting place, the village of Kanythar, before we pressed on to our final destination the next morning.

Before darkness surrounded our vehicle, I had plenty of time to watch the world of India go by. As I have written in my other India books, it is like watching a *National Geographic* Special through the front windshield of your car. One of the great thrills for me is seeing an elephant. I am sure you have figured that out by now! It was on this trip into Tamil Nadu that I saw my first Tamil elephant. We were driving through one of a countless number of tiny towns when I spotted her just ahead. By the time of this trip into Tamil I was pretty good in not only spotting an elephant, but recognizing its gender. What made this sighting so interesting was what the female elephant was doing. The local Hindu temple uses the elephant to get donations. This elephant was working its way by a series of small shops searching for gifts. As we flew by, I turned my head to watch the elephant for as long as possible. My last glimpse was the elephant extending its trunk to receive some kind of gift from the shop owner sitting by his rustic shack. What a thrill! I would learn in my travels through central Tamil Nadu that the state is known for its spectacular temples. Many of the towns and villages have the prefix "Tiru" which means sacred and indicates the presence of a major religious site. My eye caught a glimpse of a few of these temple complexes as we worked our way towards Erunelveli.

One of the things I like best about India and Indians is they are busy but never hurried. We certainly were on a tight schedule with this side trip into Tamil Nadu, especially when you consider we were traveling in the opposite direction of where we were to be in just a short thirty-six hours—on a plane for the Punjab. Shibu never seemed to be in a hurry despite a limited timeframe. He seemed to know there was just enough time to do what God wanted him to do. I am learning no more time is needed than that by anyone! I must admit I was getting a bit nervous thinking maybe we had bitten off more than we could chew, but I had to remind myself that I wasn't in charge and that Shibu knew best. What gets us into a fuss is being encumbered by our timing versus God's timing. If you study Jesus' life carefully, you will note a man at leisure, whether sleeping in the midst of a storm or taking time off from his divine schedule to rest a while (Mark 6:31). I know I don't always get the balance right, but in India I seem to be forced to yield to that blessed balance. I like what Vance Havner once wrote on this topic. *"When God allots us our mission for Him, He allows time in which to perform it. He does not favour loafing but He does not frown on resting."* As the darkness fell on our journey, I had one final flash, a sudden moment to experience before Tamil Nadu was complete shut-off except for the dim lights (there are no bright places in India after dark) that try to fight off the deep, dark blackness that is India at night!

We had gotten to a section of the main road through western Tamil Nadu where the going was straight for an extended period. Something you never experience in Kerala. As I watched the roadside scenery pass by, I spotted her. I had seen her sisters and daughters and mothers all over India, and I was still touched by the sight. To this day, nearly six months after the sighting, I can still remember the site. After we passed, I got out my calendar book and wrote in the back where I was putting down suggestions for the names of chapters in this book, and I wrote—a woman on the way. She was sitting in a pile of dirt by the asphalt highway we were traveling on. Behind her was an open field that was barren of anything (perhaps they were in-between plantings) but the appearance of a plowing. There was a shrub next to her possibly giving her a bit of shade when the sun was up. For her, I think it was a strategic position for her purpose, and what was that purpose? I couldn't be sure, but if she was like the others I had seen in my trips through the states of India, she was trying to sell something to the passing traveler. Most Indian vendors have small huts near the road, but the single lady with only a few things to sell sits alone hoping somebody will be interested in her wares. On the city streets, I have seen similar ladies selling coconuts, small flowers, or hair ribbons. But this lady was different for me because it wasn't what she was selling that drew my attention. Remember, I am traveling in a car racing along at nearly sixty miles an hour. The light is fading in the western sky. Deep, dark shadows are now engulfing the roadside, and yet in that moment, that fleeting second, I spot her. She raises her head for a glimpse of an unknown car flying by, a car she knows that would never stop and yet, in that second, our eyes met.

It was a link to a life and a lifestyle I couldn't even imagine. I have written in every book about India of the plight of women and girls. Each encounter has touched my soul and stirred my spirit. I knew deep down I couldn't help. We wouldn't stop, just another woman by the way, but for me I had to pray. I don't know her name, but my God does. How many have lifted her up to the Almighty in prayer? Why is it that so many get multitudes of prayers for their needs while others, like this woman by the way, gets one and only one because a traveling American pastor was working his way to his third graduation in three days. I still ask the Lord why He pointed her out to me. Of the thousands we had already passed along the way, I had been unaffected, and in a split-second, a lone lady sitting by the road became all-consuming to me. I still think of her often, the imprinted image in my mind that won't leave. Who is she? What is her name? Why was she really there that day? These are unanswered questions to this day, and I dare say the rest of my life. Paul wrote to Timothy this profound truth. "The Lord knoweth them that are His!" (II Timothy 2:19) Oh, that this woman by the way would become one of His—that our brief encounter on a Tamil Nadu way was the link that through prayer might have at least one praying for her, petitioning for her, supplicating for her at the throne of grace!

23

Baptism in a Water Trough

We arrived safely in Erunelveli, Tamil Nadu around 10:00 on the evening of March 12, 2016. Our resting place for our only night in Tamil Nadu would be the MNH Royal Park Motel. This hotel was located in a downtown side alley and was very nice by Indian standards. Besides the motel area there was a huge banqueting and conference center attached to the complex. They even had a security guard to watch over your car. Four stories high, the rooms were spacious and comfortable. The room had a private bath. In many Indian hotels you have to share. It was nice to take a cool shower after the busyness of the last two days and the heat of travel. It took us nearly five hours to go one hundred and five miles. We averaged barely twenty miles an hour. Didn't I say car travel in India was slow? After my shower, I got my trip journal caught up to date and had a bag of Lays Potato Chips, one of my favorite Indian treats, for a snack before heading off to bed. The room was air-conditioned, and I even had to use a blanket in the middle of the night, a rare event in my many Indian nights. I paid for three rooms for the six of us at a cost of 4545 rupees, or $67.83. I challenge you to find a better rate in the good, old USA! The rest was wonderfully refreshing and marvelously reinvigorating and definitely needed because I would not sleep again for nearly thirty-six hours.

I was up by 6:00 and on the road again by 7:00. We only had about a twelve-mile drive to get to our first stop of the day, so we took time to shop at a roadside restaurant for breakfast. To my surprise, waiting for us were three professors and the business manager of Kerala Baptist Bible College.

They had traveled through the night to be with us at the Tamil Nadu KBBC Extension graduation that afternoon. While they ate plenty of India food, I ate an apple. After a lengthy Malayalam conversation and discussion, college professors are always debating something, I paid the bill. Are you ready for this? Eleven people for an Indian breakfast cost me 770 rupees or $11.49 and that included my apple! To my surprise before I left, the manager came up to me and told me that I had been over charged for the meals and he took off 100 rupees. So the meals cost 670 rupees or $9.85! Before we left, my traveling companions stopped by a coffee stand for a morning shot of java, and it was there I learned that even Joshua, the Simon's young son, had taken up the habit. I am no coffee drinker, but I was fascinated by the way an Indian cools his coffee. Served in a small cup sitting in a larger cup, they pour the coffee back and forth between the cups until it is cool enough to drink. Stomachs full and with their coffee fix we were off to the Believers Church at Kanythar. This church was part of a denomination of churches in Tamil called The Church of Believers—a Pentecostal kind of group and very fundamental in their doctrine. This was my first surprise of the day.

Because the churches of the IGBC in Tamil Nadu don't have any building in the area, the college rents the small church in Kanythar to conduct their classes. This building would also be the site for the graduation that afternoon. Our schedule was to gather at the church and then go off to a morning service with Pastor Benjamin at his home church site on the other side of town. As we drove into the modest yard, I could see that a small crowd had gathered. I thought they were there to greet me, but I soon realized something more important was happening that morning. It was then Shibu told me I was going to be a witness to an Indian baptism. In 2006, during my first trip to India, I had the honor of participating in my first Indian baptism. What is unique about an Indian baptism is the location they choose. Most churches don't have baptisteries, and water is very scarce. My first baptism in India took place in a small stream about a mile from the IGBC mission. There was hardly enough water to get the baptismal candidates immersed. We found a deep hole in the Big Stream, and I had the honor of baptizing six of twenty-two. Even though I would only be a witness to this baptism, I was thrilled to be a part of it, but my first question was where would this baptism take place?

Behind the small church sanctuary was a series of fields that had been planted in tapioca trees, rice fields, and rubber trees. I could see a few goats and cows grazing in other meadows. The small farm was a checkerboard and in the middle of this small farm they had dug a wide well. The key to farming anywhere in India is a water source. The owners of this corner of Tamil Nadu had found a great body of water, and over the years they had dug deep into the bedrock creating a small pond. Measuring about thirty feet square, the water was pumped up to the surface and fed into a series of troughs which in turn could be opened up to flood the small fields or to water the animals. It was to the largest of these watering troughs I was led and told this would be the site of the morning baptism. Needless to say, I had never been to a more unique baptismal site! As I watched the group gather and the pastors start the service, I remembered the question of the Ethiopian eunuch, "And as they went on their way, they came unto a certain water: and the eunuch said, See, here is water; what doth hinder me to be baptized." (Acts 8:36) Here was water, yes, water in an animal's drinking trough, but water nonetheless. Why couldn't there be a baptism here?

The first person I recognized was Pastor R. Lorance, the senior pastor of the Tamil Nadu churches. He had traveled up from southern Tamil Nadu to baptized four people: Parasemo Laxmi, a man who had gotten gloriously saved after worshipping demons, Maha Laxmi, a lady who defied her husband in salvation and baptism—a real rarity, Subho Laxmi, wife of the man getting baptized, and Sundari, which means "beauty". Sundari was a beautiful young lady with a faith to match. What a thrill to witness the baptism of believers in an open and public place! In America, a baptism is such a routine event few take notice, but a baptism in the heart of Hinduism is another matter. In our day of shallow Christianity, it is refreshing to go to a place where a stand for Christ through baptism is something special. As I watched Pastor Lorance try to get the four people under the water, I thought again how the mode of baptism isn't seen as important in many parts of the world. I am a Baptist for a reason, and one of those reasons is baptism by immersion—John's and Jesus' method—Matthew 3:13-17. The Indian candidates had to literally kneel in order for them to go under the water. The concrete trough was only about three feet deep. Each gave testimony of his or her faith, prayers were said, and songs were sung. It was a joyous half hour around a cattle trough, witnessing the second greatest service in the church, second only to the communion service for me. Of course, I am of the belief that Jesus only gave us two ordinances: baptism and communion. We worship every week and pray daily, but baptism is still rare enough for me to see it as unique and special. Such was the experience that second Sunday in India. A surprise baptism that brought me back to my own in 1965 and reminded me of the many I had witnessed and conducted. One of the great privileges of the pastorate is the baptisms—forty-six for me and one hundred ninety-two individuals baptized in forty-three years—and the places I have performed them: church baptisteries, brooks, ponds and lakes, swimming pools, and the Atlantic Ocean. But without a doubt, the most unique for me has to be the day I was one of the witnesses to a baptism in a watering trough in the small village of Kanythar, Tamil Nadu India!

24

What a Blessen

It was a blessed walk back to the sanctuary of the Believer's Church in Kanythar after my first watering trough baptism. As we strolled above the small pattie fields, I kept looking at a young man who had joined our group when Pastor Lorance arrived. He looked familiar, but I could not place him. Having never been to that area in Tamil Nadu before, I quickly dismissed my thoughts as only a look-a-like. I was enjoying more the unhurried pace of my first, full day in Tamil. How we Americans can learn from our Indian brethren about the pace of our Sabbath!

I was barely three hours into my day and I had already experienced one of the great wonders of the Church, a baptism. Now I was in fellowship with distance cousins in the faith. I could have never imagined I would spend a Lord's Day with them. Our conversation was of the beauty of the baptism and the beauty of the place. Before I left the outdoor baptistery, I had wandered by the well pond and caught a glimpse of some fish swimming close to the surface of the water. How they got there I know not, but I did think, "If only I had my fly fishing rod!" I then took a small walk deeper into the series of rice patties just beyond the well. I took a series of pictures of the willow-like trees outlining the fields and a flock of white birds looking for food in the newly irrigated fields. It was a picture out of a heavenly scene. The sun hadn't gotten high and hot yet, and a cooler breeze was blowing making it an almost perfect morning in India. I knew my ride to the Kanythar Baptist Church would soon be leaving, so I left my celestial spot and wandered back to my starting point. When I arrived back to the church building, I was approached by the young man that I had been eyeing earlier. His first words to me in perfect English were, "You don't know me, do you?" He answered his own question, "I am Blessen!"

Blessen, I thought, do I know a Blessen? It was then a light in my memory came on and I asked, "Are you the Blessen I baptized in Big Stream in 2006?" The name was the only one I remembered, but that was ten years before. But sure enough we made the connection. I mentioned in the last chapter the joy I had in 2006 to have been able to participate in an IGBC baptism at their annual convention in January. When we got to the place of baptism, I was asked to help four other pastors baptize the twenty-two individuals seeking water baptism. As we stood in a circle around a deep hole in the brook, one by one those seeking a believer's baptism came forward. There was no order other than when one pastor was free he would take the next in line. The banks of the stream were crowded with nearly two hundred watching the proceedings. Eventually I would baptize Julie Simon's mother Daisy and Shibu's grandfather George and some other individuals whose names I have forgotten. However, I will always remember the young man who came to my side and said his name was Blessen. It was a unique name and an appropriate name given the circumstance. I would see Blessen one more time in my 2006 trip, but after that I would lose track of him. It wasn't until that morning in Kanythar that we would catch up.

The first surprise was the fact that Blessen was Pastor Lorance's son. I had actually visited Pastor Lorance's home in 2010, but only met his mother. Blessen was away at school. I would see his parents again at the dedication of the new Venmony Baptist Church financed through a gift by my church in Maine. I had kept up with the ministry of the Lorances in Tamil Nadu, but never once heard about their son Blessen. After I baptized Blessen in 2006, he had finished his education including Bible School and had returned to assist his father in the mission outreach of the Associated Missions of the IGBC. At the time of our getting reacquainted, he was reopening a church in southern Tamil Nadu and helping his father with the administration of the work including the Tamil Nadu Extension ministry of KBBC. The skinny teenager had grown into a fine young man, a man soon to be married, and a vital minister in the ongoing work of evangelizing Tamil Nadu with the Gospel of Jesus Christ. All I could think about was this phrase out of John's epistle, "I have no greater joy (blessing) than to hear that my children walk in truth." (III John 4) I was not Blessen's spiritual father, but I did have a unique connection to his spiritual growth that being the one chosen to baptize him as he made his public profession of faith in the waters of baptism.

That one event will forever link us if we never see each other again this side of eternity.

I am one that, like other generations before me, has spent a few sleepless nights worrying about who would follow in the Lord's footsteps. The longer I live, the less I see of the newer generation having aspirations for ministry and missions. I am encouraged now because of encounters like the one I had at Kanythar with Blessen. I am confident that the Lord is raising up individuals like Blessen to take over. Pastor Lorance had just retired from the Indian railroad and had been able to give his son his old job. Despite the fact they have secular jobs, their commitment to the Gospel is still very clear. New churches are being opened like the one we were now heading for. New Christians were being trained to open other churches through the work of the extension ministry of KBBC. The future is bright because a new generation is coming on line, men and women to replace the current leadership in Tamil Nadu when their departure comes. That morning in Kanythar "my faith caught the joyful sound, the song of saints on higher ground!" The Lord brought me to Tamil Nadu not only to witness this new generation, but also to get reacquainted with those I had known for ten years. What I didn't know was the Lord was raising them in my midst. Often we forget that that just because we don't see the Lord's hand or hear the Lord's voice it doesn't mean He is not working behind the scenes. I relearned this truth in hearing again the testimony of a young man named Blessen.

Blessen and I would have one more encounter before I headed back to Kerala and that plane ride to the Punjab. The Lorance boys would be at the graduation and would participate in the exciting ceremony. One of the last events was a time for picture taking with the graduates and their families and those of us who were a part of the celebration. Before the picture taking was over, I asked to have my picture taken with Lorance on one side and Blessen on the other. I still cherish that photograph as symbol of the three men in the picture. Me standing between two generations of Indian servants, and the link I have been privileged enough to be a part of. I knew in my very first visit to India that I would be a middleman at best, an avenue between the saints of America and the saints of India. One of the most blessed ministries of my lifetime has been the one that has connected the believers, whether being used to build a church structure or baptize a young man that would grow in grace and hear the Lord's call on his life. So many are so afraid to climb the tree, they never get out on the limb. The tree is missions and the limb is India. I won't say that it is an easy place, but the blessings are beyond imagination. The sad truth is some Christians would rather miss a Blessen than leave the comfort of their closet Christianity. As I got into Shibu's car for the short trip to our next engagement, I looked back into the face of Pastor Blessen and said a simple prayer thanking the Good Lord that He had once again encouraged my hope for the future Church. For as long as He delays His return, my dream is to return to Tamil Nadu again and see how Blessen is doing.

25

In the Shadow of Hinduism

After a short visit with Blessen and his dad following the early morning baptism, we were off to my very first church service in Tamil Nadu. I had visited Tamil Nadu two times before but never had an official service in Kerala's neighboring state. A short car ride took us to a small village just outside of the bigger town of Kanythar to the home of one of the believers of Pastor Benjamin's house church. When we arrived, the backyard of the house was already decorated for the meeting. A cloth canopy had been raised to keep off the hot, late morning sun. A small fan had also been set up to help with the heat, but it didn't! We were greeted by about twenty members of the church with cold water and some fruit. The alley, where we were meeting among a number of homes, was full of playing children. The first thing I noticed was the loud music coming from behind a low-lying fence. It was then I realized our service was going to take place next door to a Hindu temple just beginning their daily worship service.

    I have never liked a back-seat driver, and I have never liked sitting in the back seat. Rare is the individual who has been able to act graciously in life's back seat. I will admit that on that Sunday morning in Tamil Nadu that is exactly how I felt. We were small in number, maybe thirty at the most, and I could tell by the volume of sounds coming over the fence they numbered in the hundreds. We had no amplifiers to increase our singing and preaching, but they appeared to have several loudspeakers doing just that. Despite our focus, the din coming from the temple would be a part of our worship service whether we liked it or not. So what was I going to do about it? I couldn't stop it, and I certainly wasn't going to ask them to quiet down. Besides, I was in their country, in their backyard, invading their culture, and yet I believed that I could still proclaim the Gospel of Jesus Christ in the shadow of Hinduism.

I first recalled the Biblical examples of Samuel and John the Baptist when they had to take a second seat, a back seat to Saul and Jesus. Their gracious acceptance of the change of dispensations reminded me that sometimes we have to yield to others or other circumstances, but that doesn't mean we stop doing what we have been called to do. Samuel continued his prophesying, and John continued his preaching, and so would I. If the Good Lord has gifted me with any ability, it is the ability to speak above another noise or distraction. I still remember one of my first preaching services in a nursing home in Georgia while going to school in South Carolina. Halfway through the message, a lady in the back of the room fainted. The nursing home staff came in with a stretcher to take her out. There was a lot of commotion and noise, but I kept on preaching. After the service, we found out that all the activity wasn't because the resident had fainted, but because she had died! I learned then and there to block out all distractions and focus completely on the task at hand, sharing the Word of God.

Our worship in Tamil Nadu was similar to worship in Kerala. There were plenty of songs sung and plenty of prayers offered. Unlike Kerala, there were a number of testimonials. I was left in the dark for most of the service except when Shibu would whisper in my ear something that had been said, and all the time in my other ear I was hearing the chanting and drumming from behind me. People were worshiping there as well, but their worship was to dead gods and goddesses. They made a lot of noise, but before me were a few people making a lot of sense. The sincerity of heart and mind could be seen on their faces, and the genuine nature of their actions could be seen each and every time a song was sung, a prayer was prayed, and a testimony was shared. Then it was my turn to speak above the Hindu worshippers.

The title of my message was "God Loves Even Me" from I John 4:19. "We love Him, because He first loved us." I read the context first—I John 4:8-10. Then I shared with them these three points:

1. This kind of sentimental love gives us TRUTH—John 17:17, reminding them that truth wasn't a precept, it was a PERSON. The question that Pilate asked, "What is Truth?" (John 18:38) was the wrong question. A better question is "Who is Truth?"
2. This kind of universal love gives us JUSTICE—II Timothy 4:1, reminding them that justice has only one source. When we stand before the Almighty Judge, we want a loving Judge (John 3:16).

3. This kind of eternal love gives us SACRIFICE—John 15:13, "Greater love hath no man than this that a man lay down his life . . ." No matter what other world religions might teach, Christianity has the only faith in which its founder died for them.

The interesting twist to this message was the fact that I had prepared this message during my last time in India in 2012. I was traveling back to Kerala with Shibu from a weeklong mission's trip to the churches in Orissa. We had a seven-hour layover in Hyderabad Airport, and after a week visiting the persecuted believers, I saw firsthand what the love of God could do in the shadow of Hinduism, or Islam, or Buddhism.

After my message, the group shared communion together, another blessing saints can enjoy even in the shadow of Hinduism. It was my first communion in Tamil Nadu but not my first in India. Lunch was served afterwards, including the best-fried chicken I have ever had in India. Then we were off to visit the pastor's home outside the city. Located on an open piece of land in the middle of a large field, the house was modest like most Indian homes, and the hospitality was sweet. We were actually passing time before the afternoon graduation ceremonies began, but what a sweet passing of time. I got a chance to meet Pastor Benjamin's wife and two daughters and to learn a bit more about the pastor. He was in actuality a lay-pastor, one of the graduates of the extension school and a local businessman. Despite his many hats, his focus was in winning his neighbors to the Lord. I realized that I had met another Samuel and another John in Kanythar.

Despite being in an entirely different social structure, Benjamin was content about playing second fiddle and sitting in the second seat. He was no back seat driver. One of the dark shadows of Hinduism is the caste system. One of the difficulties facing Christianity in India is that system. It is so hard for your average Hindu to understand the truth, "For as many of you as have been baptized into Christ have put on Christ. There is neither Jew nor Greek, there is neither bond or free, there is neither male nor female: for ye are all one in Christ Jesus." (Galatians 3:27-28) John the Baptist said it best when he said, "He must increase but I must decrease." (John 3:30) Few people, even Christians, have learned to take the second place, even to Jesus. In America and in India, I have found many like Diotrephes. Remember he was the Christian that "loved the preeminence" III John 9. But in Pastor Benjamin, I found a "Demetrius (who) hath good report of all men, and of the truth itself . . ." III John 12. In a day where most businessmen are looking to climb the social ladder and reach the topmost rung, it is refreshing to meet men like Benjamin who are not even scrambling for the chief seats in the Church, but are, like their Saviour, humbling themselves by taking a back seat, in a backwater town, and under the shadow of Hinduism seeking those who are lost. Blessed is the man who can take a back seat to his fellowman, his Saviour, and even to those who gather behind a house-church.

26

Tamil Nadu Extension Program

There is one thing I can say about a Tamil Nadu meeting that rarely happens anywhere else in India. They start on time! At exactly 3:00, the KBBC Tamil Nadu Extension graduation program began. It was the first and hopefully not the last of its kind. This would be my third and last graduation in three days. Though the others were a blessing, this one would be special because of the people that were there. Let me share with you the order of service of this graduation and highlight and underline the memories of the honor of being asked to be the first graduation speaker for this ceremony.

A. Opening Prayer by Pastor S. Michael—This was the pastor of the church building that was used for the classes from the summer of 2015 to the winter of 2016. Despite being of a different denomination, the pastor and people of the assembly were more than encouraging and helpful in the teaching of others in the things of the Lord and in His Word and the use of His structures.

B. Scripture Reading by Blessen Lorance—This is the young man I had the privilege of baptizing in 2006 and is now helping his father lead the work of the IGBC in Tamil Nadu. As I sat and watched the maturing of this young man over the years, I was reminded of others I had crossed paths with years before that I have yet to re-meet. Blessen will always be remembered as one of the Lord's blessed successes!

C. Second Scripture Reading by Mr. Johnson P. J.—The business manager of Kerala Baptist Bible College had traveled down with a number of the professors to attend the first graduation. I had met P. J. in 2006 and, as with Blessen, have watched this young man grow into a valuable minister in the area of finances. If I have learned anything in the ministry over my four decades it is the need of men like Johnson to help men like Shibu in the Lord's work.

D. Welcome and Introduction by Professor S. James who is one of the young professors at KBBC. This young man has become one of the best-liked college professors for his sweet spirit and easy-going manner. James was at the school when I taught there in 2012. It was nice to be ministering with him again. He had been one of the professors that had traveled down to Tamil Nadu from Kerala through the academic year. The smile on his face for his students was memorable.

E. Presentation of Graduates by Professor Sabu C. Andrews, the Academic Dean of KBBC and Shibu's righthand man at the college. Sabu had also traveled south during the extension years and was there to hand out the certificates to the graduates of the Tamil Nadu Extension Program. Of all the professors, I have known Andrews the longest. A bit reserved and standoffish in the early years (2006-2007), but, during my last three trips, our friendship has only grown. He and his wife were some of the first to welcome me into their home this trip.

F. Conferring of the Degrees by Rev. T. Sackson Simon. I call him Shibu, and he has become my best friend in India. I have many friends in the sub-continent, but I have spent more time with Shibu in India than any other man. Our special journeys together throughout India have become the highlight of my trips to India, and after the graduation ceremony, we would be off on another adventure!

G. Prayer of Dedication by Pastor R. Lorance, the director of the churches of the IGBC in Tamil Nadu and the director of the extension program. Our paths have crossed a number of times before in Kerala, like the dedication of the new church sanctuary and parsonage at Venmony. However, the morning baptism in the cow trough will go down as the best ever. To be with him and his son one more time at the graduation was an extra bonus for me.

H. The Charge by Barry Blackstone—I shared a message on "How God Calls His Workers" based on I Corinthians 1:26-29. At the heart of my sermon was this thought— *"God doesn't call the qualified; He qualifies the called!"* I shared that each of the graduates was a perfect candidate in light of the qualification given by Paul in the text. I spoke for about twenty minutes to a crowd that had grown as the service continued. When we started there were about forty people in the congregation, but, by the time I had finished, there were nearly eighty, too big for the small sanctuary to hold.

I. A Special Musical Number by the Graduation Class: Benjamin A, the pastor of the Kanythar Baptist Church that I shared about in the last chapter, Geetha John, one of the ladies of Pastor Michael's Believer's Church, Kamaraj, another young lady from the Believer's Church, Iyannar Noah, another small businessman from Kanythar, and Suitha Nishon, the fifth member of the class, but not the last. They sang their song in memory of Israel, the sixth member of the class who passed away unexpectedly before graduation. His family received his degree.

J. Closing Prayer by Professor Biju Devasia, the last member of the teaching staff of the extension school. I had met Biju in 2012 and struck up an immediate relationship both on an academic level as well as a spiritual level. His commitment to the Word of God and its instruction is beyond description.

By 4:00 PM the ceremony was over. All that was left to do was take a few pictures and pack up for our trip back to Kerala. Shibu and I were on a tight schedule with our Punjab flight leaving in the morning. We still had a six-hour drive back to Shibu's house then a three-hour drive to Kochi Airport, but we couldn't rush the goodbyes.

I have gotten nervous a few times in India feeling that delays would make us late, but as I looked at my watch and calculated where we needed to be and when we needed to be there, I must admit these three phrases were repeated often by my hosts: 1) "We will go when we go" 2) "We will get there when we get there" and 3) "We will start when we start!" Shibu had warned me about the next ten-days of our lives. We were going to travel further than we had ever traveled in our other mission's trips. Those other two trips had started with a number of days of rest, but our Punjab trip was going to start after a world-wind trip to Tamil Nadu and back. At best we might get an hour or two between road trips. I was ready to go, but like all Indians I have found in India nobody seems to watch their watch. Even when we did get on the road at 4:45 PM, we hadn't gotten out of Kanythar before we made our first stop at a roadside vegetable stand. I watched as the group bartered over the price of onions, potatoes, and a variety of other fruits and vegetables. We then traveled until nearly dark when we stopped again to wait for the professor's car to catch up with us. They had gotten lost; another event that doesn't bother them! By the time we were back to Edayappara, it was 10:45

PM. I climbed the stairs to my second floor bedroom with these words in my ear, "We will leave for the airport at one!" The first half of my fifth India trip was over. Three graduations in three days in two states, and yet the best was before me. All I thought was what I would be doing and where I would be going had been scheduled. Little did I know that my traveling companion had another set of plans totally unknown to me!

27

The Story Continues
I Had Fainted Unless

Before I start recording my Punjab adventure, let me share another chapter in my "a tale that is told" series. It's like a book within this book. Remember, as I turned sixty-five in India, I decided to take my free moments and write a short autobiography of my life, the story before my India expeditions. I had found in India a great place for reflection: the mind is clearer and ready for self-examination, the heart is more open to personal evaluation, and the soul is geared to meditation. As you can see, it has been awhile since I added a chapter because of the busyness of the three graduation ceremonies. Let me pick up my tale here.

"As a great man of God once said, *"Even God can't fill what is already full!"* One of my struggles in the ministry has been being too full of Barry things. Granted, Barry things had mostly to do with ministry, other people, spiritual works, not personal things, as is the case with some people. I filled my days, weeks, months, and years with church things. Because of my upbringing on a working family farm, it wasn't strange or hard to work seven days a week, 12-hours a day, and rare was the year I didn't work 300 days in that year! For those that think this is impossible or simply crazy, I can only say I have the record books to prove it! I have for most of my life had good health and an energizer-bunny metabolism, so work came easy. God created us to work, but even I admit I over did it. One of the commands I have highlighted all my life is "Six days shalt thou labour, and do all thy work." (Exodus 20:9) My goal was always to only take fifty-two days off a year—a day a week average, to fulfill what I thought was God's command. I would note that also included all vacation time—only fifty-two days. Since I started keeping track, I still have one hundred and thirty-four days coming to me. If I took off four straight months, I would only be even with a 52-days-in-a-year rest. Even I see there is something wrong with this math, and I have come to believe that even my God doesn't demand such servitude. I would have fainted unless the Good Lord in all His grace and mercy hadn't sustained me in the midst of my stupidity. While others experienced illnesses and sicknesses, I experienced the strength and power to press-on through difficult days, difficult pastorates, and difficult family problems. My daughter was born with a birth defect, my wife had breast cancer, my father-in-law died of lung and liver cancer, and at thirty-nine my son died of the same thing. Yet, through it all, I maintained an aggressive ministerial work ethic. Some might ask how this was possible, and my simple answer comes from the Psalmist who wrote, ". . . for so he giveth his beloved sleep." (Psalm 127:2) Give me nine to ten hours of rest, and that doesn't necessarily mean sleep, and I can do anything the next day, any day, for as many days in a row that is needed. I have worked months in a row without a day off and granted I am not digging ditches or doing hard manual labor most of those days. But for those of us who have used our minds more than our hands over the years, you can still get tired! I believe my regiment of rest and the Good Lord's giving me rest has allowed decades of daily labor. I had fainted unless . . . I have not been the first, nor will I be the last, that got caught in what I call spiritual workaholism. In my attempt to serve the Lord, I forgot even His own instruction to His disciples after a busy period of time dealing with the unending needs of people. "And He said unto them, Come ye yourselves apart into a desert place, and rest awhile: for there were many coming and going, and they had no leisure so much as to eat!" (Mark 6:31) Vance Havner once put it this way: "You better come apart or you will come apart!" Oh, the stories I could tell of missed meals in the ministry, and many of them were of my own doing not because of another. If the Son of God rested when He didn't have to, then who was this rest for? His disciples! We forget, ". . . He that keepeth thee will not slumber. Behold, He that keepeth Israel shall neither slumber nor sleep!" (Psalm 121:3-4) Jesus could have not rested, but He also knew His disciples would soon burn-out without it. Do you see now why the Good Lord has been so merciful to me? Why He has been so gracious to me over the years? I should have a body that should have broken down years ago, but at sixty-five I feel like Caleb at eighty-five. "As yet I am as strong this day as I was in the day that Moses sent me. As my strength was then (at age forty), even so is my strength now, for war, both to go out, and to come in." (Joshua 14:10-11) Granted, I don't feel forty at the end of my days now, but I feel forty at the beginning after a good night's rest. What has bothered me most in my old-age revelation is what I could have been doing if I had observed a day of rest every seven days. God created us with a need to work, but also a need to rest. I always convinced myself that I was helping others, doing what nobody else could do or would do. I, like Jesus, have come to the conclusion there will always be needs and the needy and no matter if you work 24-7, you will never meet all the needs. If anyone could Jesus would have, and yet instead of a 24-7 life style, Jesus was always seen resting awhile—going into the hills away from the crowds to rest. I don't challenge people with my example, for I haven't given such a good example in this category. Every man must be fully persuaded in his own mind (Romans 14:5) and work out a system in line with his own make-up and limitations and drive. We can't start out too fast lest we burnout before the Good Lord brings us out. My life has never been a sprint, though I have at times acted like it was, but I see now after sixty-five years it is a marathon. Did Jesus not ask the question, "Are there not twelve hours in the day?" (John 11:9) I am learning in old age that it is important to recognize the limits of the day and to realize that God will give you enough time in any day, any week, any month, any year to do His will and nothing more. Years ago I heard the argument, "Well, the Devil doesn't take a vacation!" I was guilty of believing the statement. It took me years to realize I wasn't working for the Devil, but the Lord. I am not to follow the example of Satan, but my Saviour. My dear wife has been preaching this doctrine to me for years, but I fear like many who I preach to, I wasn't listening. Coleen deserves a whole chapter in my autobiography, and I will give it to her in the next installment. Wise is the young preacher that learns this lesson early in his ministry. Don't wait like this old preacher in old age. I warn you it is hard to change the pattern. Over the last two years I have tried my hardest to live by the Biblical standard, but I struggle at times. Last year it was the Good Lord laying me flat out with a series of kidney stones and a series of infections forcing me to take nearly eighty days off. The year of this writing, it was the cancer of my son that forced me to lay aside my ministry to care for him and still I will only have taken around eighty days off. I am cutting into those one hundred and thirty-four days, but even if I continue on this pace I will still have one hundred and ten days in the bank. I am more aware of the need to follow the Lord's command and the Lord's example as I near threescore and ten. I could and would go home to heaven today if the Lord wills it, but it appears that I have some years left to serve. I want to serve Him with the best body, the best abilities and skills, so that when it is all said and done I will not be found lazy, but faithful. I will not be found overdoing it, but simply doing it. Solomon told us years ago, "To everything there is a season and a time to every purpose under heaven . . ." (Ecclesiastes 3:1) I believe he left one out—a time to rest. He speaks of work in Ecclesiastes 3:2-3, but he too must have been a workaholic, for where is the rest?

28

North to the Punjab

After just an hour and a half turn-a-round, Shibu and I were on the road again for the airport in Kochi. Robin and Lalu were our drivers. It was one of the fastest trips I have ever made to the Kochi Airport. In just two and a half hours later, Shibu and I were entering the newest terminal of this ever-expanding hub of Indian air transportation. By 4:00 in the morning on March 14, 2016, we were through customs waiting our Indigo #6E561 flight to Delhi. I was a bit disappointed because I had thought our flight to the Punjab would be through Mumbai, but instead we would be heading for India's capital city. Right on time, as all of my Indian flights have been, we left Kochi for Delhi.

The 1200-mile flight took us from 6:00 to 9:00 that morning and then an hour layover at Delhi International. We didn't get off the plane as we waited for our final leg to Chandigarh, Punjab. It was only one hundred and eighty miles away; we left at 10:00 and were in the Punjab by 11:00. As with my other travels around India, I had no fears or frets through these first legs of our mission trip to northwest India. Despite parts of India being quite primitive, the parts of India I was journeying through now were quite modern. As a matter of fact, the airport at Chandigarh was brand-new, state-of-the-art, and better than anything I had experienced in the States. My heart was excited that I was in the Punjab, but my soul was a bit disappointed because it was more American-like than Indian-like. I was soon to discover that on this mission trip I wasn't heading for another out-back place of India or another rural India as I experienced in Andrah Pardesh and Orissa in my two previous Indian missions' trips. I was heading to the teeming masses of some of India's biggest metropolises. Where I had numbered the population of the towns and villages in the hundreds and thousands in my other expeditions, this trip I was going to cities of millions and tens of millions!

Sometimes we need to travel outside our comfort zone and test our faith in the multitudes. Sometimes like Moses we have to leave the desert (Andrah Pardesh) for the big city of Egypt (Delhi). Sometimes we simply need to quit what we are doing to start doing something else. But whatever it is, we need to do it to the honor of God and stop wasting our time worrying whether we will fit in or that it will work out. If I had learned anything from my other trips within India's States it is to trust my guide (Shibu) and my Lord. I had prayed for this trip for months. I had desired to visit the Punjab for years, and now I was here and it was nothing like what I had imagined, but that didn't make it wrong. I thought I was coming to the bread basket of India, and I had, but what I didn't realize is that the State had also become an industrial hub as well. I would get to the country-side eventually, but it would be in the great cities of the Punjab I would spend the bulk of my time. Every once in a while in the course of my meanderings and journeys, I find a place like Chandigarh, the shared capital of both the States of Punjab and Haryana, a place of great size and diversity. I am a country boy by heart, but the Good Lord in His divine providence sometimes leads me into a city (like Ellsworth where I live now). I still remember my ten days in Melbourne, Australia on my way to six weeks in the western outback of the Gibson Desert. The population then was over a million (1972) and, though my cousin Bob and I had only planned to pass through the big town, the Lord stopped us in our tracks by a railroad strike and forced us to stay in the city. And despite the size and the unfamiliarity with city life, Bob and I had a grand time with the saints of the Kew People's Church. I would discover, like with Melbourne, the big cities of India also contain some precious saints worth stopping in and seeing, despite where they live.

What I liked best in the Punjab—which I never had in Andrah Pardesh or in Orissa—was the freedom to roam at will. My first two mission's trips into the interior of India had come with plenty of restrictions, as I felt in Kerala at times. The boys were very protective of their American friend, and they kept close supervision on me. I don't know what it was about the Punjab, but from the first minutes in the Punjab, Shibu let me go. He didn't seem to be as concerned with my safety there as in other places. I was allowed to stroll and what I found best about the Punjab was the weather. As we flew northward, the temperature decreased and the humidity decreased and the climate turned mild, more Maine-like. You could actually stand outside without sweating a bucket or two. I discovered that immediately as we waited for our ride from the Chandigarh Airport into the city of Mohali. Our driver was late, something that would be a continuing theme during our four days in the Punjab. Oh, well, we did make all our schedule starts and stops; more about that later! Despite the delay, the weather was spectacular, and I said to myself, "I might have come to a city, but the weather is divine, country-like!"

While I waited, I learned that we were on the vast plains that stretched from the River Indus to the Gangetic belt, a series of foothills just before the great Himalayan range of mountains. I would soon discover nothing but flat-land in the Punjab. I don't remember seeing a significant hill in all my travels, and in our travels we would cross the entire width of the Punjab. The region is considered the granary of India producing half of all the wheat, rice, and millet grown in the entire country. The state also has a flourishing dairy, and to my heart's delight, I saw more potato fields in the Punjab than I have ever seen in my home state of Maine. What I learned in the crowded metropolises of the Punjab was that like in the country, you could find the simple things that satisfy and please. I found good-natured people and breathable air and enough newness to wet my imagination and stir my interest. I had come to a new culture and a different people to get acquainted with a different part of the Body of Christ. I found that I could find brothers and sisters in Christ in the back alleys (literally-as you will see) of these big places and, despite the masses and the multitudes; there were still individuals that I could get to know.

The last thing I realized in the vastness of the Punjab was that God was just as near there as anywhere in India. Despite the pagan culture that dominated the State (Sikhs), there was still the Church of God in the Punjab. Smaller in number than the Sikhs certainly, but alive and well and expanding every day. As with the rest of God's Church Universal, He was adding "to the Church daily such as should be saved". (Acts 2:47) His peace and joy and eternal life are not limited to America or Andrah Pardesh. I don't wonder that Jesus loved Jerusalem and weep over it despite the fact He, like me, came from a small town. He spent His time in the country, in the desert places, and in the small places, but periodically He came to the big city. I had come to a big city for the same reason. There were people there who needed the Lord. The city man and the countryman can meet on occasion, and it was on that occasion that I had traveled north to the Punjab that early spring day in March to not only meet the saints but also share the Gospel with unsaved Sikhs. Blessed is the man or woman who knows to divide his or her time between Edayappara and Chandigarh, the metropolis and the mountain, Eastport (my country church) and Ellsworth (my city church), the teeming masses and the dusty lane. I would experience both sides in my

Punjab adventure, but in the end, it wasn't the culture or the climate or the cuisine or the countryside that I enjoyed most in the Punjab, but Christ's Christians, and what people they turned out to be, as you will see!

29

Still, Soft, Slow Songs

As Shibu and I waited for our ride outside the Chandigarh Airport, I thanked the Lord for another opportunity to visit one of the "earth's farthest bounds". I knew for the citizens of the Punjab this was home; their Jerusalem, but for a Maine boy I was a long way from my coast. To this point in my travels, I had passed the 10,000-mile marker. My trip to Australia in 1972 had been my farthest trek from home, but now the Punjab was second on that list. Even my previous trips into the interior of India had not taken me this far afield, and I was still not at the end of the line, the Pakistan/India border. I was brought back to reality when a small car pulled up beside Shibu and me and our luggage. It was our ride, and the driver was the director of the Punjab ministry for the Associated Missions of India (the IGBC mission's arm), Shaju Philipp.

We got into the Pastor's car and headed into town. The airport, like most airports, was located outside the twin cities of Chandigarh and Mohali, like Minneapolis/Saint Paul. Our first stop was at the Crown West Hotel where we would spend the night to start our travels in the Punjab and end our last night in the Punjab. This four-story hotel was located at Plot No. 359, Bulk Market, and Phase XI in Mohali. Note the description of the address because I would soon learn that the twin cities had a unique history. The makeup of the cities is nothing like anything I had ever experienced. The hotel was located very close to the tech center of the city. It was Punjab's version of Silicon Valley, though it was on a plain. That was a surprise. Some in India call it the Hyderabad (India's great commercial hub in central India) of the North. The hotel's greatest drawing card, according to the brochure I was given, was that it was located only ten minutes from the renowned PCA Cricket Stadium! India is crazy about cricket, but more about that later. Besides the very modern rooms, the hotel had a 78-seat restaurant and a 275-seat banquet hall. I thought I had been in some nice Indian motels and hotels up to this point in my Indian adventures, but this Punjab trip would change that, and the best was yet to come!

We settled into our fancy digs and Shibu and Shaju talked shop a bit before we headed across town for lunch at the Philipp's apartment. The highways were American-like, the streets and boulevards were wide and well planned, so unlike Kerala! There was room to expand because of the flat land for as far as you could see. The roads were congested with plenty of cars, trucks, and autos, but unlike Kerala fewer pedestrians and fewer animals, another surprise. Mohali was modern! The town was booming with new streets and new high-rises going up everywhere, which was causing a problem in the rise of rents and the cost of ministering in the Punjab. The Philipp's had a third story apartment on one of the numerous tenant complexes on the edge of the city. When we arrived at the modest structure, Shaju's two girls, Joanna and Jamma, were just getting home from school. Jesse was upstairs preparing lunch, and, of course, my first thought was how the meals would be. Before the Punjab I had traveled to four other states in India, and the food in each state was drastically different from one another. I figured I was in for a totally different dining experience in the Punjab, and I was. But what a pleasant surprise!

When we walked into the four-room apartment, another little girl greeted us. I thought the Philipps had three daughters until I was introduced to Febin Finney's daughter Evon. Febin was the pastor of the Chandigarh Baptist Church, and his wife was having their second child. The Philipps were caring for Evon during the delivery. It would be at Finney's church we were to have our first Punjab meeting that evening. We sat down to a wonderful meal of potatoes (no rice in sight) and chicken cutlets. I tasted no spices; if I didn't know it, my wife Coleen could have prepared the meal. I said in my heart, "I think I am going to like the cuisine of the Punjab!" Our fellowship was sweet; the feast was Indian, and the friendships in the Punjab were beginning. The Philipps were transplants from Kerala through Philipp's father, the man I met at the graduation at Vision Bible College. Shaju's dad had been a missionary in the Punjab since Shaju had been a boy. It was an easy match when the Simons were looking for someone to head up the new mission outreach. Shaju already knew the Punjabi language and the culture. The work was new, just a few years, but it had already multiplied to two churches in the east and two churches in the west. By the fall, an extension ministry of KBBC would be started. Much like the extension in Tamil Nadu, this extension would train the next batch of pastors for the ever expanding Punjab Mission.

We returned to our hotel after lunch for a little downtime and an afternoon nap of one and a half hours. Shibu got in three hours as I got up to prepare a sermon that was on my heart. We needed to recharge our batteries after the whirlwind of the last twenty-four hours. Just think twenty-four hours before we were still in Tamil Nadu in the most southeasterly part of India and now we were in the most northwesterly part of India! By 5:30 PM we were back on the road heading to Chandigarh for a 6:00 evening service at Pastor Febin Finney's church in a small community center in the heart of town, nine miles away. As we worked our way through the maze of streets and alleys, I recognized that it was to the masses Philipp and Finney had come. We eventually stopped in a parking garage and walked the rest of the way to a small room in the city center. When we got there, we were greeting by a group of about forty adults and kids. It was there I first meet Febin Finney and his two youthful helpers: Samuel John and Johanna Christ, Bible students at a local school who helped Finney with the music. It was also there I learned of the vast work ahead for these two young thirty-year-olds. There are 1.2 million people in the twin cities!

The first difference I heard as this service began was the kind of music being sung. Most Indian worship music it loud to say the least with plenty of volume. With a keyboard, guitar, and a small drum, the congregation of the Chandigarh Baptist Church sang slow songs, soft hymns, and choruses. I was shocked, but I enjoyed it—my kind of spiritual songs. I preached on *"It is not what is in your hand that counts, but what is in your heart!"* By 10:00 we were back to the hotel with our Punjab mission trip well underway. By 8:00 the next morning, we were heading west to visit the two churches there before returning to have our last meeting at Finney's church. As I pondered my first impression of the Punjab work, I was reminded of something that I had been taught very early in my ministry. I too had started a pioneer work in my twenties and was under the prevailing delusion that says a pastor must be judged by the size of his congregation—bigger being better and smaller meaning failure! Granted, there are those of every generation that are able to attract the multitudes, but they are few compared to the vast majority of preachers. Some would say that Finney and Philipp were not doing well if they could only draw forty people out of 1.2 million to a Gospel meeting. Not true! This concept of worshiping the crowd is a part of modern philosophy, not Biblical truth: "For who hath despised the day of the small thing?" (Zechariah 4:10) Figures can lie! It has become all about the statistics instead of watching for souls. God is looking for quality not quantity, and I found a great quality in the Punjab Christians. Remember, even Jesus ended with a few. God keeps the books!

30

The Tale Continues
A Good Wife

Unable to go right to sleep after my first Punjab service, I began to think again of my autobiography and a short description of my life up until India. One of the things I noticed most in my Indian adventures were the wives (like Jesse) that help, support, and minister with their husbands. Then I thought of my good wife in America. Solomon said it best when he wrote, "Whoso findeth a wife findeth a good thing, and obtaineth favor of the Lord." (Proverbs 18:22) My first glimpse of Coleen was just a passing glance as she walked into the First Baptist Church of Perham, Maine. She was new to the assembly, while I had been in the church since my first days of life. Coleen's family was from Washburn, seven miles away, while I lived just up the road and around a few corners from the little white church in the vale. Our Pastor was very evangelistic and was always looking for a new spiritual project, and the Meister family was one of his projects. He started with the father, Stacy, an alcoholic, and the mother, Opal, a beautician, but it was with the two girls, Coleen and Kim, he had his first success. Over a few months, the family, from where I went to high school, started to attend regularly and their oldest daughter started to attend our youth group—the BYF (Baptist Youth Fellowship). I rarely gave her a look as I was focused on my friends and playing baseball in the spring and basketball in the winter. I was not impressed at first, but you ask my wife and she had an eye for me from the beginning. Toward the end of my senior year and Coleen's junior year, there were a series of school activities that usually required a date: Junior Exhibition for the juniors and Senior Banquet for the seniors. One Sunday Coleen finally got the nerve to ask me to her Junior Ex, to which I replied, if she would go to my Senior Banquet. We spent the final days of my high school career together and by graduation we were going steady. The summer of 1969 was spent getting to know each other and falling in love. By fall I was off to college in South Carolina and letters were our only contact except for Christmas break. By the fall of 1970, Coleen was off to college with me, and over the next three years, we had our ups and downs—even breaking up for a few hours, but deep down knowing God had brought us together. Unlike many of the young people of today, we looked at life in a more practical way: college first then marriage. I would finish my degree in 1973 while Coleen finished her associate degree in 1972. My last year at Bob Jones University saw us separated again, including the summer before as I spend my summer in Australia working with an Aboriginal tribe in the Gibson Desert of Western Australia. But our times apart only drew us closer together, so by Christmas 1972 the question had been asked, the ring had been placed on her finger, and the date had been set for our wedding. I had learned through our four-year long courtship that if I was going into full-time Christian service I needed a friend for friendship, a companion for companionship, and a fellow (kindred spirit) for fellowship, and I had found all three in Coleen. Besides, she was a great cook, a gifted Bible teacher to kids, and a person who could find a bargain! Going into small church ministries she would need that skill above and beyond all others. I do not want you to envision cheap when I write a bargain shopper. Coleen is a genius when it comes to finding something inexpensive but still looks like a million bucks! By the summer of 1973, I had also learned another precept from Solomon, "Two are better than one: because they have a good reward for their labour. For if they fall, the one will lift up his fellow: but woe to him that is alone when he falleth; for he hath not another to help him up. Again, if two lie together, then they have heat: but how can one be warm alone? And if one prevails against him, two shall withstand him . . ." (Ecclesiastes 4:12) I had found an old-fashioned girl who made up her mind very early that she was not going to follow the crowd. Despite the fact she didn't come at first from a Christian home, she became the first Christian in her home. So after a long four years in which we were separated for nearly half of that time, we were joined as one on June 21, 1973, and in the same service we dedicated ourselves to the Lord's work. We would be rarely separated again! Since that day nearly forty-seven years have passed. To say we haven't had our ups and downs would be a lie, but no matter the challenge, the church, the children, the crisis, or the changes in our lives we have always stayed together. One of the best things about our relationship is that we have never been down together. When I am down she has been up, and when she is down I have been able to be up. I have thanked my good wife over and over again for one thing above another though I have much to thank my good wife for! That one thing being the sanctuary she has made out of our home. We have now lived in seven different houses, but each of those houses has been a refuge home for me, and the reason they have can be contributed to one person: Coleen, the lady of the house. Coleen is always busy with pots and pans, handiwork, helping others, and church activities. She loves and keeps a clean house and decorates it as if by a professional. Ask any lady of our churches! Coleen is not only the lady of the house, but the pastor's wife as well. If anybody lives in a fish bowl, it is the pastor's wife—the lady of the church, always under the public gaze. She is in a constant stage of readjusting to the changing list of parishioners, but never allowed to adjust because if there is a glass house in any town it is the parsonage! Coleen, for the majority of her life, has been able to keep a balance between our home life, our children's lives, and the church lifestyle. While I have been able to minister at will, spend the bulk of my time caring and sharing with others, Coleen has majored on the minor, the thousand and one things it take to keep a household going. Rare has it been that I have planned a meal, bought my kids clothes (as a matter of fact my own clothes), the toothpaste, the salt for the shaker, the sheets for the bed or seeing the clothes are washed, dried, and laid out for wearing. I know this might sound terrible, but for forty-six years of Sundays, my wife has laid out my suit for the Sabbath. My wife is the shopper for the house, the errand runner, and the caretaker of her mother's affairs and health for over eleven years now. Her care of her children has been legendary, in my opinion. For the years in our house, and now at the writing of this chapter, she is at it again as she has been tasked with the love and care of the final months of her beloved son's life as he dies of liver and lung cancer. A task she fears, but a task she will willingly fulfill with the greatest form of grace. When I think of the good wife the Lord gave me, I can summarize her in three Biblical words: '. . . *keepers at home* . . .' (Titus 2:5) She created a home out of a trailer in the New Hampshire hills overlooking Suncook, before making a home in the woods of Chichester, New Hampshire where she brought home our firstborn son, Scott, into our home. She then fashioned a home out of a rental property in my hometown of Perham in between our first two pastorates. After that she remodeled three parsonages (Calvary Baptist in Westfield, Washington Street Baptist in Eastport, and Emmanuel Baptist in Ellsworth) into lovely homes; the last we have lived in for twenty-nine years. She even took my grandparents' home and turned it into a vacation, cottage home. My good wife has prayed for me, sat and listened to more of my sermons than any other mortal man, and cut my hair. Coleen has been my barber for over forty years now. Coleen has always seen her place as a divine calling, and a divine wife is what she is!

31

India/Pakistan Border

I woke in a far off place on March 15, 2016. My night in the CrownWest Hotel in Mohali was pleasant and peaceful. I slept like a baby after traveling from the southeast corner to the northwest corner of India in just 24-hours, a 1500 mile trek! Both Shibu and I were up at 6:30 AM excited about our second day in the Punjab; Shibu's goal was to journey from eastern Punjab to western Punjab and finishes our day at the India/Pakistan border 168 miles away. But before we could leave we had to have breakfast. I am not a breakfast person, but Shibu is. So we headed downstairs to the hotel restaurant before Shaju picked us up for our travels west. I was pleasantly surprised to find a lot of American breakfast selections on the buffet counter. There was even a chef that would cook you an omelet or your eggs anyway you wanted. It was then I found out just how far afield I had come. I asked the man for two eggs over-easy. I got a blank stare back. Shibu was behind me and saw the dilemma and tried to explain what I wanted. I will never forget the expression on the chef's face with he replied in perfect English, *"Oh, you want half-fried eggs!"* Thereafter I knew what to ask for. I added some toast to my order and then the most wonderful surprise of the culinary part of my Punjab adventure, milk and even hot chocolate. Real cow's milk is a rare thing (lots of water buffalo milk and goat's milk) in Kerala and in the other parts of India I have traveled to, but in the Punjab I found it everywhere. To the son of sixth generations of dairy farmers, I was thrilled; it wasn't Maine, Blackstone milk, but it was the best milk I had discovered in India.

Shortly after 8:00 AM, Shaju arrived with Arood, our taxi driver for the trip across central Punjab. This was my third taxi driver in India: I had a Moslem (Shamash) in Andrah Pardesh, a Hindu (Jara) in Orissa, and a Sikh in the Punjab who was a Christian. After filling the car with gas costing 2000 rupees (about $30), we headed north through the province of Rupnagar, west through the province of Nawanshahr until we hit Route One, the main highway through the Punjab. This was a toll road with a number of toll plazas. The most we paid was 44 rupees about 75 cents. A few were just 25 rupee tolls. The highways, even the country roads, were very modern and smooth most of the time. What impressed me most were the fields of potatoes we passed and the tractor and trailer loads of potatoes on the roads heading for warehouse in the villages we passed through. The potatoes were in burlap bags, exactly like the burlap bags we used to ship our potatoes in during my days on the family Maine homestead in the 1950s and 1960s. In addition to the potato fields, we saw many fields of rice and sugar cane. About half way into our five-hour trip, we stopped for a midmorning snack at a roadside restaurant. The boys had to have their tea! I was more fascinated with a man wrapping his turban around his head. I knew that I was in a faraway place for sure. I walked around the parking lot and took in the beauty of the surrounding area as the boys talked and drank their tea. The temperature was around a glorious 75 and the sun was warming up. The smell of spring was divine. I remembered what Isaiah once wrote, "Thine eyes shall see the king in his beauty: they shall behold the land that is very far off." (Isaiah 33:17) Each and every time I take one of these mission trips for my King to a far off place, I see new things: a different world, a different people, and a different culture. It has been beautiful every time for me.

As we motored westward, we went through a myriad of towns, villages, and cities. India doesn't believe in bypasses. Between cities the travel was quick, but going through the bigger towns and cities, like Jalandhar, slowed us down. But, in comparison to Kerala we were flying! Our goal was the city of Amritsar and the two church plants on either side of the 1.5 million Sikhs that lived there. I was watching another *National Geographic* documentary through the front windshield of Arood's car with each twist and turn. The twists and turns were few because the land was so flat. All the time we traveled, Arood, Shaju, and Shibu were talking about the challenges of ministering among the Sikhs. One of the interesting bits of information I gleaned was the five things a pure Sikh always carries with him:

1. A sword—representing that he is always ready to defend his faith
2. A comb (which is part of his turban)—symbolizing that he is always ready to look good

3. A pair of long pants—representing his covering to maintain his purity
4. Long hair—which he can never cut but must always cover
5. A bracelet—representing his faith that he is willing to stand for

We arrived in Amritsar a little after 1:00 PM and immediately headed for Pastor M. Singh's house in the suburb town of Khasa and the Praise Baptist Church. After meeting the pastor and his family and seeing the new sanctuary they had built on the roof of his home where we were to have our first service that evening, Shibu told me he had a treat in store of me for the rest of our afternoon. We were going afar—afield again. Did I know that we were only six miles from one of the most heavily guarded borders in the world and one of the most famous border crossings at Wagha? I didn't!

As we traveled from Pastor Singh's house to the India/Pakistan border, we passed one Indian military base after another. I counted at least six including infantry and tank bases. One mile from the border we were stopped at a checkpoint, which allowed few, if any cars to pass through, and we were not one of them. We would have to walk the rest of the way. The checkpoints and the bodily searches were intimidating to say the least as we walked with a multitude of people heading for the border. The double walls topped by barbed wire were also impressive and intimidating. Every day in the evening there is a ceremony that marks the 1947 split of the Punjab between India and Pakistan with the Sikhs to the Indian side and the Moslems to the Pakistani side. Each sunset, a bugler from each side sounds the last post, and two immaculate, uniformed soldiers (B.S.F. soldiers on the India side and Sutlej Rangers on the Pakistan side) on either side of the border goose-step across to the flagpole to lower their respective national flags. Their motions are so perfectly matched they seem to mirror each other, I was told. There is great pride in who can kick higher and perform the ceremony the best. Thousands watch this performance each day, and grandstands have been built for the large crowds. Some liken it to the ceremony in London of the changing of the Royal Guard. As we neared the spot of the show, I could see more people were filling the grandstands. Because we had a service planned for 7:00, we couldn't stay and watch, but I had a chance to get my picture taken with the captain of the guard and a couple of his soldiers. I could see across the border into Pakistan, and I was less than 200 miles from Islamabad, the capital of Pakistan. I was at the end of my afar.

It took us three hours to walk the mile and back though security checks and looking around. When we got back to the car, I looked up again at the massive sign over the road that indicated we were a mile from the border. I also noted that we were 15 miles from a place called Lahore. It meant nothing to me at the time that is until I got home for Easter and the news reported a massacre of Christians in Lahore, Pakistan. Then I realized just how dangerous a place I had been to. For me, however, I began to sing the grand hymn that states, "Anywhere with Jesus I can safely go; anywhere He leads me in this world below . . ." including one of the most dangerous border crossings in the world!

32

The Tale Continues
In Journeyings Often

As we traveled back from the India/Pakistan border to our evening service at the Praise Baptist Church in Khasa, I realized that I had reached another of "earth's farthest bounds" for me. In every trip I have taken from my home in Maine, I have come to some end, a place in which I go no farther and a place from which I will retrace my steps back home. Paul, in his great explanation of the events he endured in the service of the Lord, writes of 'in journeying's often' (II Corinthians 11:26). This is the theme of the next installment of my remembering my past as I relive my fifth adventure in India:

"Remember, I came from a very small hamlet in Northern Maine, a sanctuary that I rarely left in my childhood, but I still have memories of special journeys I would like to recount and recall for you. In my first eighteen years of life, I only remember traveling away from home once. When I was twelve, our Little League coach Mac Holts took the team to Boston to a Red Sox game to reward us for winning our league. I played shortstop on that team, and the experience away from home was eye opening. We had traveled nearly 400 miles from home; I thought I had traveled to another planet. I still remember coming up out of the subway a few block from Fenway Park. My eyes couldn't take it all in, the vastness of a city. Perham contained a few hundred people at best, and we saw more people than that just walking to the ballpark. When we got into Fenway, it was by far the largest gathering of people I would see for a long time to come. Our trek ended at the Green Monster, and then we retraced our steps back north. The year was 1963. I wouldn't take another trip out of town until the fall of 1969 when I headed off for college in South Carolina. Once again my journey left from Perham, and I reached the end of that trek at Bob Jones University. Over the next four years, I would retrace those steps many times, but it was during that stay at college I would take my longest expedition to a far off end. In 1972, my cousin Bob and I took my first short-term mission's trip to Australia. I literally flew half way around the world ending my journey at, of all places, a deserted, desert mining town called Blackstone! Our place of ministry was in an Aboriginal town called Warbunton, but one day Bob and I and an aboriginal guide traveled 134-miles northeast of Warbunton to see the place named after our family name. It would be the end of our journey despite the fact we were still hundreds of miles from two of Australia's most recognized sites: Alice Springs and Ayers Rock. One of the things I have learned in traveling to earth's farthest bounds is that there is always someplace beyond that you desire to see, or to go to, but you have reached the end of your journey. From Blackstone, Bob and I retraced our steps back to Maine. Interestingly, 40 years after this adventure, I published a book on this earth's farthest bounds under the title of *The Region Beyond!* Between my Australia journey in 1972 and my next interesting journey to Paris, France in 2001 were countless small trips up and down the east coast of the United States and into eastern Canada. These included family vacations and fishing trips and ministry trips to summer camps. These mini-journeys were exciting if not adventurous, and each had a beginning and an ending. It was only after my wife and I got our primary ministry finished, the raising of our son and daughter did the Good Lord decided it was time for more journeys to more of earth's farthest bounds! The first took place because my daughter Marnie decided to go to Togo, West Africa for a summer ministering with a Child Evangelism Fellowship missionary. Marnie had spent a couple of her summers as a teenager working for CEF of Maine, so it was a logical next step in her desire to be a missionary. The summer went well until Marnie picked up a parasite and then malaria. She was in a hospital for ten days gaining her strength, then the problem arose did she have enough strength to return to Maine alone? The decision was made for me to travel to Togo and bring her home. Because of the difficulties of getting in and out (Marnie's story of getting out of Togo is a book in itself) of the West African country, the best we could do was to *Rendezvous in Paris,* which we did. I published a book of this adventure with the same title. Because we had a few hours between flights, Marnie and I took a trip into downtown Paris and our journey ended at the Eiffel Tower. I was hoping to go to the Arc de Triomphe and Notre

Dame Cathedral, but both were beyond our effort for that journey. Marnie and I retraced our steps through the maze of Paris, got back to Charles De Gaulle Aero Port and flew home. Within two years (2003), my wife and I were on another journey to the British Isles. Since our marriage we had dreamed of a second honeymoon to England, Scotland, and Wales. For our 30th wedding anniversary we made that trip. I even wrote of our adventures in a book that was published under the title of *Scotland Journey*. Our travels took us through the sites of London Town, Stonehenge, Salisbury, Chester, Edinburg, York, and Cambridge. Because both our families have roots in Scotland, it was at the famous Firth of Forth Bridge that our journey ended. It has been our hope to return to the land of our ancestors and visit the places beyond our first end, but despite our wish to see around our last corner, our last bend in our British Isle journey, we had to return south to London and then back to Maine. 2006 started my India journeys as I traveled as far as Edayappara, Kerala before my joureney ended, and I had to return home. In 2007 I returned to India and got as far as the hills of eastern Kerala before my journey ended. By 2010, I was back to India but this time my journey took me as far afield as the State of Andrah Pardesh in central India and the small village of Kalyandurg before I had to retrace my steps by way of the Indian Rail System to Kerala and home. Then within two months of my return, I was on another journey (the best of them all) to Israel with my daughter Marnie on a Dallas Theological Seminary extension trip to the Promised Land. What a journey our Palestine trip was, but like with all previous journeys there was an end, a stoppage when in reality I wished to go further. We got to Bethlehem but were not able to go to Hebron. We got to Beersheba but were not able to go to Ashdod. We got to Eilat but were not able to go on to Petra. We got to Dan but never got to Damascus. Our 19-days in the Lord's Land were amazing, beyond description, though I did write of my observations in a book I got published entitled *From Dan to Beersheba and Beyond*. With each twist in the road we came near a Biblical place I wanted to visit but time and the restriction on the West Bank stopped us. Palestinian controlled areas were too dangerous to explore at that time. Our official end was on top of Mount Gerizim looking down on the ancient city of Shechem before we turned around, returned to Jerusalem and eventually home. I desire to take that Israeli journey again to go 'beyond' the end to other sites and sights we missed the first time. Within two years of Israel, I was back in India to travel again to an earth's farthest bounds in the State of Orissa and the town of Phulbani before returning the way I came. Now I am in the Punjab returning from this end of the road. I still have a ways to go to get back home, but for now, I have reached the farthest I will go on this journey. How many more journeys I have in this life I know not, but this I know: "in journeying's often" the Lord has been with me every step of the way and has determined both my beginnings and my endings", even when, like in the Punjab, I was sad. I wanted to go to the Khyber Pass!"

33

Punjab Praise

Before going to Pastor Singh's Praise Baptist Church for an evening of fellowship, we drove back into Amritsar to check in at our hotel room. If I thought the CrownWest was nice in Mohali, I couldn't believe it when we pulled up in front of the Golden Tulip Motel of Amritsar. I thought Shibu had gone out of his mind. This place would surely do great damage to our trip budget! I had never heard of the hotel chain before, but I learned the Golden Tulip was in 40 countries and in 200 locations around the world. They specialize in famous tourist attractions, and, sure enough, we were less than two miles from the greatest tourist attraction in the entire Punjab, The Sikh Golden Temple. As we checked in, Shibu told me that he had found the hotel on line, and they were having a special. We could stay there for actually less money than we had spent at the CrownWest. The five-story building was elaborately decorated, and the facility might just be the best I have ever stayed in, not just in India but also in the States! Despite the five floors there were only 52 rooms. I got this off a Golden Tulip brochure: "All rooms and suites are equipped with minibar, LCD television, including air temperature control, satellite channels, hair dyer, in-room tea and coffee maker, Wi-Fi broadband connectively, electronic safe, and DVD player." And you thought India was a third world country! It is in parts of India but not at the Golden Tulip. There was even a pool on the roof. Of course it had a fine dining restaurant where I would, the next morning, get the best American breakfast I ever had in India, including my half-fried eggs. We settled in and by 6:00 Arood and Shagu picked us up for the half-hour ride to where the Christians of western Punjab were gathering.

We arrived at the small church after walking down a couple of narrow lanes to Pastor M. Singh's house. The mission had built another room on top of the Singh house to create a small sanctuary, which would comfortably accommodate about 40 people, but that night nearly 60 crammed themselves into the room with a few having to sit outside the door on a ledge. I instantly got a great feeling as I entered the room and began to greet the people. There was quite a mixture of young and old and everyone in between. They were all smiling and excited to see an American; a few even spoke English. The typical Indian greetings were offered to Shibu, Shagu, Arood, and me. We were all guests and would be treated as such. The one big difference was in the formal form of the greeting. In Kerala, Andrah Pardesh, and Orissa I usually ended up with some form of flower arrangement around my neck, both artificial and real. But in the Punjab what they put around my neck was money! The banner was made using ten-rupee bills attached to a colorful garland cord that was placed around our necks. The decoration looked like a badge of honor or respect. Despite the poverty I saw everywhere, I graciously received the token, but all I thought was how could I give the gift back to them?

As I sat back in only one of three chairs in the entire room, I looked again in the faces of the pastor and his people. We live in a land where the pastor is more often than not judged by the size of his congregation. This is a delusion manufactured by who knows who, probably the Devil himself, but it has become so standard in judging a work for the Lord. In America a 50-person congregation is seen as a failure, but I sat amazed that this uneducated, simple man could effectively raise a congregation this size in the heart of Sikh country. This worship of the crowd is falsehood. Granted, at times, Jesus even had crowds, but they were crowds for miracles and healings. When he began to teach, why He had come, even his disciples began to leave (John 6:66). Christ would trod this road and He would have the multitudes (Matthew 5:1), but the closer He got to the cross the smaller the multitude. I have come to the conclusion as a small congregation pastor for nearly 45 years, the fewer the people often the better the quality of people! The modern church has fallen in love with big statistics, quantity over quality, and mass movements. What I found in the Punjab was small in statistics, but big in spirituality!

The music was a bit more up-beat than the Chandigarh Baptist Church, but still very nice. The song I remember best was their version of "He is Lord". I have always been surprised when an American hymn or chorus is sung on earth's farthest bounds. Granted I knew not the Punjabi they sang, but the tune was unmistakable. I preached that night of "What manner of . . . .Lord, Love, and Life" from John's first epistle. After the praise, I preached. What I remember best about my sermon was a young man in the front row that seemed to react to my words before Shagu translated them into Punjabi. I meet him after the service and realized he could speak better English than I could. After the preaching and prayers, I was able to mingle with the crowd. The first person I was introduced to was a baby named Believe! His parents wanted me to hold him and pray for him. This is not unusual in India, for I had done it many times before, but it became a special blessing when I heard their story. It seems they had lost a young son, and it appeared they would be having no other children. Of course, their family who were still following the Sikh faith said, "I told you so (American phrase)!" But they stayed true and started praying for another son. Remember, no matter where you travel in India a son is the greatest blessing a couple can have. Sure enough, God answered their supplication just like he did for Hannah (I Samuel 1-2) and in answer to that prayer they called their son Believe!

I shook everyone's hand, but they hung on. Even after a few hours as we were heading back to the motel, we were asked to stop by another home in the village for a special prayer. The Singh (not the pastor, I was learning that many have the name Singh as you will see) family was a family of seven (six kids and a father). The mother had just died in her 30s, and the father wanted special prayer to care for the kids. A motherless home in India is a tragedy because of the role she plays in rearing the children. It was hard to leave. Even after we had the prayer, they wanted us to stay for supper even though they didn't have much. The pastor got us out only to have us return to his home. He wanted us to pray for his wife who was sickly, his mother who was elderly, and that they might have another child. Their first was a girl, a beautiful little girl, a little lady anybody would love. I know they loved her, but they wanted a boy.

We didn't get back to the Golden Tulip until 10:00 PM. The boys were still hungry so they went off by themselves for a late supper. I stayed back in our room to get my journal caught up and thank the Good Lord for the marvelous second day. I had already been told of our third day and the late night trip back to Mohali, but before I hit the hay (as we say in Maine) I had one more blessing on this day. That morning I had missed a call from my wife, but at 11:30 that night we reconnected. It still amazes me that one can talk to a loved one in Maine when you are in the Punjab. It has happened numerous times that no matter how far the earth's farthest bounds are a call is possible. It was great to hear her voice, and I know she was grateful to hear my voice. Coleen has always been concerned on my adventures to the ends of the earth. She knows that I have no fear and can get myself into some dangerous situations. Her California trip was just what she needed to recharge her batteries especially when her grandson son started calling her Gee-Gee!

34

Cycle Rickshaw and Auto Rides in Amritsar

My third day in the Punjab started at 7:00 AM. The view of Amritsar from our fourth- story window was otherworldly. A huge city stretched out before my eyes. My modern surroundings at the plush Golden Tulip was in sharp contrast to what I was witnessing below: horse carts traveling alongside tractor trailers, a cycle rickshaw competing for space with a Land Rover, and three-wheeled autos dodging modern construction equipment trying to finish a future train line that will ferry passengers from one end of the city to the other. Even at 7:00 AM the street vendors were setting up their carts in front of the buildings that line the main road through that part of Amritsar City. I watched the dust rising from the half-paved, four lane street as hundreds of vehicles and thousands of pedestrians traveled back and forth in their daily dance to survive another day in the Punjab. My eye only left the organized chaos when Shibu called for breakfast. And what a breakfast! It was an American breakfast of French toast, pancakes, sausage, toast, and cornflakes with COLD MILK to put on top. Wow!

As Shibu and I left the motel for our morning expedition to the Golden Temple, we realized that we had a bit of extra time before Philipp and Arood were to meet us. They had stayed at a smaller motel down the road from the Golden Tulip. The weather was ideal for me, in the 70s. The activity of a big Indian city was as I have mentioned before—like watching a *National Geographic* Special. My eye caught a group of gypsies trying to cross between

CYCLE RICKSHAW AND AUTO RIDES IN AMRITSAR 137

the barriers that separated the street from the railway construction zone in the middle. It appeared they were trying to reverse their direction and had found a small gap in the median. The group included three wagons pulled by horses and bullocks, about twenty people from small kids to elderly adults, a few cows, and a couple of dogs. They were poor in their appearance, and as I pondered their lifestyle Shibu asked, "Have you ever been on a cycle rickshaw ride?" Brought back from my daydreaming, I answered, "No!" The next thing I knew Shibu was hailing down one of a score of cycle rickshaw drivers that are the taxi drivers of Amritsar. In Kerala it is the auto taxi, but I saw more cycle rickshaws than autoes in the Punjab.

Within seconds a tall (by India standards) muscular man stopped beside us. His rickshaw was simple but sturdy. Shibu asked a price for a small ride around the area, and the man seemed to agree quickly as if he needed the job. The bike with the double seat cart attached was well worn as Shibu and I loaded up. My first thought was for the driver, a man who looked to be near forty. Will he be able to pull the two of us? Combined we weighted over 400 pounds, so how would this Punjabi do? I must admit I felt very Oriental as I settled into my seat, and we started off. Shibu and I took a selfie to record the adventure. I was amazed at the power of the man as he peddled us through early morning traffic. It was a bit scary as we crossed traffic for a side street on the other side of the road, but we made it to a quieter lane. Our original intent was for just a fifteen-minute ride, but something must have been lost in translation because we were over half an hour traveling some of the side streets and back alleys of Amritsar. We even made it up a small incline seemingly effortlessly. When we arrived back in front of the Golden Tulip, we were well pleased with our little adventure. Our cycle rickshaw drive had worked up a sweat, but I was in a sweat when I noticed that Shibu only gave him 100 rupees. I questioned the amount and he said it was normal, but I gave the man a 100 rupee tip, and even with that the cycle rickshaw ride cost us less than four dollars!

Despite the extra time on the rickshaw ride, we still had to wait a few more minutes for Philipp and Arood to show up. When they did they had a Sikh auto driver in tow to take us on our ride to the Golden Temple and, to our surprise, Pastor M. Singh from the Praise Baptist Church joined us on the adventure. It was then I started to add up the number of passengers for this small auto. There were five of us besides the driver, and could I say all big guys? I had ridden in autoes before but with the most, two other people. I thought to myself, "This ought to be interesting!" Philipp and Shibu and I climbed in the back seat and Arood and Singh settled in beside the driver, one on each side. I was told we were just a couple miles from the famous temple, but the trip might take us some time depending on traffic, and there was plenty of traffic as there always is in India.

We soon left the main street about a block from our motel. It seemed the farther we traveled the more congested the streets. Again, my eyes were on the hundreds of new sights I was seeing: the milling crowds around every shop, the countless cycle rickshaws and cars, and in-between every one were people simply walking and, of course, a cow or two, dogs and oxen and were those chickens running in front of us? We had just navigated around one of those circle intersections when I heard from behind me somebody yelling above the din of the city noise. At first I didn't pay any attention. It was just a louder sound in the middle of mass pandemonium. My companion also seemed uninterested in the policeman that was now running beside our auto.

It was then the reality of the situation became clear to the auto driver and Pastor Singh and anyone else that could understand Punjabi. *Our auto was on fire!* Sure enough from under the back cover of the auto a column of smoke was exiting just a few inches from where Shibu and Philipp and I were sitting. We quickly abandoned the auto as the driver brought his machine to a sudden stop. Quickly the driver removed the cover and sure enough the engine was on fire; too much weight? The traffic cop who had warned us was also back by this time with some water in a jug. The flames were quickly put out, but our ride to the Golden Temple was over or at least in that auto. What surprised me more was just how quickly another driver came along to take us on our journey. This auto looked different than the others. I was about ready to take my first ride in an electric auto!

We paid the first auto driver his fare and piled into the second auto. Because there was no big engine, there was a bit more space in the electric auto. But once again, I wondered if the motor had the power to pull the six of us along. It did! The drive through the traffic and pedestrians was slow but no more fires. The bedlam only increased the closer we got to the temple and about half a mile from the entrance we stopped again. I was told no vehicles were permitted any further. We would have to walk the rest of the way, a prospect that I thought was great. Over my many days in India, few have been those days that I have been able to walk among the masses. To walk freely and openly was a rare privilege for me in India, so as we exited the electric auto and headed down a side street in downtown Amritsar, I was in heaven.

Our walk to the Golden Temple took another fifteen minutes. I was again a country boy gazing and gawking at the wonders of a big city. The streets were congested with pilgrims, and I realized once again that one of the greatest joys of going to a special place was the journey getting to that special place. I came around a corner and there it was, not the Golden Temple but the courtyard surrounding the temple. If what was beyond those walls was anything like what was before those walls, I was in for a very special treat!

35

The Golden Temple of the Sikhs

Throughout my many trips to India, I have always had a desire to visit a Hindu temple or an Islamic mosque or both. Despite traveling by many of these structures, the only temple I had been to before the Golden Temple was a Buddhist temple called Dhaul Shant Stupa outside the Orissa capital of Bhubaneshwar. I understood why my hosts were reluctant in letting me visit such sites; so to be walking into the courtyard of the most holy site of the Sikh religion was a dream for me! I was not there to worship as with Dhaul Shant Stupa, but that doesn't mean, as with my walk around the Buddhist temple I was not blessed. (If you haven't read my book *The Uttermost Part* you might find the thirty-fourth chapter interesting as I share the story of the unexpected blessing bestowed on me by a Buddhist priest). Before I share my impressions of the Golden Temple, let me give you a bit of history and description of this shrine:

"The spiritual centre of the Sikh, the Golden Temple was built between 1589 and 1601 and is a superb synthesis of Islamic and Hindu styles of architecture. In keeping with the syncretic tradition of those times, its foundation stone was laid by a Muslim saint, Mian Mir. It was virtually destroyed in 1781 by an Afghan invader, Ahmed Shah Abdali, but was rebuilt some years later by Maharaja Ranjit Singh, ruler of Punjab, who covered the dome in gold and embellished its interior with lavish decorations. The holiest site of the Sikhs, the three-story temple (Hari Mandir), decorated with superb pietra dura is where the Holy Book is kept. The Holy Book (Guru Granth Sahib) is covered with a jeweled canopy and lies in the Durbar Sabib (Court of the Lord). The lower walls and foundation of the temple are made of white marble while the upper walls are covered in pure gold, whereby it gets its name. The holy shrine is surrounded by a maze of lanes (it was like a maze to get to the temple from where our auto driver let us off) and eighteen fortified gates. The temple complex is actually a city within a city, and the main entrance is through its northern gateway, known as the Darshani Darwaza (the entrance we took into the site). Once you enter you step down to the Parikrama (marble pathway) which encircles the Amrit Sarovar (pool of nectar-where the Sikhs are baptized and was built in 1577 by Ram Das, the 4th guru). There is a causeway that leads from the Parikrama to the temple which sits on an island in the middle of the pool. The causeway is 197 feet long and is flanked by nine gilded lamps on each side. The Darshani Deorhi is the gateway into the temple and it containing two massive silver doors."

I think it is time to take a walk with me around the Golden Temple. Note, around, because we never actually got to go in it!

Upon reaching the plaza in front of the Darshani Darwaza and Clock-Tower, we first had to remove our shoes. That was the first amazing thing to me, how they were able to keep track of all the pilgrims' shoes. We gave ours to a check-in lady, and she gave us a number and, sure enough, after our two-hour tour we got our shoes back! We then had to cover our heads with a turban. You could buy one (as far back as where our auto driver dropped us off, the salesmen of turbans had tried to sell us one) or simply pick out one from a bin just in front of the gate. I picked out a blue one and Shibu picked out an orange one. We took a selfie of the two imitation Sikhs. Our third requirement for entrance was the walking through a pool of water to wash our feet. To enter the gate you must wade through about four inches of water. Until then we had seen nothing but the elaborate plaza with a fountain in the middle and the 60 foot high white granite walls that surround the entire complex. Only when we got within the gate did the panorama vista of the Golden Temple in the middle of a body of water come into view. We walked down a series of steep steps to finally reach the interior of the temple area.

I stood for a few moments to take in the grandeur of the site. It was massive. It was like an inner courtyard of high walls and a granite walkway all around a five-acre lake and there in the middle was the Golden Temple. It was certainly golden; even more golden, in my opinion, than the golden Dome of the Rock in Jerusalem! The next thing that caught my attention were the fish (like giant gold fish) swimming near to the steps that led down into the water. It was then I saw, for the first time, a person entering into the water to be self-baptized. The doctrine is if you wash in the pool surrounding the Golden Temple your sins will be washed away. It was here I got my first picture taken with the Sikh ceremonial guards. I think a size requirement was necessary, for every guard we saw seemed to be six foot four and weigh 250 pounds. They were huge men all decked out in their ancient temple garb including their impressive spears. After the picture, we began to wander around the pool counter-clockwise with the hundreds if not thousands of others—mostly Sikhs worshiping, but there were a few like us just sight-seeing.

Our first stop was at the Athsath Tirath (or 68 shrines). I must admit my eyes were mostly turned to the pool and the multitude of fish swimming near the surface of the water. As we turned the first corner, I saw a man in the pool with what looked like a cleaning rod, like you would see a pool man have to clean a swimming pool. Then it hit me; sure the pool needed to be clean if all those people get into it for baptism. It was also on that corner we saw a series of booths that people, especially women, could use to baptize in private. It was then Philipp came up to us and asked if we wanted to see the feeding operation at the Golden Temple. It seems that every individual that comes into the temple area is fed or is at least offered a meal. We walked through the dining hall area where scores of people were preparing bread and vegetables and other foods I didn't even ask about. The operation was on an impressive scale as hundreds of people could be feed at once. It was then I realized that the Sikh religion was all about good works. Every person I saw working was not an employee but a volunteer. Ordinary Sikh gave their time to the temple to pay for good favor. Young and old alike serve others as a way of serving themselves. I watched a young man making the flat bread that was the cornerstone of the meal. I watched young ladies buttering the bread before it was sent off to the huge bins where the pilgrims could pick it up. I watched scores of people cutting up carrots and onions and potatoes to be added to the mixture of curries that would make up the rest of the meal. Then I watched the scores of dishwashers (no mechanical dishwashers at the Golden Temple) hand wash every metal plate and metal cup!

Before we left the dining area of the Golden Temple, I stopped a minute by the pool before we continued our walk to consider just how damning a "works" religion can be. I have come to the believe other than Christianity many are trapped into the falsehood of a religion of good works. Unfortunately, I am afraid certain segments of my faith also have been trapped in the falsehood of works. The fundamental tenant of my faith are these words from the pen of Paul to the Ephesians, "For by grace are ye saved through faith; *and that not of yourselves*: it is a gift of God: *not of works*, lest any man should boast." (Ephesians 2:8-9) A Sikh can do a lot of boasting if he spends just one day at the Golden Temple serving. Some of the most devote and gracious people I met in my walking tour are seen through the food preparation quarter of the Golden Temple!

36

The Trees of the Golden Temple

As Shibu and I left the food preparers and the food eaters, the rest of our party seemed to head off in other directions leaving Shibu and me to finish the circling of the temple on the Parikrama on our own. The eating arrangements at the Golden Temple were impressive. Guru ka Langar is the meal provided for the pilgrims. The kitchen and dining hall can feed up to 10,000 people a day and seat 3,000 people at a time—and I mean seat 3,000 people at a time. We didn't stop to be part of the food eaters and partake in the simple meal of dal-roti—lentil curry and bread. Periodically we would stop by the pool's edge and take a picture with the temple behind us. I couldn't pass a temple guard without snapping a photograph. I was impressed with their costumes, their size, and their spears. We slowly worked our way to the other side of the lake having for a few minutes walked up the side lane to the assembly hall. The late morning sun was high overhead when we finally arrived at the entrance to the causeway that would take us to the temple. It was then we realized we didn't have enough time in our tour to actually wait to go in. The crowd was that large. It reminded me of the day I was in Bethlehem at the Church of the Nativity and wanting to visit the grotto they claim to be the birthplace of Jesus. As with the Golden Temple, the line was too long to wait because of our schedule. The same thing happened when Marnie and I arrived at the Holy Sepulcher Church in Jerusalem and a chance to visit Golgotha—too long a line. That seems to be my fate at times when I reach a famous site and find more people want to see it than there is time for me to see it! So what do you do when you can't make the trek into the Sikh's holiest site? You go to Arjun Dev's Tree!

For nearly half an hour, Shibu and I stood outside the Darshani Deorhi, the only entrance to the Golden Temple, by one of only two trees in the entire complex. It not only provided me with a wonderful place to watch the happenings of the temple pilgrims, but it gave me a bit of shade in the warming day in the Punjab. I learned long ago that any shade is better than no shade under a tropical sun. With the Psalmist I believe this about my God, "... *the Lord is thy shade upon they right hand*" (Psalm 121:5). The Arjun Dev's Tree stands right in front of the Akal Takht, a building directly across from the Darshani Deorhi. The Akal Takht is the seat of the supreme religious order of the Sikhs; it also houses the gurus' swords and flagstaffs, as well as the Holy Book at night. The sixth guru, Guru Hargobind, completed its construction when he began organizing the Sikh community into a political entity. As part of the daily ritual at the Golden Temple, the Holy Book of the Sikhs is carried out of the Akal Takht to the Hari Mandir (Golden Temple) at daybreak. The head priest then opens it for the vaq, the message for the day. From dawn until late at night, the temple echoes with the music of ragis, musicians employed by the temple to sing verses from the Holy Book. While Shibu and I stood under the Arjun Dev's Tree, there was a group of about a dozen musicians doing that very thing. Just to the right of them was also a group of priests proclaiming the truths of the Holy Book. It hit me after a while that I was in the middle of a Sikh worship service and that was even before one gets into the temple.

It was then Shibu whispered in my ear, "Do you know what they do in the temple?" I thought for a moment. If the singing is done outside and the preaching is done outside what is there left to do? Then it hit me what the Golden Temple was for—offerings! Then Shibu told me that every visitor (including non-Sikhs) is given a dollop of sweet prasad (holy offering). But for most they bring their own offering and people come from all over the world to give an offering in the Golden Temple. The temple is nothing other than an offering plate, a collection box. According to Shibu, the Sikh religion is one of the wealthiest in the world. People give gold and silver, gems and jewels, and just about anything of value and that is why there are no admission fees and no cost for the Guru ka Langar-the holy meal at the Golden Temple.

This is all a part of the Sikh doctrine of kar-seva. We mentioned in our last chapter about the voluntary manual labour for the cause, the giving of yourself and your time to the service of the temple. Tasks like sweeping the grounds, cleaning the pool, cooking the langar, looking after the pilgrims' shoes, and standing guard duty are all done as either a penance or an act of worship, and then there is giving of something valuable. I saw only enthusiastic acts going on under and around the Arjun Dev's Tree. These people were not being beaten or shamed into these acts of service, but they were eagerly doing what they saw as their duty. They told me that around 9:45 PM after evening prayers, the Holy Book is reverently closed and carried in a silver palanquin back to the Akal Takht. The floors of the Hari Mandir are then washed with milk and water and the silver doors of the Darshani Deorhi are close for the night. The next morning the whole ritual is repeated again. My spiritual soul started to cry for this proud, hospitable, and open people, the best in India, in my opinion. I thought the Hindus were gracious. Blinded by the god of good works, they were doing everything they could to gain their own salvation. They were working harder than most I have seen, and as I turned the final corner back to where we had entered, I came face to face with another falsehood of good works.

They called it the Dukh Bhanjani Ber or the shrine tree. The story behind this tree was the miraculous powers it was said to have for healing all manner of diseases. One of the lessons I have learned about any so-called divine healer, human or tree, is what is required to get that healing. More often than not some payment is required. *Have you ever noticed that when Jesus healed anybody from anything that He never demanded anyone to pay?* All that was needed was faith. Faith and not works is the key to healing. As James put it, ". . . the prayer of faith shall save the sick . . ." (James 5:15) I know of only one healing tree and that tree is in Heaven (Revelation 22:2) not Amritsar, Punjab, India! We passed the Dukh Bhanjani Ber on our left as we finished our stroll around the Parikrama, and like with every other shrine in the Golden Temple complex, there were a group of people surrounding the tree—touching it and praying to it and wondering if they would be the one that would be healed. It reminded me of the myth of the troubled waters at Bethesda (John 5:4). How I wish I could have gone up to the people of Punjab at the shrine tree and tell them that healing doesn't come from a tree but from a tree on top of Calvary! I saw no healings, and I knew that the temple was just another way in which the Wicked One was blinding the eyes of those that would not see (II Corinthians 4:4).

Before I left the Golden Temple, I did have one unexpected blessing. As I reached the stairs leading back to the plaza and our waiting friends, a little boy about twelve years of age with a white turban on his head came up to me. In perfect English he asked if he might have his picture taken with me. If this was the first time it had happened in India I might have been surprised, but it wasn't. What was such a blessing was the way in which this lad approached me. Remember where I was and the crowd of people there. I could see his father at a distance, but the little boy boldly approached me on his own. He reminded me of the lad and his lunch (John 6:9) and the great miracle of the feeding of the five thousand. Jesus fed the multitudes with that lad's lunch, but I was in a place where a multitude was trying to feed the masses themselves. I ask—who serves the greater God?

37

Barry Singh

By the middle of my third day in the Punjab, I had done enough Punjabi things that my companions were calling me Barry Singh. Singh is the most prominent last name in the Punjab as you have seen, and there is more to come. We left the Golden Temple and pretty much retraced our steps back through the masses to the circle intersection where we had been dropped off mid-morning. I was surprised to see a McDonald's around the first corner from the Golden Temple plaza. I had missed it coming in, but my American stomach was growling. I thought it is lunch time so why not treat the boys to an American meal? My suggestion was quickly rejected, not by my companions, but by me when I discovered that in a Punjab McDonald's there is no meat. Years ago there was a famous American commercial with the catch phrase, "Where's the beef?" It seems that beef is outlawed in the Punjab, a direct religious connection to the Sikh faith. When I found out this reality, I decided not to find out what was behind the Golden Arches!

Once we got back to the place where we could pick up a ride back to the Golden Tulip, the mid-day traffic was insane. I was glad I was with someone who knew what he was doing. Within a short time, Arood had hired another auto to get us back to his car. I was informed that an unexpected meeting in an independent church had been arranged. Shibu thought it might give me a taste of Christianity outside the mission. I was game for any circumstance or situation where I would get a chance to preach. The meeting was set for 1:00 PM so we had to hurry to get there on time. The trip back through central Amritsar was thrilling, like a bumper-car ride without the bumping though you wonder why in the tight spaces of the narrow streets there were not more accidents. We finally got back to Arood's car, and we immediately loaded up for our cross-city trip to the New Life Church of Amritsar and Pastor Suraj Ganguly, a former Hindu with a good government job. Pastor Ganguly pastors three house churches each Sunday. More of a lay pastor, this friendly man had heard of our visit and wanted to meet us. The invitation was passed on through Pastor M. Singh, and within half an hour we were parking on an overpass and walking down a side alley to a high rise about a hundred yards off the street.

When we arrived, I quickly realized we were in an apartment complex with many rooms and on the third floor there with a central living area. I immediately noticed a meal was being prepared and plenty of people were gathering. Shibu, Philipp, Arood, and I were ushered into a side room, and the door was closed. I thought that was unusual, but when in the Punjab do what the Punjabis' tell you to do. We had barely arrived on time because of a traffic issue. As we were traveling to the New Life Church, we had to cross a set of railroad tracks; when we arrived the road rods were down. Quickly the traffic backed up but there was nothing we could do until the Indian freight train into Amritsar passed. I expected the church service to begin immediately, but how wrong I was. 1:00 PM came and went then 1:30 PM. As the clock neared 2:00 we were still sitting and waiting, and then it happened. The door opened and the food poured in, and I mean poured. For the next two hours, course after course appeared, and we hadn't even seen the pastor yet. I filled up on the first course thinking that was it, but no. The boys were gracious and sampled each offering, but after the third course I stopped. Maybe, I should have tried the McDonald's?

Just before 4:00 the food stopped, the pastor and his wife arrived, and she began to lead the people in singing. It wasn't long before I realized that we were in the midst of a Pentecostal-style service rather than a Baptist-style of worship, but I didn't mind. The room and the area outside the door were packed with plenty of people. They sang for about fifteen minutes then I was introduced and preached a short message on checking your spiritual eye sight from II Corinthians 4:18. Is there anything that harms us more than the loss of our eyesight? I have known a few blind people over my years. At the present time, we have a member of our church in Ellsworth that has been blind since middle age. I visit him often and have found him one of the most interesting parishioners I have ever had. I admire his willingness, despite his handicap, to live life to the fullest. What I have been most impressed with in his testimony was his cross-country trip by bus with only his seeing-eye dog as his guide! I impressed on the folks of New Life Church it is important that we have a guide even when we have our sight. In this world, our eyes can be deceived. We can see mirages, things we think we see but there is nothing there. The god of this world is trying to constantly blind us (II Corinthians 4:4). There is no point in asking the Good Lord to open our spiritual eyes when we already have them focused on something else. I told them to, *"turn their eyes upon Jesus, and look full into His wonderful face, and only then will the things of this world grow strangely dim in the light of His glory and grace!"*

After the service was over the congregation swarmed all over me. I think I had my picture taken with every member of the church especially the women. I might just as well have been Barry Singh that day. It was hard to get away, for as we left the church family followed us to our car. Unable to understand a word spoken, I simply followed the lead of Philipp. We still had a few stops to make before heading out for our last service at Glory Baptist Church and Pastor G. Singh's fellowship and then off overnight back to Mohali. So we walked as they talked, and because Shibu and I couldn't understand a word, we talked about our day. It was then I learned that it had cost each of us 50 rupees to travel to the Golden Temple; that is about 80 cents. That the oranges the street vendors were selling were called tangerines, and you could buy two for thirty rupees. I know these simple facts of life in Amritsar might not be interesting to you, but they were helpful for an outsider who was trying to fit in. Each and every time I go to a place like Amritsar I have tried to apply the teachings of Paul on the matter. "And unto the Jew I became as a Jew, that I might gain the Jew; to them that are under the law, as under the law, that I might gain them that are under the law; to them that are without the law, as without law, (being not without law to God, but under the law to Christ,) that I might gain them that are without law. To the weak became I as weak, that I might gain the weak: I am made all things to all men that I might by all means save some. And this I do for the Gospel's sake, that I might be partakers thereof with you." (I Corinthians 9:20-23)

Perhaps, that is why the Good Lord directed me to walk away from that McDonald's, so that I might have an afternoon meal with my Punjabi brethren, to worship with my Punjabi sisters, and be called by my Punjabi name, Barry Singh. One thing I have never had trouble doing in earth's farthest bounds is blending in, accepting that when in Israel do as the Israelis do. When in Australia do as the Auzzies do, and when in the Punjab do as the Punjabi do. I might have visited the Sikh temple, but within a few hours I had visited the true temple of God: "Know ye not that ye are the temple of God, and that the Spirit of God dwelleth in you?" (I Corinthians 3:16) Yes, and in Barry Singh as well!

38

Manohar Singh

I would like to introduce you to a Punjabi man by first reminding you of an encounter Jesus had with an unnamed centurion in Capernaum. "And when Jesus was entered into Capernaum, there came unto him a centurion, beseeching him, and saying, Lord, my servant lieth at home sick of the palsy, grievously tormented. And Jesus saith unto him, I will come and heal him. The centurion answered and said, Lord, I am not worthy that thou shouldest come under my roof: but speak the world only, and my servant shall be healed. For I am a man under authority, having soldiers under me: and I say to this man, Go, and he goeth; and to another, Come, and he cometh; and to my servant, Do this, and he doeth it. When Jesus heard it, he marveled, and said to them that followed, Verily I say unto you, I have not found so great faith, no, not in Israel. And I say unto you, that many shall come from the east and west, and shall sit down with Abraham, and Isaac, and Jacob, in the kingdom of heaven. But the children of the kingdom shall be cast out into outer darkness: there shall be weeping and gnashing of teeth. And Jesus said unto the centurion, Go thy way; and as thou hast believed, so be it done unto thee. And his servant was healed in the selfsame hour." (Matthew 8:5-13) May I share with you the story of Manohar Singh, a man of great faith in Amritsar, Punjab!

We left the New Life Church late in the afternoon of March 16, 2016. As we traveled back through the crowded streets of Amritsar, Philipp told us we had a quick stop to make before we returned to our motels to checkout. A member of Pastor M. Singh's church wanted a visit because he and his family were not able to make the meeting the night before. Philipp told me that I would be interested in his story. We weaved our way through a series of roads and lanes before we came to a modest home in a side alley on the edge of town. There to greet us were four people: a father (Manohar), a son (Rahul), a mother (Amanpreet), and a daughter-in-law, whose name I never got. They looked at first like a typical Punjabi family, and what impressed me most about Manohar was the huge red turban on his head. It made him look a foot taller than he was, and I must admit I have always been fascinated with men who have the self-confidence to wear a sheet around their heads. We were invited into the living room of their home with all the hospitality and graciousness of any Indian. Immediately the refreshment began to arrive against our protest (remember, we had just endured a two-hour meal and we were full), but nothing could deter the Singh family from entertaining us with soda, fruit, candy, and dessert!

As we sat around and talked, the amazing testimony of Manohar Singh began to emerge from the casual conversation that was taking place around the sitting area. Manohar's life was changed when in middle age he heard for the first time the story of Jesus, and a rare thing in the Punjab took place. He was converted. A devout Sikh, Manohar had for most of his life tried to work his way into the good graces of his god, but with no satisfaction. That is until he met the Christ. He was gloriously saved, and his family of two boys and a wife soon followed. Manohar had become very successful and had worked his way up through governmental service until he held an important job with all the worldly benefits to go with that job. He owned a great house and could send his children to the finest schools. But two and a half years before my visit, Manohar had a Job-like trial of his faith. Manohar's son Rahul was involved in a serious motorcycle accident, literally every bone in his body was broken. A young man full of life and one of the best cricket players in the area was now in a hospital, a stay that would last for a year and a half. It was a miracle he even lived, but Manohar and his family took up the challenge to nurse Rahul back to health. The first problem was that in order to get Rahul the best of care, they had to move him into a private rehab center. India runs a government supported health care system, but the care is limited but paid for. Private pay systems (eventually Rahul's bill reached 6 ½ million rupees) are better but expensive. Manohar choose to go the private route and within a short time had run through all his savings. As the time in the rehab center lengthened, he had to sell his big house to pay the bills. He was hoping the settlement over the accident (another person was at fault) would come through, but the India court system is very slow and at the writing of this chapter, 3 ½ years after the accident, the case still has to be settled. Because the India health system, both public and private, demands a lot of help from the family (in some case bringing in food and helping with rehab) Manohar took so much time off from his good job to care for Rahul that he lost his job!

Also there was the attack from his family and friends, still in the Sikh faith, that told Manohar if he would reconvert this would go away, and Rahul would be healed. Despite the assaults and attacks, Manohar never once lost his faith. Like Job he was hanging on the day I met him and heard his sweet story of trust. God had answered their prayers and Rahul was home, but still unable to work, yet the family continues to believe that Rahul will be completely healed and that one day the 25-year-old son will be back to work. Rahul's older brother, the husband of the daughter-in-law I met that day was away working helping to support the family. Manohar believes that like with Job (Job 42) God will one day give him everything back and, like the centurion's servant, his son will be completely healed! ". . . I have not found so great faith, no, not in . . ." the Punjab and may I add perhaps ever in the context of such a severe trial!

Despite the seriousness of the story, perhaps the funniest event of my entire India trip also took place at Manohar Singh's house. After hearing Manohar's amazing story, we began to try and leave. We still had to get back to the motel and pack up for our trip back across the Punjab. There was also the travel to our last service in western Punjab in New Amritsar, a ways outside of Amritsar City. Time was slipping away, but we couldn't seem to leave. Every time we headed for the door there was another treat brought in by Amanpreet. Finally Philipp asked if I might prayer for the Singh family, the situation with the court, and Rahul's health to which I readily agreed and bowed my head for prayer. As I paused for a moment, I could still hear the conversation continuing so I thought that I might have misunderstood my instruction. It was then I opened my eyes and before my face was a bowl of bananas. In my moments of pre-pray, Mrs. Singh had returned from the kitchen and was presenting her honored guest with another snack. I guess the expression on my face was so shocking that the whole room erupted in laughter. Later Shibu told me that the look on my face on seeing more food was priceless. We all had a good laugh, and we did eventually get to pray. Just before dusk, we did leave the Manohar Singh house, but our fellowship would not be over because later that evening at the Gospel Baptist Church one of the late arrivals to the service was the Singh family.

As I ponder the lesson of Manohar Singh, I realized something else in Jesus' story, the centurion, and the Manohar story. Jesus said that there would be many that would come from the east and the west to be a part of His kingdom. Well, I think I know someone from the east. A man can talk and brag about his faith, but until that faith is tried (I Peter 1:6-7) one never really knows just would kind of faith he has.

39

Magnum Bars in the Punjab

By 7:00 PM we were at the Glory Baptist Church for an evening service. This would be our farewell meeting in Western Punjab. The mission outreach in that part of the Punjab was strategically located as two bookends are on a shelf: Pastor Manjeet Singh's Praise Baptist Church is located on the western side of Amritsar in the village of Khasa and Pastor Giurjit Singh's Glory Baptist Church is located on the eastern side of Amritsar in the village of New Amritsar. These villages were but a part of the mega-city eighteen miles across. So as Pastor Philipp told me, *"We now have the city surrounded and we will see what the Good Lord will do in the middle!"*

As with the Praise Church building, the Glory Church building was actually a build-on. Remember at Praise, they added a room on top of Pastor Singh's home. At Glory they actually added a roof over the alley way between the Singh homes. The compound was a collection of small houses of one family with Pastor Giurjit Singh's dad's home being the first. As is often the case in India, families stay together and when a new generation grows up they simply build next door and often the buildings are connected. The simple answer for a sanctuary for the Glory Church was to connect the roofs of the three homes in the triangle. What was created was a long, narrow room, a lane really. Giurjit house was at the peak of the triangle while his brother's house and his father's house formed the other two points. A staircase was built up to the roof that added more space, and sure enough, I found when I climbed the staircase women on the roof preparing another meal. Yes, we would eat again before we headed back across the Punjab!

While the congregation and guests gathered, I was invited by Giurjit's father to see his horse and cart. This elderly man was one of hundreds of horse-cart drivers I had seen on the streets and back lanes of Amritsar. He boarded his horse behind his house, and I found it fascinating the story he told me through Philipp's translation. I asked of his day, and he told me he had one job that day. That task was to transport a load of goods three miles across town. I never asked what the load consisted of. He drove his horse and cart from his house to pick up the goods in town then drove three miles to the delivery spot on another side of town and back home for a total of over ten miles. How much did he get for his day's work-500 rupees ($7.35)! What touched me most was the fact that it cost him 200 rupees ($2.94) just for the fuel (hay), so for the day's work this man earned just $4.41! Another reminder of just how hard people work in India for very little in return. I could, however, sense the pride this man had in his work and his horse. As darkness engulfed Mr. Singh's backyard, I patted his horse and I admired his cart. Actually there were two horses and two carts in the yard. The other owned by a neighbor. We went back inside for the evening service and, as we did, I praised the Good Lord for reaching down and saving another family in the heart of Sikh country!

Once again I was sitting in only one of four chairs with everybody else sitting on the concrete street and up the stairs of the staircase to the roof. I counted about 70 individuals. But what was so exciting to me was that half of them were under fifteen years of age, and they were sitting literally at my feet. I hardly had room to stand, but the intimacy was special as they began to sing. They sang 45 minutes non-stop, but they only sang four songs! I preached for about an hour with translation time. The service stopped around nine, but the ministry had just begun. How these people loved to be prayed for! After the final public prayer and in-between the service and the supper, people came up to me for personal prayer. It was the kids first and then the adults. There were prayers for healing and school work and an unsaved friend. I had a chance during lunch time to pray for the Manohar Singh family needs. Rahul was there with his father and mother, and I prayed for his complete healing. I ate very little of the big meal Pastor Singh's wife and the ladies of the church prepared. I was still full from our afternoon meal. I was enjoying the sweet fellowship with the saints of Amritsar. Over and over again they asked if I would return, but will I? Only the Good Lord knows if I will and my prayer is that I will, but as I told them whether here or there we will be together again someday!

Finally around 10:00 PM we left the Glory Baptist Church family and headed east down the same roads and highways and country lanes that had brought us to the western side of the Punjab. Arood drove us through the darkened towns and villages scattered in-between the bigger cities of central Punjab. As we rode, we talked of the wonderful assemblies of believers that were shining lights in a pagan land. I had come to the conclusion early on in my time in the Punjab that its people made tremendous saints: strong, faithful, and dedicated. I also came to the conclusion that it was the daily testing of these saints that made them so strong and committed. Though they faced no physical persecution like their brethren in Orissa and other parts of India, there was that constant social pressure on men like Manohar that turned their beginning faith into great faith. They firmly and without questioned believed that the battle is the Lord's (I Samuel 17:47) and despite being outnumbered in the number of devoted Sikh believers they were not outclassed in the struggle to win the Punjab to Christ. These were a group of ordinary people that were doing extraordinary things in the name of Jesus.

About halfway through our return trip, a trip that only took us four hours in the dark compared to the five hour in the light, Arood pulled his car into what looked like an American-style truck stop. It was a little after midnight, but the service area was hopping and hooping. There were places you could gas up, but there was also a mini-mall with all the stores still open for business. There were places to eat and places for kids to play besides the tourist traps. We wandered around the central plaza, a mini-museum of the kinds of work done in the area plus the history of the village. The creators had made concrete images of the local hero and mockups of the kinds of occupation. In the middle of the area was a fountain, a pleasant place to take a break from travel. As I got my picture taken with a door-man with a bright yellow turban by one of the shops, Shibu was off exploring. When I looked around for him, I caught a glimpse of his back around the backside of the plaza. I walked towards him and found him in front of Kuality Wall's, an ice cream stand. He saw me coming and asked if I wanted an ice cream. Granted, we hadn't eaten in three hours, but it was a new day and when I saw they had magnum bars I immediately said "Sure"! I had my very first magnum bar (my favorite ice cream bar now) with my daughter Marnie just after we climbed through Hezekiah's Tunnel in Jerusalem. Ever since that day I have associated that marvelous treat with special occasions. Before this India trip was through, I would have another special event with a magnum bar with Shibu, but you will have to wait on that story. Shibu would buy four magnum bars in total, one for me, one for Philipp, and one for Arood besides himself. As we ate our treats in the cool air of central Punjab, we began to notice the truck stop shutting down. They must have had a curfew time (1:00 AM), for before we finished our bars most of the people had left, the shops were closed, and the lights were turned off. It was time to finish our trek back to Mohali with the energy provide by a magnum bar!

40

Kentucky Fried Chicken Indian Style

It was good to sleep in until 8:30 AM, but remember, I hadn't gotten back from the Western Punjab part of our mission's trip until 2:30 on the morning of our fourth day in the Punjab. We returned to the wonderful accommodations of the Hotel Crownwest where we had spent our first two nights. Shibu was up even earlier than I for breakfast. (Remember, I am not a big breakfast-kind-of-a-guy, so if I have a chance to miss one, India or America, I will) He was with Pastor Philipps on an early morning mission to find a suitable room for the Punjab Extension Program sponsored by Kerala Baptist Bible College. Patterned after the Tamil Nadu Extension Program, this training project was going to give the local pastors, who had never been to Bible College, a chance to study under the tutorage of a college professor. So as Philipps and Shibu hunted for a rental, I got my Punjab journal caught up.

The next event on my Punjab calendar was a luncheon meeting with all the current Punjab pastors, and we were also to be joined by the new leader of the extension work Shijil Samuel who was traveling in from Haryana (the State just south of the Punjab) where he had been working as a missionary. Even the Singh boys were traveling into Chandigarh from Amritsar by train. How early had they started seeing we never left them until around 10:00 the night before? This would be the first time that all the Punjab team would be getting together, and I would join them, but where?

Around 1:00 Philipps and Shibu returned to the hotel. They didn't find the place they were looking for, but they had some good leads.—Postscript:

KENTUCKY FRIED CHICKEN INDIAN STYLE

As I write this chapter in my fifth India book, I have recently been sent a photograph of a session of the new extension group; the classes started about four months after I left. It was then I heard a phrase by Shibu that has helped me understand the cautious and deliberate actions of this man of God—*"Shortcuts That Cut You Short"!* Ponder that the next time you are in a hurry to do something for the Lord. Shibu has always seemed to have the patience to wait on the Lord and to never make a decision about something before its time, including a rental room for an extension program that would not start for a few months. As we discussed the pros and cons of the rental properties they had visited, I asked where we were going for lunch and some familiar words come out of Shibu's mouth, "Kentucky Fried Chicken!"

By a little after 2:00 PM the seven of us (Shibu, Febon, Shijil, Manjeet, Giurjit, Shiju, and I) had gathered at the local KFC. It looked like your typical KFC, Indian or American. I had been in another KFC in Hyderabad on my last trip to India in 2012, so I was expecting some of the same, small portions but that classic flavor. The reason Philipps and Shibu had chosen the site was the fact that the pastors from Western Punjab had never been to a KFC before. They wanted to give them a treat. We entered the store and got in line at the counter. The minute I saw the menu on the board above the counter I realized that this wasn't your typical KFC. There was hot chicken and not so hot chicken, but the extra crispy and the original recipe weren't even on the menu, but why? Before we left that afternoon I was able to speak to the manager, not because I sought him out because he sought me out. He had few westerners for customers, and he wanted my opinion on his restaurant. I asked why not the traditional chicken and he told me they had started the KFC with the American menu, but soon found out that the chicken was too bland for the Indian palate, so they had to spice it up a bit. I found that even though the chicken we chose to eat, a bucket of spicy and a bucket of mild, it wasn't hot enough for the boys. The meal for seven, my treat, cost me just over twenty bucks! I might not have enjoyed the meal myself, but I enjoyed watching six Indians eat an American meal Indian style.

As we sat and ate, I listened to the chatter that happens around a bucket of chicken. Granted, most of the conversation was in Punjabi, but on occasion they would talk in broken English and I could pick up a few words. It wasn't so much the content of the conversations around that KJC table that drew my attention, but the realization of the mission of these men and my opportunity to sharpen their ax. Do you remember the amazing story from the life of the prophet Elisha where he was able to miraculously make an ax-head swim? (II Kings 6:6) I was raised on an old farm where the ax was still an important instrument. I never was a good ax-man, and my father never allowed me to sharpen the ax, a very delicate operation that good skilled hands. I, like the man in the Bible story, broke more ax-handles than the average, but I never was close enough to a stream to actually lose an ax-head. All you have to do is cut wood with a dull ax-head and then chop wood with a sharp ax-head and you will know the difference.

I can still see in my mind's eye Dad holding the ax and me turning the grindstone. Later a small motor was attached to the stone so I would only watch. Anybody can turn the grindstone, or turn the motor on, but it takes great ability and judgment and a gentle touch to hold the ax just right to put an edge on a dull ax. What a satisfying moment when Dad would touch the edge of the ax with his finger and declare it was now ready for cutting. The years have passed and Dad long ago laid down the ax for the final time. I no longer use an ax but for the rarest of occasions, but as I sat and watched the Punjab five eat Kentucky Fried Chicken, I realized I was still turning the grindstone and turning on the motor for the sharpening of Punjabi axes. Our interaction was a kind of grinding, a kind of sharpening of the instrument that would be used to cut through the hardness of the Punjabi spiritually. I have come to believe the lesson of the ax-head story in the life of Elisha was the symbolic loss of spiritual power. What good is an ax-handle without the ax-head? Or what use is a dull ax-head in chopping of wood? Oh, some progress can be accomplished, but it will take more time with a poorer product! I like what Vance Havner once wrote on this subject, *"The spiritual edge of our lives may be blunted, and as a consequence the chopping will be laborious and the chips few!"*

Someone has written, "He who waits on God loses no time!" I could see that was the philosophy of Shibu in the Punjab outreach. Some would throw these men immediately into the battlefield with little training and instruction. Shibu believed in taking the time to sharpen the axes of these men. That is why he brought in Shijil Samuel and that is why he was taking the time to start the Punjab Extension Program; it all had to do with sharpening the ax of these men so they could be more effective faster! The man who takes time to sharpen his spiritual ax is a wise man. Some feel that to keep on chopping is the best even if the ax is dull. I still remember watching my Uncle Clayton stop and sharpen his chain saw while I kept on cutting thinking I would get more done. It was a waste of time seeing the saw was still cutting. But I often noticed at the end of the day that Uncle Clayton always got more wood sawed. Did not Jesus tell the early disciples to wait on the sharpening of the Holy Spirit before evangelizing Jerusalem? As I watched and listened to Shibu sharpening a group of young pastors around a bucket of KFC chicken, I realized that it does pay to take the time to sharpen the spiritual ax, and more grinding was in store for these men as we headed off to the Mohali Bible Church for another session.

41

A Desire without a Date Is Only a Dream

As we traveled from Chandigarh back to Mohali, I could hear the plans of this pioneer work developing in the conversation of Shibu Simon and the director of the work, Shiju Philipps. A few years before, the ministry in Kerala had been looking to expand their mission's outreach to the State of Punjab. They felt they had found their man in Philipps and Shibu was even more pleased with the results as he had visited the work a number of times. Now Shibu felt he had the five men that would change the face of the Punjab—turn the Punjab "... *upside down* . . ." (Acts 17:6) These five men were Febon Finney at Gospel Baptist in Chandigarh, Manjeet Singh at Praise Baptist in Khasa, Giurjit Singh at Glory Baptist in Amritsar, Shiju Philipps at Mohali Bible in Mohali, and the newest member of the team Shijil Samuel. Samuel came from Haryana with his wife Jini and their three children Dan, John, and Samuel and would act as a statewide evangelist and head up the new Punjab Extension Program. We eventually drove down a side street off a very busy boulevard in the eastern part of Mohali. It looked to me like a series of storage lockers were located side by side on the right-hand side of the narrow lane. Sure enough, Philipps came to the third one and unlocked a typical storage locker lock. Inside was a brightly colored church sanctuary.

On the front wall was a big sign that announced Mohali Bible Church—Jesus is Lord. It was a big locker by any standard, but still a locker. It was long and narrow but provided ample room for the Mohali fellowship.

We had gathered at the sanctuary for the formal meeting of the Punjab Outreach Ministry. The time at the KFC was the working lunch. Now it was time to get down to business, formalizing the plans for the expansion of the ministry. Before the six men broke up into individual sessions I had a chance to sharpen their axes a bit more. I shared with them a message I had prepared in Kerala to be preach in the Punjab. Shibu had warned me of this opportunity, and I was prepared with a message I called "The Creed of Caesarea" taken from the lessons Jesus gave to His disciple in Caesarea Philippi. I started out my challenge to the Punjab Five by sharing the experience I had in 2010 when I had the privilege of visiting Caesarea Philippi on my Dallas Theological Trip with my daughter Marnie. I shared with them my belief that the Church started there in its purist concept (Matthew 16:18), and its basic creed had also been established by Jesus on that spot. I gave them this simple outline for establishing their own segment of the Universal Church.

1. CONFESSION-Matthew 16:13-16. It starts with the confession that was printed on the back wall of the Mohali sanctuary—Jesus Christ is Lord. Peter made the first confession and every true believer since Peter has to make the same confession (Romans 10:9-10). Their responsibility was to share this confession with the citizens of the Punjab.

2. CHRIST-Matthew 16:16. There are a lot of people today who want Christianity without Christ, Christendom without Christ, a Church without Christ, just like now we have a Christmas without Christ. When Andrew found Jesus he told his brother Peter that he had found the Christ (John 1:41). That was the goal of the Punjab pastors—to point people to the Christ.

3. CHURCH-Matthew 16:17-18. The theology of the Church began in Caesarea and Jesus had no plan B if plan A didn't work. It has been since the first mention of the Church in Caesarea the plan of the ages (Ephesians 2:20). The pattern was established in Acts 1:8: ". . . Jerusalem (Mohali), Judaea (Chandigarh), Samaria (Amritsar), and the uttermost parts of the world (Punjab)!"

4. CROSS-Matthew 16:21-26. I pointed out the two crosses in this passage: "his"-vs. 21 and "ours"-vs. 24. Calvary began at Caesarea for the Christ and believers must have a time when they pick up their cross and follow Jesus (Luke 14:27). The Punjab was the cross of these men as they took the Cross of Christ across the State, and the cross would include some suffering.

5. COMING-Matthew 16:27-28. Jesus ended His challenge to His disciples with the wonderful truth that despite His going there would be a coming! (John 14:1-3) Over three hundred times this truth is revealed in the New Testament, more than any other doctrine. If they proclaimed these five tenets of the faith they would be fulfilling the Creed of Caesarea.

After I finished, Shibu interviewed each of the members of his Punjab Team. He sought where they were in each of their ministries and how they could be of support to the other members of the team. Our stay at Mohali Bible lasted well into the afternoon. We still had one more service in the Punjab before we headed for Haryana to catch a train for Delhi, or so I thought. As Shibu interviewed, I had a few minutes to ponder again the men of the Punjab that God had called to reach their own people with the Gospel of Christ. It was the Good Gospel and still is, and the Gospel was and still is the cornerstone of the Church. What I liked best about the Punjab was the absence of denominationalism. Despite the fact the Punjab Boys (like with the Orissa Boys the reason I call them boys is the simple fact of just how young these men are—more my son's age than mine) were Baptists in their theology, the heart of their message was "prepare to meet thy God"! These men were not enamored with the modern ways of evangelism nor were they caught up in the liberal philosophy that somehow the Sikh religion and the Christian religion where somehow compatible. They preached a choice as Elijah challenged the people of his day (I Kings 18:21).

Sometimes people wait until they can cross all their T's and dot all their I's before setting out on a course. What I like about Shibu and his style of ministry and the style of ministry he instilled in the ministries of the mission is summarized in the title of this chapter. Have you pondered its truth yet, or have you waited until now to read what I mean by this proverb title, *"A desire without a date is only a dream"*? Shibu encouraged his men to not wait for a better time. They were to reach forth and step forward with plans of expansion. Don't wait a moment. They did that—setting dates for up and coming events that would challenge the Sikhs with an opportunity to choose Christ. They would make Christ the issue. He is the issue of salvation (Acts 4:12) and He is the issue of separation from Sikhism. Most of them had come either from Sikhism or Hinduism, and they had come to the day that Paul challenged us all, "For he saith, I have heard thee in a time accepted, and in the day of salvation have I succoured thee: behold, now is the accepted time: behold, now is the day of salvation." (II Corinthians 6:2) This is the best date of them all! It is time we all get weary of the planned projects that never happen, the grand ideas that never materialize, and the wonderful dreams that remain dreams. Shibu had set in motion in the Punjab a desire and a dream, but unlike so many before him he also set a date. Date setters might fail, but people who never set dates will never accomplish anything!

42

Farewell to the Punjab

After the pastor's meeting at the Mohali Bible Church storage locker, we headed across town to pack up our things at the CrownWest Hotel. As we drove the few miles through rush-hour traffic, I commented again on the strange layout of the city and the lack of names anywhere. The brainchild of a German engineer, the cities of Mohali and Chandigarh were laid out in sections and phases. Only numbers were used to give direction whether on streets, boulevards, or roadways. All the massive high-rises and condos were numbered as well. I found it very strange and unusual, but Philipps seemed to know how to get around a city by the numbers. We stopped to get some gas and some air in a tire and, like the old days, there were servicemen for each. We would be leaving the Punjab for Haryana to catch our train south, so Philipps wanted everything to be in order with his car. We had a tight window between the evening service and the departing overnight train, so there would be no time to stop for gas or other things.

Just before 7:00, Philipps picked Shibu and me up with our luggage for a ride over to Febon Finney's house for a Thursday night cottage prayer meeting service. We parked the car in a large parking garage under the high-rise Finney lived in. We had to climb at least four flights of stairs to get on the floor where the Finney apartment was located. When we got there, we were greeted by a handful of people already gathered for the meeting. As with the other Punjab assemblies, I was impressed with the number of young people and young couples. While we waited for the rest of the church to arrive, I noticed a meal was being prepared. Surprised? I also got a chance to meet Febon's wife. If you have forgotten she was in the hospital delivering a baby when we arrived four days before. I got a chance to visit with the new mother and hold Timothy. It has been a thrill of mine just how many children I have been able to greet that someday I hope will be the continuation of ministry until the Lord's return. The service actually got started around 7:30 with a few songs and a few prayers, but as always I was given the bulk of the time to share the Word. My final (hopefully not my final, final message, for my desire is to return again) sermon in the Punjab was entitled "What Are You Looking For?" The message was based on the great encounter Jesus had with the palsy man at the Pool of Bethesda (John 5:1-9). I gave them this outline:

1. What are you looking for—*a moving*—John 5:4? A fairy tale can be a powerful thing to desperate people. The lame man was looking for the moving of the water for his healing because he thought it was his only hope, and when you remember he had a physical handicap for 38 years (John 5:5), he was grasping for a straw! Many today, and I saw a lot of it in the Punjab, are looking for the supernatural, a sign. I warned them to be very careful in putting their faith in a movement. Sikhism is a movement that gives a hope that can't be delivered on, especially one that believes in angels over God (Colossians 2:18) like Mormonism.

2. What are you looking for—*a man*—John 5:7? The palsy man just wanted someone to help him to the pool at the troubling of the water, an assistant, a helper, someone to do what he couldn't do. Man looking to man for the cure. We live in such a time, and in my four days in the Punjab, I recognized the symptoms of this fatal flaw on mankind. Note the text, "no man", and ultimately man will fail man just like they did with this man. Why? Read carefully I Corinthians 2:11-14!

3. What should he have been looking for?—*the master*—John 5:8. Jesus was there all the time, right in front of his face, but like so many today he missed him at first. Jesus was the Master of all Maladies. (Matthew 23:10) We, like the Church at Corinth (I Corinthians 1:12), have chosen other men to focus our attention on instead of going to Jesus, asking Jesus, letting Jesus take our burdens. Whether the man at the pool or the men of the Punjab—"Jesus is the answer, what a Friend is He, God's beloved Son who died on Calvary. He gives my life meaning and I want to share the love of Jesus with my friends everywhere!"

I finished my message around 8:30, but we couldn't just rush off. There was that meal to eat! I must admit I was a bit nervous because I knew how driving in India can be, but Philipps kept saying we had plenty of time.

We eventually left Febon's flat around nine. Our thirty-mile trip to Ambala took us about an hour, which is great time for India. Most of the way we traveled a very nice interstate highway over the border of the States of Punjab and Haryana. Within a half hour we said goodbye to the Punjab, and I entered the seventh Indian State I had actually traveled through. I had flown over a few others and would a few more before I returned to Kerala, but Haryana was the seventh actual state (Kerala, Tamil Nadu, Andrah Pardesh, Karnataka, Orissa, and Punjab). It was a lighting ride to the railhead at Ambala as Philipps proved again that if an Indian driver has some open road he can cover a lot of ground in a short time but because of the congestion they rarely do.

I was still in the dark as to why we were taking a train to Delhi, but I wasn't complaining because I have had only pleasant experiences on the infamous Indian Rail System. This would be my fifth trip (two going back and forth between Kerala and Andrah Pardesh, and two traveling around Orissa), a ten-hour overnight trip from Ambala to Delhi, or so I thought. The train station was typical Indian: crowded, smelly, and noisy. Philipps and Samuel stayed with us until our train arrived, a bit late but I had experienced worse delays. I was never at a lost for what to do on those delays because there was always plenty to see. And if nothing new, a few small recollections that filter down through the memory of other train platforms in Kottayam, Guntaka, Titlagarh, Bhawanipatna, and now Ambala. Isn't memory an amazing creation of God? Get me on an Indian train platform and my mind instantly focuses on other similar times I was waiting for a train in India. I still remember my first as I set off for a week tour of Andrah Pardesh by way of a train: that trip took us twenty-four hours. Or the time I set off to visit the persecuted church in the hinterland of central Orissa: that trip took us eight hours. Now I was getting ready for another adventure. Little did I know that I would be remembering this train trip for the rest of my life, a trip, perhaps, to top all the others including my two train trips across Australia? Such memories are not earned by payment or learned from a book, but entered into by just being you. You actually have to go where these memories are made, experienced, and shared with another. Shibu and I had already been on some amazing side trips together in India, but little did I know until I boarded a train for Delhi in Ambala, Haryana that Delhi was not our destination at all. We were off to another train platform south of Delhi that would add to my memories of India. So as we bid farewell, I knew if Shibu planned it there would be a marvelous sight and site waiting for me at the end of the line!

43

The Tale Continues
A Church of a Lifetime

As Shibu and I settled into our berth on our way out of northwest India, I began to think again of another chapter in my life's story that I had been remembering on this trip:

"I should have been happy to be called to the pastorate of a city church with a congregation large enough to support my family of four at the age of forty, but I was not! My wife and children were happy to leave the coastal village of Eastport, a place my wife described as *"not being the end of the earth, but you could see it from there"*, but I was reluctant. As my wife and children gladly packed and prepared for the big move rejoicing in the change, I was nervous. This would be my fourth pastorate in eighteen years, and to say the first two had been difficult would be an understatement. But the third was quiet and relatively peaceful and the laidback character of the congregation was to my liking. Eastport was called a city, and it might have been years before. But while I lived there it was just a sleepy, coastal community at best with a little over a thousand people swimming in a city that could have held four thousand. I liked Eastport because it was a status quo church. After two brutal church experiences, was I ready to face the politics of a troubled church again? Perhaps I feared that Emmanuel would be the same-old, same-old of my first two churches. But after a three to one vote of the family counsel and with no good reason to reject the call to Emmanuel, I like the old-time preacher who in a sermon was describing Paul's shipwreck, yielded to the call with the philosophy: *"If you can't swim, get on a board!"* (Acts 27:44)

My family and I arrived in the big city of Ellsworth on the first week of the summer of 1991. I was immediately taken aback because, before my first sermon, I had a wedding on the Saturday before my first official service was scheduled. That Sunday I looked out on a packed sanctuary, something that had never happened in eighteen years in my three previous churches! I saw a mixture of mill workers, school teachers, fire fighters, engineers, retirees, small businessmen, big families and small families, and a mix bag of church skippers and the spiritually wounded from tragic church affairs around Hancock County. In the early days, I had over twenty different communities represented at Emmanuel. I hadn't come to a city church but a county church. There was also a mixture of at least four generations with the most being in the old age category. Everything seemed peaceful, but there was a spirit of restlessness in the congregation. As I would describe later, *"I sensed a group of people with one foot under the pew and one foot in the aisle ready to leave at the slightest hint of trouble!"* Outside there was a calming tranquility and the patriotic service (just before the 4th of July) was emotional and uplifting, but I felt out of place. There was not a farmer or fishermen in the place, the kind of people I had given nearly fourteen years of my life to before Emmanuel. Could I even understand city people?

I made the mistake of saying in some of my opening remarks that the congregation would have to pray for their new pastor because he didn't know how he was going to survive in the big city. I couldn't shake off the haunting uneasiness of being outside my comfort zone. I was a fish out of water, and I knew it. It was then the Lord in His good humor did something that helped change my attitude, at least for a while. My family and I had only visited Emmanuel once two months before when we had visited the church in early May. Called within a couple of weeks, we decided the kids needed to finish their schooling before we moved. After the service was over and I was shaking hands and greeting people at the door, something happened. Other than a few deacons we had visited with a few times throughout the process, I recognized very few of the over one hundred and twenty people that had come to my first service. So I was totally ignorant when two very tall men approached me in the lobby of the sanctuary and asked if they might have a word with me in my study. I first thought they might be seeking counsel, but within a short time a sick feeling came to my stomach as I thought I might have already made my first blunder as the pastor of the Emanuel Baptist Church.

I shut the door behind them as we entered the pastor's study just off the lobby. It was then I noticed the serious expression on their faces, and

I knew that I had offended a couple of members of the church on my first official day at the post. The taller of the two spoke first as he told me they had stayed back after the service to debate with me my meaning of big city. At first I was stunned and confused by the question, "Big city?" When in my message had I mentioned big city? Then I noticed a slight smile coming on the lips of the other man. Within a few seconds, both men had big grins on their faces, but I was still in the dark. My mind was in overdrive trying to figure out what these two inquiring gentlemen wanted or meant by the phrase 'big city'! It was then the second man said this, "We are here to debate your use of the phrase big city in the prayer request you asked of the church. We are vacationing in Ellsworth, visiting from Hartford, Connecticut and this town of yours wouldn't even be considered a hamlet in our city!" By this time both men were laughing out loud and I had my first smile on my face. I realized that I was not in trouble with the membership, and my two brethren from out-of-state had tried to put my dilemma into a different perspective to calm my reservations.

By the time I arrived at Emmanuel, I had been a Christian over thirty years. I was not young in the Lord, but I knew that Emmanuel was going to be a challenge, big city or not. Its history of splits, legalism, and disunity was only multiplied by the community it resided in (Ellsworth) and the county it ministered in (Hancock). Both were known for a very dysfunctional Church. By the time the last decade of the twentieth century began, the Emmanuel Baptist Church and its sister churches were far from an example of the first century Church. Modern Christianity, complacent Christendom, and the discontented Christian were as the old preacher put it, *"We are so subnormal that to be normal we would be counted abnormal!"* But could one man make a difference in a church where the average pastorate was only a little over three years (twelve pastors in forty years)? Would I stay very long? I had discovered that three pastorates in eighteen years, six years my average, wasn't much time to affect a difference. It was then, despite not liking the city culture, I determined that I would tackle Emmanuel differently. I wouldn't approach Emmanuel from a second-hand standpoint (canned vegetables versus garden vegetables), not from what had happened with the other pastors, but as a first-hander. I would seek those who felt like me— that church can be different, that fellowships don't have to be a wrestling match, that believers can live together in unity if they submit themselves one to the other (Ephesians 5:21), and that we need to be an organism not an organization. It wasn't as if I hadn't tried this before. I left Bible College with a dream to do it differently, to get back to the basics, to live the Christian experience as Christ did, and to reestablish the Church as it once was.

In three attempts I had failed. Why did I think a middle-aged man could change an old age church? I didn't know it then, but twenty-nine years later I recognize the key ingredient that is necessary for such an event—you need 'a church of a lifetime'!"

44

Overnight Train to Agra

My mind continued to drift between my life's story and the story I was on, a story in which I didn't yet know the plot line or the punch line. Shibu was keeping this part of our journey close to his vest for some reason, but I couldn't figure out why. We certainly had more comfortable accommodations on this train (four people in our berth versus six to eight on my other Indian trains), and it appeared, by my observation, that it was a much more modern train than the other Indian trains I had been on. It was only when I got our trip ticket for my journal (after the conductor had punched it) that I realized that our destination was not Delhi but Agra. Agra? Why did I know that name? I pondered and pondered as I read the information off the ticket stub: two males, one forty-five and the other sixty-five, Ambala to Agra-1665 rupees ($26.42). Agra? Why did I know that name?

We officially left Ambala Station at 10:20 PM in the evening of March 17, 2016. Once Shibu saw I knew the final destination of our train, he began to open up just a bit about our mysterious side trip. He told me instead of spending the day in Delhi we were going to spend the day in Agra and would drive up to Delhi after our tourist day. Wow! I began to remember my other tourist days with Shibu—to Thakkadi and the Periyar National Park, to Kodanadu and the elephant rescue center, to Kumarakom and the house boat ride on Kerala's largest lake, and to Munnar and the wild goats of Eravikulam National Park. What could top these adventures with Shibu into the natural wonders of India? I was brought back from my mediations of past expeditions into the out-of-the-way places of India when I heard Shibu say, "And Johnson's (the mission's manager) brother is going to meet us at Agra Station to be our tour guide." Why did we need a guide, and what is in Agra that would be worth seeing?

Shibu went on to explain the day before us. We would tour Agra, over a hundred miles southeast of Delhi, for most of the day, and then travel back north by taxi to stay overnight in an Indian hostel before catching our next plane ride. It seemed pretty straight forward, but why Agra and not Delhi? Delhi has been on my to-see list. I have never been a big city kind of guy, though I have visited LA, Dallas, New York, and Boston, my share of megacities. Delhi would be considered a mega-city, too big really to see, even for a week, and we just had a day. So as I settled into my bed around 11:00, my mind was still racing about the bits of information I had been given. Shibu has always been a secretive and surprising person, so I was not taken aback by the lack of information being given me as our train rattled south. My other tourist days in India had been spectacular, to say the least, and I knew Shibu wouldn't disappoint.

Just about the time we were switching days, my mind finally figured out why I had heard the name Agra—Taj Mahal! Was Shibu taking me to see the Taj Mahal? Wow! It was then my imagination began to run wild. Few in the world get to visit some of the world's most striking sites. I still remember the morning my daughter and I walked up Mount Moriah to see the Dome of the Rock in Jerusalem, iconic places that you see pictures of and watch documentaries of on television but never get to actually visit. If I was really heading for the Taj Mahal then I was in for another special treat—places everybody knows about simply by the mention of their name: Lady Liberty in New York Harbor, Gettysburg in Pennsylvania, Yosemite in California, Mount McKinley in Alaska, Big Ben in London, Stonehenge on Salisbury Plain, Bunker Hill in Boston, Arlington Cemetery in Washington, Bethlehem in Israel, and now the Taj Mahal in Agra!

Before I slipped off to sleep on that overnight train to Agra, I rehearsed in my mind the few things I remember reading about the Taj Mahal. I knew that the story of Agra, the home of the Taj, was shrouded in mystery and obscurity. Some feel the site was developed in 1131, but there are only a few references in Indian literature until 1501 when Sikandar Lodi made Agra the capital of the Mughal Empire and built a fort there and laid out the design for a city. Then along came the famous Mughal, Babar, followed by the equally famous Akbar, his grandson, who made the city the centerpiece of their kingdom. He built Agra Fort, but the crown jewel of Agra would be a memorial to an undying love between Shah Jahan and Mumtaz Mahal, the lady of the Taj. Born in 1593, Mahal was the daughter of a brother to the Prime Minister of India. Raised in royal court, she was very beautiful and attracted the interest of the Prince of the Land. Even in childhood they were inseparable and would eventually marry, but unlike most marital relationship of that day, theirs was a love affair of the ages or so the story is told. Mahal died after giving birth to the couple's fourteenth child. As tradition tells it, on her deathbed she asked Jahan to build a beautiful monument over her grave as a token of their love. In December of 1631, the body of his beloved Mahal was buried in a garden on the banks of the Jamuna (Yamuna) River. The emperor then announced that a memorial would be built in memory of his wife. He sought out the most famous architects from around the world, and eventually Jahan chose the work of Ustad Isa Afandi of Turkey for the final design. The work on the Taj Mahal began. The Taj Mahal was not finished until the year 1648, seventeen years later, but five more years were needed to finish the gardens and walls around the complex. The twenty-two small domes on the main entrance are said to have represented the twenty-two years of construction. The Taj, called a dream in marble and some say the most beautiful building ever construction on the planet, is made of white marble from Rajasthan, an Indian state southwest of the site. The walls around the memorial were constructed of red stone like the fort. There is also yellow and black marble on site, but after that my mind went blank.

    I will admit that the Taj Mahal was never on my bucket list, but as our Ambala train covered the ten-hour trip to Agra, I put it on my list. Shibu hadn't confirmed my suspicions, but the more I thought about it the more I was convinced of our secret stop. I will admit I had a hard time getting to sleep that night as I thought more about our possible destination. It is like hoping and wishing you might see something you never expected to see, and all of a sudden you are brought face to face with the reality that today might be the day of the sighting. I will admit that I have had very few days like March 18, 2016. For most of my life, I have lived in the simple places of this planet, places that you would have to want to go there to be there. I never imagined in my wildest imagination on our trip to the Punjab that I would be on a train to Agra. My focus was on the missionary side of the trip, not the tourist side. Did I enjoy visiting the Golden Temple? I did, but I enjoyed more visiting the churches of the Punjab. I didn't know what the Taj Mahal would do for me, but I have long since discovered that when God takes you on an unexpected detour there will be a very important lesson to learn. I drifted off to sleep around 1:00 in the morning, and slept until 7:00. When I awoke, I realized we still were not in Agra. On the way, we did pass through Delhi Station, but I slept through that as well. As I woke, Shibu also woke up. I smiled at him as he realized that I had figured it out. "We are going to the Taj Mahal, aren't we?" I asked. To which he simply replied, "Yes!" It was then I learned he had never been to the Taj Mahal either!

45

Taj Mahal
Closed?

Shibu and I arrived at Agra on my grandson's seventh-month birthday. I was excited to say the least. We were actually 140 miles southeast of Delhi, and it had been ten hours since we left Ambala Station in Haryana. I thought we were going to only travel through Haryana State to Delhi, but we would travel through Utter Pradesh State as well in our overnight trip south out of the Punjab. It was 10:20 in the morning of March 18, 2016 when we got off the train. There to meet us was Johnson's (the business manager of KBBC) brother John Philipps with a taxi. He had actually driven down from Delhi that morning to pick us up, take us on a tour of Agra, and return with us to Delhi later that day. I was, according to my hosts, only six miles away from the world most famous mausoleum!

Instead of heading straight for the Taj, we stopped at the hotel Taj Vilas for breakfast and a wash up. I was too excited to eat much—cornflakes with cold milk and toast off the breakfast menu, but my companion dug into the variety of foods as if they hadn't eaten in a week. This, of course, took time. Time I felt I didn't have. Little did I know! The breakfast cost me 900 rupees, about thirteen dollars, for four big guys. I will admit it was nice to go into the washroom and clean up a bit. Indian trains don't have much for bathroom facilities, whereas the Taj Vilas was first class no matter what country you were in. I was the first out the door after paying the bill and excited to see the Taj. The boys lingered awhile as the huskers descended on me. There was anything and everything to buy with the Taj on it: pins and plates and books and tee shirts. Merchants and merchandise surrounded me—young and old trying to get my rupees. I decided to wait until I got closer to the no doubt countless opportunities near the Taj. As I warded off the waves of salesmen, I noticed that Shibu and John and our taxi driver were huddled near our car. I have learned in my many trips to the subcontinent that Indians in a circle talking in whispers isn't a good situation. My instincts would soon prove to be true. I really knew something was wrong when Shibu approached me with a very sad face.

It was then I was told that the Taj Mahal was closed every Friday. Guess what day March 18, 2016 fell on? Shibu didn't know, and John didn't know because they had never been there before. It was a simple mistake, nobody's fault, but the bottom line was the Taj was closed, plain and simple. Could I even see it from afar? You must understand a very high red granite wall surrounds the Taj Mahal. There are very few places outside the wall even to see the Taj. I would soon learn before the year was out that 2016 would go down in history for me as the year of "the closed". Perhaps an explanation is in order. By the time I had gotten six miles from the Taj, I had traveled over 11,000 miles. Granted, I didn't know that I was ultimately going to the Taj Mahal, but the truth is the truth. That many miles and I was not going to be able to go in? Five months later, I was in California after traveling 3000 miles to visit my grandson, Judah Alan, for his first birthday. His parents decided after the celebration we ought to take a vacation together into Yosemite National Park. I was excited, really excited to see the natural wonders of one of the great national parks of America. I had seen pictures of the mountains, valley, and the waterfalls, but more importantly the sequoia trees. I wanted to see a sequoia up close and personal. A long story short, the day we arrived California was in the midst of a historic drought. When we arrived at the falls they were all dry, not a drop of water flowing over their granite ridges. I was disappointed, but there was still the sequoia, right? The greatest and best known grove of the giants is Mariposa. As we drove up to the entrance of the Mariposa Grove, there were those demoralizing six letters: C-L-O-S-E-D, the same letters I saw on the gate into the Taj Mahal in Agra, India five months before. Postscript: My son-in-law Josue was able, before we left Yosemite, to find a small grove of sequoias near where we were staying at Bass Lake, so I did get to see a few giants, but not the giants of the giants! So what do you do when the Taj is closed? We decided to travel the six miles and try to find a place where we could at least see the Taj. Little did we realize just how difficult that would be!

Our trip to the walls of the Taj took us through quiet traffic. I was surprised, and then it hit me. Taj closed, so no tourists, and sure enough that is what we found when our taxi driver dropped us off a mile from the front gate. It seems this is the closest they allow vehicles, so Shibu and John and I would have to walk the final mile to try and get a glimpse of the white memorial. On our way through the tree-lined path leading toward the Taj we passed a leper colony, my first. I was told that the Taj had become a healing center, a kind of a "troubling of the waters" (John 5:4) place, if you know what I mean. We didn't go near, though I would have liked to, to give me a better understanding of the leper stories in the Bible, but we pressed on toward the massive red wall rising before us. Because of the trees in the park sections we were walking through, we saw nothing. It seemed we had the lane to ourselves with only the occasional individual either walking towards us or with us. It seems there were a few others that didn't know the Taj was closed on Friday! As we neared the massive first of many gates, a row of shops had been set up. Tourist traps we call them in Maine, but most were closed. Wow! I just still couldn't believe it, but the signs were all pointing to the one unchanging fact: the Taj Mahal was closed to Barry Blackstone. I must admit I whispered a simple question to the Lord, "Surely, Lord I haven't come all this way, and Shibu hasn't planned this surprise for nothing."

As I pondered the reality that the Taj was closed to me, I had a plan. Even though we had promised a shopkeeper we would come back on the way, we passed the few shops that were open and headed straight to the gate. There, beside the gate were two guard posts and a few soldiers. It was then Shibu decided, with my encouragement, to plead our case to the soldiers. Maybe they would just open the gate so we could see her. As of yet, we hadn't even had a glimpse. That is how high the walls were. We knew that just a few hundred yards beyond the wall was the Taj and the iconic Lotus Pool in front of it, but both were completely blocked from our view. It wasn't long before Shibu came back to John and me with that all too familiar sad face. There would be no exception for a man from Maine. The Taj Mahal was closed to one and all, but if we wanted an outside view we were to walk down the length of the wall until we came to the river. So walk we did. The walk to the river was nearly half a mile. On the way we came to gate after gate, but they all were closed. I did get my picture taken by one just to highlight and underline the irony of getting to the Taj Mahal, but not being able to get in. We saw a number of work parties replacing section of the old red wall. It appears they work on the Taj on Friday but don't allow visitors. It was a warm walk. The day was heating up, but the closer we got to the Yamuna River, the second most holy river in India behind the Ganges, the breezes off the river were really pleasant.

And then it happened! I must admit I was more focused on the Yamuna thinking that the red barrier ran all the way around the property. Little did I know that the giant red wall only runs along three sides of the Taj Mahal, but the river wall is very short!

46

God's Plan B at the Taj

Just when you think your perfect day has been ruined by an unplanned event—an unexpected closure—that is when the Good Lord has the ability to work all things for good to them that love him and trust in His plan. (Romans 8:28) This is exactly what happened on the day Shibu and I was going to tour the Taj Mahal in Agra, India.

When I turned the corner on the gigantic red wall separating me from the Taj Mahal, I couldn't believe my eyes. I might have not been able to enter the Taj Mahal plaza, but that didn't mean I wasn't going to see the Taj in all of its glory. As I stood gazing up at one of the four 131-foot tall minarets that highlights the corners of the Taj, I was less than 100 feet away. The wall that was hiding the Taj from our view was now barely a wall at all along the river bank, maybe ten feet tall. The Taj was created as a garden tomb on the banks of the Yamuna River, and the Taj was close to the river. In Maine we now have laws restricting construction close to bodies of water: a lake, a river, or the ocean, but the Taj was built right on the bank. It didn't look like more than fifty feet between the back wall of the structure and the short retaining wall called the plinth. The waves of the river could be heard lapping against that wall. Shibu took a picture of me with the Taj in the background, a keepsake. I took in the glory of the dome, 144 feet up on the top of the building, the snow-white granite of its walls, and the impressive architecture creating the shapes making a perfect symmetry in marble. Granted, we couldn't see the famous Lotus Pool (but I would, eventually) out front or the vast garden area, but the two sides we could see gave me enough to understand the splendor of the structure. Supposedly built after the imaginary garden of paradise of the Islamic faith, the Taj Mahal itself, not the other structures, was built by 20,000 workers in 12 years, from 1631, the year of the princess's death, to 1643. You could see that no expense was considered in the costly material, but as we talked along the banks I was told that the Taj was just a shell of its former self. Over the years, most of its fancy interior had been taken. It has only been in recent years that the Indian government protected one of its jewels. A gem is a perfect way to describe the Taj. I found this observation in a pamphlet I bought at a gift shop outside the walls. *"For every hour of the day and for every atmospheric condition the Taj has its own colour values, from the soft dreaminess at dawn, and the dazzling whiteness at midday to its cold splendor in the moonlight. Yet none of these effects can equal those few fleeting moments when, softly illuminated by the brief Indian afterglow, it assumes the enchanting tint of some pale and lively rose."*

I did see the white rose on the banks of the Yamuna River in the late morning sun of our walking tour along the walls of the enclosure. Then it happened. Don't you believe as I do that the Good Lord knew the Taj Mahal was closed on Fridays? So if He knew then why did He allow us to be so disappointed? After a few pictures of the Taj, I worked my way down to the banks of the Yamuna to get another angle on the Taj. Meanwhile, my companions worked their way around the small plaza that had been built to allow people like us to at least get a view of the great, white structure. You might even call it a small park. There were a few other people with us that day eating their lunch and enjoying the warm sun and cool breeze off the river. I was about ready to head back to the taxi when I noticed Shibu talking to a man by the shore. He owned a simple craft with low sides and seating both front and aft. After a short conversation, Shibu approached me with a simple question. "How would like to go on a boat ride and see the Taj from the river?" It didn't take me very long to recognized God's plan B at the Taj!

Shibu, John, and I got into the simple boat, and the boatman poled us out into the river. Immediately I realized that if we would have gotten through the front gate we would have never seen the Taj from this angle. The more we drew away from the shore the more we were able to see inside the complex. Granted, we were further away but the mere size of the structure made up for the distance. Eventually the boatman took us across the river to the other side. It seems he was there every day providing a service for those who wanted to cross the river, not only to view the Taj from across the Yamuna, but also to visit a shrine on that side of the river. We didn't visit the shrine, but we did get some wonderful shots of the Taj from a completely different perspective. Little did I know I would get another such perspective when we stopped at another famous site in Agra for a truly spectacular sight of the Taj from upriver?

I sat in the bow of the river man's craft with the breeze against my back and the Taj Mahal in front of me. We drifted back and forth across the Yamuna for about forty-five minutes. It was a glorious interlude after what I thought was going to be a bitter disappointment. Shibu and I would talk later, and we both came to the same conclusion. God is still the best planner. Shibu had planned a wonderful surprise for his friend from Maine, but God had overruled and planned a surprise both for Shibu and me. When we finally landed, paid the boatman, and headed back to the taxi, we realized that God's Plan B was much better than our Plan A. I will be honest with you. Would I have liked to see the inside? Yes! But when the place is closed and you don't think you will even get to see the inside, a boat ride is an amazing compromise! You will never be disappointed when you allow the Almighty to be your tour guide. Now I know that the Lord did direct our steps that morning in Agra and as the Psalmist so fitly wrote, "The steps of a good man are ordered by the Lord: and he delighteth in his way." (Psalm 37:23) As Shibu and John and I walked back along that tall, red wall, we certainly were delighting in the way the Lord had directed us that morning. If someone would have asked me how I would like to have toured the Taj Mahal, the last thing I would have said was by boat!

On the way back to the taxi, we meet a brahma bull in the side lane beside the red wall. We gave him a wide birth. We also meet a group of young boys playing cricket, and we stopped to watch a few balls. As we rounded the corner at the first gate, we stopped at an open souvenir shop. I picked up a book on the Taj Mahal, a small jewelry box for Coleen made out of the same granite that created the Taj, and a few postcards, which cost me 1200 rupees, or about eighteen dollars. We walked into the afternoon, and it was then Shibu told me of another reason why it is best to let the Good Lord plan your days off. Shibu's original plan was to tour the Taj and head for Delhi, but because we didn't get to go inside the Taj, we still had a few hours to stay in Agra and make one more stop before heading for our overnight stay in Delhi. When he told me where we were going, I realized that the Lord knew his servant. A fort was a better choice than a mausoleum. If Shibu's plan had happened, then I would never have gotten to visit Agra Fort. For some I know this might sound strange, but the best stop in Agra wasn't the Taj Mahal, but Agra Fort. Built between 1565 and 1573, this imposing red sandstone rampart forms a crescent shaped fortification along a high bank of the Yamuna River, just up-river to the Taj Mahal. A deep moat surrounds the landside of the mega-fortress which only makes the impressive walls that more impressive, and I might have missed it!

47

Agra Fort

I once heard of a medical report that suggested we should relax on a daily basis instead of trying to save up our relaxing time for a vacation. In order words, we need to learn how to take an inside vacation every day! People talk about getting away from it all, but in reality they unusually take it all with them. I have made relaxing my goal for most of my life. Even when I take a vacation day while doing my vocation, like the day Shibu and I had after our whirlwind four-day tour of the Punjab in the historic city of Agra. The afternoon of our Agra stop was both an inside vacation, one of the best relaxing times I have had in India, and an outside vacation for me personally. Our drive over to Agra Fort from the Taj Mahal only took us about fifteen minutes, despite the increase of afternoon traffic. The minute we drove into the parking lot across from Agra Fort I knew I was in historic heaven. Not since seeing the Ottoman Walls of Jerusalem had I seen anything more architecturally amazing and militarily impressive. I knew my military nature was in for a visual treat, a mental feast, and this time I could go inside, walking through the main gate. The fort was not closed on Friday!

Shibu, John, and I walked through the Nagina Masjid, the main entrance also called the Amar Singh Gate. The only other gate was the Delhi Gate. We entered a three-chamber gate system (Amar, Water, and Darshni gates). I hadn't witnessed one of these since Israel and the Solomonic triple gate complex at Megiddo. Unlike Megiddo, Agra Fort was still standing in all of its sixteenth century glory. The complex of fortification was still functional as half of the fort was still being used by the Indian military to this day. The gates were solid, the arches high, and the walls thick. This is what I learned about the fort as we walked through the three gate areas that gradually took us higher up into the palace areas of the fortress. The mighty Mughal emperor, Akbar the Great, built this threatening fortification. It is an amalgamation of official buildings, palaces, and fortifications constructed, reconstructed, and added to by four other emperors of the Mughal Empire. Situated on the high ground on the right side of the Jamuna River, Akbar actually built the fort on the old Badalgarh Fort of the Rajput rulers that once ruled the area. Once we got inside and looked back, we realized that there were two ditch systems, an outer ditch that once contained water filled with deadly crocodiles and an inner dry ditch that made the access to the fort that much more difficult to overcome. Once you are able to get through each gate complex, you finally arrive in the area known as the Courtyard of the Diwan-i-Aam, the largest open area in the fort.

I found this short history of the fort. After it was finished in 1573, it served as a seat of power for the Mughal leaders. In 1639 Nadir Shah attacked and actually captured the fortress. I couldn't see how! Over the next two hundred years, it faced numerous attacks from the mighty Marathas and the Jats as a power struggle eventually ended with the coming of the British. Even the fort felt the wrath of the Mutineers of 1857 when the Europeans used the fort for a shelter. I was told the fort had lost its glamour and grandeur, but I couldn't believe that as we began to explore the various structures within the interior of the fortification. What I especially liked were the high ramparts that allowed us to look out across the river, back into the city, and as far down river as the Taj Mahal. That is the history, now for the grand tour.

After passing through the three gates, we came to a long ramp that led us first into the grape garden (Anguri Bagh). In the garden was one of the largest stone bathtubs I have ever seen. The grass was green and the flowers were beautiful leading us to the Jahangir Palace, the first huge stone building situated along the ridgeline overlooking the river. Akbar himself built a double-storied building of red sandstone for his son. There were still plenty of colored ceiling tiles and walls to give you a sense of its former glory. Right next to it was the Khas Mahal, another white marble structure. This was for the harem. Each of these buildings had porches overlooking the massive walls of the fort as well as the river. The next building was the Diwan-i-Khas, the hall of the private and dignified audience. Also made of white marble, this two-hall complex also looked out over the river. It is said that the emperor loved to sit on the terrace and watch elephants fight below on the river's edge. It was from here I got my first look at the Taj Mahal in the distance, about three miles away. Because of the height of the fortress, I got my first complete look at the Taj, the building, the minarets, the Lotus

Pool, the surrounding wall, and the gardens! It is said the same artisans that built the Taj built the Diwan-i-Khas.

We then explored the Sheesh Mahal, the dressing rooms for the harem of the emperor and the royal baths. They told us at one time the walls were made of mirrors. This whole time we had been going from building to building all located on the ramparts towards the river. Eventually we came to the last, the Kala Takht, and I found from its windows the best view of the Taj. We turned inward to the Nageena Masjid. This was the prayer building for the harem, and I was told it was once constructed of red sandstone, but Emperor Aurangzeb had the red sandstone replaced with white marble in 1668, which was how we saw it. Situated along our walk were these very informative benches giving us details of where we were and what happened where we were and what we were seeing where we were. Then it was off to the Diwan-e-Aam, the hall of Public Audience, a massive courtyard around a huge hall. It was here in the courtyard I found my first and only cannon. I simply asked, "Where is all the artillery?" A great throne (the fabled Peacock Throne) was set on the stage of the pavilion so the emperor could meet his people. To the right of this complex was the Meena Mosque and Bazaar, and on the other side was the Moti Masjid (the pearl mosque) and then there was the Nagina Masjid (the jewel mosque). By this time, we had made the rounds into and through the major structures within the fortification, but we were not allowed to go through the working part.

We slowly made our way back through the three-gate complex. I stopped to have Shibu take a picture of John and me at the mouth of the massive wooden entrance. I could tell the boys wanted to press on because we still had a three-hour ride back to Delhi, but I lingered. I dragged my feet; I didn't want to leave. I wanted to explore the moats and the outside walls, but the day was hurrying by. I did stop the boys long enough to buy them a soda just outside the main gate, just after the second moat. You have to walk across a bridge to get to the street. That allowed me a few more minutes to gaze upon the third greatest fortress I have had the privilege of exploring: third behind Edinburgh Castle in Scotland and old Jerusalem in Israel. The series of gates, halls, courtyards, galleries, pavilions, dungeons, gardens, and palaces were impressive as well as restful, relaxing, and refreshing. Jesus said a long, long time ago, "Come unto me and I will give you rest . . ." (Matthew 11:28) Sometimes He gives us rest by allowing us a down day, but *"His rest,"* as Vance Havner once said: *"is not for loafers but for learners, for as we learn, we are enlightened."* It is a foretaste of glory divine each and every time we get a chance to see an earthly marvel and imagine just how much more glorious the New Jerusalem (Revelation 21:10) is going to be, a walled city (Revelation 21:17) beyond imagination.

48

The Tale Continues
Forget Not All His Benefits

After the disappointments and delights of Agra, I drifted back to my past. As we drove back to Delhi, I began to count my blessings not my disappointments. I have always liked Johnson Oatman's hymn "Count Your Blessings". You know the one that goes: "When upon life's billows (it was certainly a blow to find the Taj Mahal closed on the only day I probably will ever be in Agra, India) you are tempest tossed, when you are discouraged, thinking all is lost, count your many blessings, name them one by one, and it will surprise you what the Lord has done!" In this chapter I would ". . . forget not all His benefits . . ." (Psalm 103:2)—His blessings to me in my life. Could I summarize and count my blessings this way? I take as a benefit and a blessing from God the following:

1. I was born in this country. I am so proud to be called an American, even when I am at times ashamed of my native land. Even though American is a byword, a swear word, a curse word in many parts of the world, I still count it an honor and a privilege to be called an American. God made the chose for me in which country I would be born, and I thank Him for choosing America for me. I believe it still the best country on this planet to live in! "My country tis of thee, sweet land of liberty, of thee I sing: land where my fathers died (my dad is 93 now and at his passing (February 20017) he will be the eighth generation to have died in our native land since its birth

in 1776), land of the pilgrim's pride, from every mountain side let freedom ring!"

2. I was raised in this country—Aroostook County that is! The most northern county in Maine is sometimes simply called "The County" by those of us who were born there. I have cared little for anything south of the Mason-Dixon Line, even though I spent four years there, or west of the Mississippi, though I have taken a few trips there. I count it a blessing that I was raised away from the "maddening crowd's ignoble strife", but on a family homestead that was planted in the North Maine Woods in 1861. The four seasons and the open spaces were to my liking and still are. Over the years I have learned to love every moment I get to spend in the wild and the wilderness of God's wonderful away places, away from that maddening crowd! "My native county, thee, land of the noble free, thy name I love; I love thy rocks and rills, thy woods and templed hills, my heart with rapture thrills like that above."

3. I was nurtured in a Christian home. I wonder, on occasion, what it would be like today if I hadn't been raised by godly parents and grandparents, among people that believed in Ephesians 6:4 and surrounded by Christian ideals and examples. I feel strongly that I would never have accepted Christ as my Saviour at age seven and that I would never have accepted His call into the ministry at nineteen. Granted, "there were foes to face and floods to stem, and this poor world was no friend to grace to help us on to God", but like Noah, my family built an ark in the Person of Christ to the saving of my soul (II Timothy 3:15). What a blessing! What a benefit it is when you are brought up in a Christian family!

4. I was married to Coleen. I have already given this lady from God a chapter in this book (the 30th), but I would be amiss in counting my blessings if I didn't mention her again. Like with being raised in a Christian family, I often wonder what my family would look like today if I hadn't married Coleen. I know I wouldn't have a wonderful son named Scott, who is at this writing dying (April 2017) of liver and lung cancer. My dear wife has become his number one caregiver, and without complaint or argument, Scott and Coleen have faced this terrible trial together, and a special daughter named Marnie, who is at this writing the mother of Judah Alan our first grandson (his sister Elena Hope would come along in February 2018). Faithful and true is what Coleen has been all these years and what a blessing!

5. I was a father to children. I have mentioned Scott and Marnie, but there was also Beven Cherith, a child we lost between Scott and Marnie. Despite most people simply calling it a miscarriage, Coleen and I have always believed that life begins at conception. So for three months, our child grew in Co's womb, but on one of those bitter days in life God decided to take Beven home with Him. As I await the departure of a second child, I still say with the deepest meaning that I was still blessed by having children. The Lord giveth and the Lord taketh away, blessed be the name of the Lord (Job 1:21). They will not come back to me, but I will go to them one day (II Samuel 12:23). Glory to His name!

6. I was a part of the church. "What a fellowship, what a joy divine!" to be a part of the family of God. (Ephesians 3:15) This blessing here on earth has been one of the greatest blessings of my life. I still remember when I realized what Jesus was talking about when he told his disciples, "But he shall receive an hundred fold now *in this time*, houses, and brethren, and sisters, and mothers, and children, and lands . . ." (Mark 10:30) He was talking about the Church. In my life, I have received a hundred-fold blessing for being a part of the Body of Christ. I have so many brothers and sisters in Christ scattered around the world it would be very hard to name them all, and yes, even mothers and grandmothers. Every place I have pastored I have found an Eastport Gramie and not just people but houses. I have lost count of just how many houses I have lived in my life, and in all of them, I have only owned two myself.

7. I was bought by Christ. I Corinthians 6:20—"For ye are bought with a price: therefore glorify God in your body, and in your spirit, which are God's." With Paul I thank the Good Lord for His unspeakable gift (II Corinthians 9:15) to me. When I meet Jesus at seven, I not only found a Saviour but a lifelong Friend. As the old church hymn goes, "I've found a Friend, O such a Friend! He loved me ere I knew Him; He drew me with the cords of love, and thus he bound me to Him!" On that day I became an heir, a joint-heir with Jesus (Romans 8:17). I still ponder how this is possible, but I believe it because the Bible says it. The benefits and blessings that came with Christ's purchase of my soul on Calvary would fill another book, but, as for now, this will have to be enough."

These are my top seven blessings, written down and remembered so that I will "forget not all Thy benefits". Have you taken time to count your blessings? Perhaps you will be traveling between two places as I was on that day I visited Agra and Delhi, India. In-between I pondered and mediated on some of the blessings of my life. Maybe, you should to. The best way to overcome a disappointment (Taj Mahal closed) or a disaster (the death of your 39-year-old son) is to "Count your blessing, name them one by one; count your blessings see what God has done. Count your blessings, named them one by one; count your many blessing see what God has done!" God has done more for you than you can count, but you should try!

49

Visiting a Childhood Friend

I was awakened from my daydreaming by an announcement from the back of the car. It seems as I was reliving my life, Shibu was trying to reach out to an old childhood classmate. As we left Agra, Shibu realized we would be passing this friend's village on our way back to Delhi. A visit was in order, and we had time. It was early afternoon and the trip back to Delhi was only about three hours long because we were traveling on the best road I had ever seen in India. You would think we were on Interstate 95 in America. It was smooth and wide with few cars or trucks to speak of, so there should be no delays in slowing our travel. About a half an hour into our journey a cellphone connection was made, an invitation to visit was offered, and a rendezvous place was set.

According to the directions given by Ponnanma, Shibu's childhood friend, we were to meet her beside the road after we came off the super highway. We exited the cloverleaf at a place called Vrindanan but saw no Ponnanma. We continued on a typical Indian rural road through crowded towns and villages for seven miles, but still no Ponnanma. Eventually we came to a tiny hamlet about the size of Edayappara. There, sitting on a motorcycle beside the road, was a middle-aged lady waving her hands. She directed us to follow her down a side lane that led out of town. We traveled about a mile when she turned into a hospital complex. Ponnanma was a midwife in a small rural hospital run by the federal government, and she lived in an apartment complex beside the hospital with the other nurses and doctors that worked there.

We drove by the simple hospital before arriving in front of the three-story apartment where Ponnanma lived with her daughter Athira, an engineer looking for a husband and a job. We arrived around 2:00, but once again you would have thought we had arrived at banqueting time. Ponnanma and her daughter had prepared a feast for us. I know some of my readers don't believe the amount of food I have been describing in this book, but at this simple afternoon luncheon there were twenty-one items on the menu! Yes, I counted them just to be sure. The apartment was simple with few luxuries, and the kitchen was small. How they prepared the spread in the time allotted I know not, but there it was and all of it was set in front of us on a long coffee table! I was the honored guest, but I only nibbled, a bit of this and a bit of that, enough to be polite. I was more interested in the conversation we were having with the adminitatrative doctor of the hospital. Ponnanma wanted the staff to meet Shibu and me. The huge meal was needed because there were at least a dozen people sandwiched tightly in Ponnanma's small living room that also doubled as a bedroom.

The doctor, whose name I heard but never recorded, spoke very good English, and I became his sounding board as he shared the dilemma he was having in his job. There is wide spread corruption in the administrative side of Indian government. Some rural hospitals are just a moneymaker for the corrupt. Kickbacks, bribes, and payoffs were a part of his life, and he hated it. Years of living with the system contributed to his drinking problem. He told of how often he almost lost his job, but nurses like Ponnanma had covered up for him. Raised a Hindu, but never content in the faith, he finally came to Christ through the example of Ponnanma and her daughter. The event that changed his life was the answer to a prayer in which the Good Lord gave him and his wife a daughter after three miscarriages. His dilemma now was how to live his faith in the corruption of his job. He felt if he made waves he would be shipped off to a distance hospital by his administrator. It was then I realized the added dimension of persecution the working Indian Christians have in their daily labor.

As we finished the mega-meal, the doctor invited me next door to see his hospital. I had never been to an Indian hospital, so I took advantage of the opportunity. What I witnessed and saw shocked me! The concrete structure was nice enough on the outside, but I have seen more equipment in an animal hospital than in this hospital. I was even more shocked when I was told that this was primarily a baby hospital, and they average between 125 and 175 deliveries a *month*! I have a sister-in-law who is an obstetric nurse in a rural hospital in northern Maine that only averages 3-6 babies a *month*. Before I left, Ponnanma told me her record for a delivery on one shift was nine babies! The doctor took me into the delivery room (there was lady in the very next room waiting to give birth) and I was shocked again. I wouldn't take my cat Eddie into that room. It was still bloody from the last delivery. They had already had three deliveries that morning. No wonder the population of India is projected to surpass China in a few years! I said nothing as this dear Christian doctor took me around, showing off his hospital as if it were the Mayo Clinic. He was proud the mortality rate was very low, and he was helping these rural mothers in a safe birth. There was a small emergency room attached to the facility, but any major illnesses or accidents were treated in a larger government hospital a few miles away. He spoke of the lack of drugs and the basic medical equipment, but, at the same time, he was proud of his building and especially proud of his staff.

As we wandered back to the apartment and our departure to Delhi, I was reminded of a story in the life of an Ethiopian of the Bible. We all are familiar with the Ethiopian eunuch that was led to Christ by the deacon Philip (Acts 8), but are you as familiar with Ebedmelech, the Ethiopian in the book of Jeremiah (Jeremiah 38) that helped the weeping prophet out of a dangerous situation? We might even say Ebedmelech saved Jeremiah's life. Jeremiah had been cast into a dungeon (Jeremiah 38:6) by his enemies because of his prophesies of the coming Babylonian victory over Jerusalem. The prison Jeremiah was in was more like a pit, for the prophet had sunk into the mire at the bottom of the hole. Ebedmelech, a eunuch in King Zedekiah's palace, pleaded with the king to help Jeremiah before he was dead. (Jeremiah 38:7-9) Ebedmelech intercession worked, and he was sent by the king to rescue Jeremiah. (Jeremiah 38:10-13) Taking ". . . old cast clouts and rotten rags . . ." and putting them under Jeremiah's armpits Ebedmelech and thirty men pulled the prophet out of "the miry clay". (Psalm 40:2) As I walked away from that Indian hospital, I thought that is what these dear people were using to help the ladies of Uttar Pardesh in their time of need. Why didn't Ebedmelech simply throw down a rope and pull the prophet out of the pit? Ebedmelech knew without the old rotten rags and cast-off clouts Jeremiah's armpits would have been bloody and bruised by the time he was pulled out. I found an Ebedmelech in India—a doctor and a nurse that didn't have much, but with great comfort and compassion made the misery of childbirth as comfortable as possible. These two are examples of the unsung heroes who only have "a cup of water" (Matthew 10:42), but they give it in Jesus' name! They make the bed smoother for the pregnant lady; they cook a meal for a visiting preacher; they wipe the brow of the laboring lady. Granted, the room might be made of concrete and there might be little medicine, but Ebedmelech is on duty with "cast-off clouts and old rotten rags"! Some have despised the ministry of rags, yet I found that work alive and well in India. Though I was taken aback by what I saw in the building, I was blessed by what I saw in the Body of Christ!

50

Snubbing the Sticks
Overnight in Delhi

After a few group pictures to remember the side trip to visit a childhood friend and an interesting visit to a primitive, rural hospital, we got back in our Delhi taxi for the final 100 miles to India's capital.

The world has for years proclaimed that the country and country folks are the backbone of society. I believe this theoretical teaching has been promoted both in America and India. I have come to believe that very few, very few indeed, city dwellers actually believe in this philosophy. Politicians speak of it while running for office, and vacationers seem to acknowledge it on vacation, but most desert the country as quickly as they can when the city lights beckon. I believe this was the problem of the prodigal son in Jesus' famous parable in Luke 15:13. I have mentioned a number of times already that my fifth trip to India was nothing like the other four. A case in point was the amount of time I spent in the great cities of India versus the amount of time I spent in big cities on my other trips to rural India. While in the Punjab, I spent most of my time in the mega-cities of Amritsar and Chandigarh/Mohali. I had just spent a day in Agra, and now I was heading to visit the nearly 15 million residents of the mega-city of Delhi. However, Delhi is only the third largest city in India! Little did I know a tour of some of India's biggest cities wouldn't be over when I left Delhi the next day. Before I got back to Kerala, I would visit two more mega-towns, Bhubaneshwar and Bangalore.

Surely by now, you have perceived that I am a country boy not a city slicker. I sometimes feel ashamed (my country roots, I think) when I spend so much time in a city versus the country. As Vance Havner once put it, *"Anybody who can live in a modern city and stay good deserves honorable mention!"* Maybe it was my rural Maine upbringing, or my ancestral foundation in all things country, but the city has had very little draw for me. Despite the scanty means and plenteous adversities, I admire the doctor and the nurse of that little hospital I had just visited more than their big city equivalent. You and I know the country way has been snubbed by most city dwellers. Hayseeds from the country have become the rising stars of the city, but sometimes they hide their origin. The yokel from the potato patch is just not seen as important to the big city citizen who believes his New York is where it is all at. It's the *"Can there any good thing come out of Nazareth?"* (John 1:46) philosophy! It is amazing to me as I read through my Bible just how many of the great men of God came from the country: Elijah, Amos, David, John the Baptist, and Jesus to name a few. I knew I was heading for the madding crowd, but I also knew I would only have to stay overnight.

Sure enough, our arrival in Delhi coincided with what we in America call rush hour, but in Delhi they might call it mass confusion! Even in our big cities there is order: streetlights, lanes, and traffic rules. What I saw in Delhi, I had seen in other smaller Indian cities, but the sheer volume of cars, trucks, autoes, and other vehicles I had never seen before on the highways and byways brought the traffic flow to a standstill numerous times as we tried to make our way to the other side of Delhi. Have you forgotten the Indian mind set is they don't believe in bypasses! We struggled to maneuver through the edge of the city. I couldn't imagine how we would get through the heart of the city. Despite the four-lane road we were on, the multitude of vehicles had turned the four-lanes into seven-lanes. Nobody stays in a lane in India. It is the survival of the fitness or in the case of India, survival of the biggest. Our car was far from being the biggest, but we were bigger than most. I watched our driver work his way from gap to gap as we emerged from one bottle neck after another. One of the goals of my companions was to get me to the Lotus Temple before dark. Also called the Baha'i House of Worship, this was one of Delhi's most innovative modern structures. Completed in 1986, the building looks like an unfurling twenty-seven-pedaled, white marble lotus flower. The edifice is surrounded by nine pools and the yard covers 227 acres. The lofty auditorium can set 1300 people, and it was something to see! I saw it from afar because when we got to the gate it was closed. We had missed it because of being delayed by traffic. Closed, a recurring theme of this trip I would say, and all because of the "madding crowd" on the roads.

I was impressed with another temple we passed because massive Redstone carved elephants surrounded it. They would have looked better at Agra Fort, I thought. I never got the name of the complex as we sped on through rush hour traffic trying to make our destination before dark. I was interested to learn that the one big river we crossed was the northern section of the Yamuna River, the same river that flows by the Taj Mahal and Agra Fort, 139 miles away. We also saw massive high-rise complexes being built to house the rapidly increasing population of the city. Delhi is your typical metropolitan center, and despite the architecture, I felt I was driving into Dallas or New York or Boston. Delhi had its sky scrapers and its overpasses, but no bypasses! We even passed the train station that Shibu and I traveled through the night before. Eventually, after nearly an hour crawling through Delhi, we arrived in a simple suburban area and to the Christian Theological Research Center just before dark, around 6:30. We paid the taxi drive 8500 rupees, about $125—not bad for a day. Remember, he had driven down from Delhi with John Philips and had taken us around Agra, the side visit to meet Shibu's friend, and back to Delhi; all total the man had been on the road for over twelve hours.

We entered the three-story house through a wide, iron gate. The building was surrounded by a high wall which was only a few feet from the next house. The caretakers greeted us and ushered us to a simple room containing two beds. It was our home for the night. We unpacked and settled in for a quiet evening of relaxing after a hectic thirty-six hours of travel and visiting. As Shibu took a shower, I counted my money. I had left with 30,000 rupees, and I was down to 3440. Good thing I was heading to Kerala tomorrow! I would have had 1000 less than that if it hadn't been for Ponnanma who gave me 1000 rupees before I left her home. I tried to resist her gift (actually it was the first I had ever received in all my India trips), but I could see she really wanted the blessing of giving me the valuable funds. I still stand amazed at the giving of poor people. They are people who can't afford to give, but they do—a widow's (nurse's) mite kind of giving (Mark 12:41-44).

After Shibu got out of the shower, he asked what I wanted for supper, maybe something American? I told him I was ok, but he left the room as I finished getting settled. About half an hour later, he came back and told me my supper was on the table, and he was going to eat with John and our hosts, Indian style. When I got to the table there was a thin crust pepperoni pizza on the table—a delivered thin crust pepperoni pizza on the table. I couldn't believe it, and it was really good. Maybe there are a few benefits to living in a city! I spent the rest of the evening reminiscing on my amazing day in India: riding on my fifth train ride, seeing one of the seven wonders of the modern world, and walking through Fort Agra. Oh, I forgot to tell you while traveling back to Delhi by way of the Indian Autobahn (a toll road), we stopped at one of the many gas plazas and guess what we found? Magnum bars—caramel over vanilla covered in chocolate. What a day!

51

Surprise Side-Trip to Orissa

After my first delivered pizza in India, I was off to bed. It had been an exhausting day. Those tiring kinds of days automatically give you a good night's sleep and a restful night to recharge. I might have been weary, but I was rejoicing in the special day my friend Shibu had planned. Though it didn't work out quite the way he intended, it still was a day that will long be remembered. I fell asleep under the covers of a comfortable bed in an air-conditioned room with a good friend. Does a day end better than that? Shibu came in after visiting with our host family, people like John Philips who had moved from Kerala to Delhi for work. Shibu and I said goodnight on what I thought would be my last night away from Kerala. How wrong I was!

I slept from 10:00 PM to 8:00 AM. I knew I needed a good rest because it was time to fly back to Kerala. We were not scheduled to leave until around 2:30 PM, so I had the morning to get to know our hosts better and to learn more about the Christian Theological Research Center. Around breakfast, I learned the ministry had been started in the 1950s by a couple from New Zealand. Originally it was a hostel to host local Christian groups on retreat. Also, I found this amazing. I learned the original house was actually in the woods far from Delhi. Over the sixty years of its existence, the city had grown until it had literally swallowed the center. Our trip into the hostel was through a densely populated area outside the main city. Even far beyond the Center, the streets and lanes stretched on for miles. The vast urban sprawl had reached far and wide, and now the Christian Theological

Research Center was just a part of the mega-metropolis. I was taken through the house and shown the large bedrooms on the third floor where groups of people could stay while having their conference. It had been added on to and built up over the years. I was taken into the cellar where there was a large library where people could come and research spiritual things. I was taken out into the garden where one could relax and enjoy the cooler air created by the wonderful trees and flowering plants. Despite being stuck on the edge of a massive city, the world behind the wall at the Christian Theological Research Center was tranquil. Even the noise of the street seemed to be blocked out by the walls and the trees. It was a relaxing oasis on the corner of urban sprawl!

The highlight of my morning at the TRACI (Theological Research and Communication Institute, its new name) hostel was a talk I had with a young man who came with his family to see Shibu. I soon discovered that many families from Kerala had moved to Delhi for jobs. While we were there, a young lady showed up who had attended the Kangazha Church before moving north. The family that came after her was also from the home church of the IGBC. I had learned that John's brother Johnson was part of a piece of my past history at the IGBC. In 2006 on my first visit, Shibu was talking about the new business manager that he had just hired from Delhi. That new business manager was Johnson! Now I know where my good friend Johnson had come from. He had once managed the hostel, and now John Philips was moving back to Kerala to join the staff of the IGBC. But my joy that morning in Delhi was in conversing with a young man named Daniel. I knew the minute the first word came out of his mouth that I could talk to him. Daniel had perfect English, a Shibu kind of English. While his parents talked to Shibu and John in the living room in Malayalam, Daniel and I talked in English about everything American and Indian. Daniel was an organizer in the field of foreign education. If you wanted to study abroad you would search out Daniel's company, and Daniel would make all the arrangements necessary for you to study in Australia, Canada, England or the States, the most popular places for Indians to study overseas. Daniel had a college decree and loved his job despite working six-days and 50 plus hours a week. The business was booming, and his employees had already opened offices in four other cities and two other countries. It seems everybody in India with a bit of money wants to get their education abroad. The other thing I found interesting is that Daniel never drives in Delhi for work (I don't blame him), but takes the local train.

I think it is time for us in America to take a fresh look at the word culture. For too long culture means a college degree, the ability to talk about art and architecture, trips overseas, and to be polite and proficient in various forms of etiquette. These things might be desirable to some and without fault, but do they really define culture? I am speaking in the same tone as Paul when he wrote this to Timothy, "But refuse profane and old wives fables, and exercise thyself rather unto godliness, for bodily exercise profiteth little, but godliness is profitable unto all things, having a promise of the life that now is, and of that which is to come." (I Timothy 4:7-8) Oh, there is profit in art and the opera, how to hold your fork and what to wear, but there is something more important. I have found in India, more than in America, the importance of the greater things over the lesser things. Oh, we are to do the lesser things as Jesus said (Matthew 23:23), but we need to be careful not to omit the "weightier matters". Daniel knew of the weightier matters.

Daniel and I spoke in Delhi that morning of how the Bible, a long time ago, proclaimed a different standard in culture. "He that is slow to anger is better than the mighty; and he that ruleth his spirit than he that taketh a city!" (Proverbs 16:32) How man loves to glory in his cities, cities like Delhi. I didn't hear that from young Daniel, for his glory was in the Lord. The cultivation of culture will never start until Christ becomes Lord of the life. Look at all the so-called cultured civilization and the many wars they have drawn the world into. The twentieth century ought to be enough proof of the poor state of culture today! I found in a young man from Delhi, a poor, plain person that had no proud markings of culture, but I found him very cultured. The intellectual and elite of our societies think themselves cultured because they are smart, or rich, or powerful, but they have no heart for true culture. When Jesus was on earth his greatest and most bitter enemies were the cultured Pharisees. They were so cultured, so holy, so spiritual they wouldn't eat an egg that was laid on Saturday. Jesus came to proclaim a different kind of culture, the kind I found in the heart of a young man from Delhi. It was a joy to spend a morning with him. The truly cultured are those who have come to Jesus Christ for eternal salvation and thereafter follow him into an uncultured world. Through Jesus' Holy Spirit the marks of true culture are produced: love, joy, peace, longsuffering, gentleness, goodness, faith, meekness, and temperance (Galatians 5:22-23), the fine characteristics I saw in Daniel and so many others including a nurse and doctor in a rural village.

We left TRACI around 1:00 for a 45-minute ride over to Delhi International Airport. The traffic was heavy, but once again our taxi drive knew how to maneuver his way through the obstacles that are part of Delhi driving. We got through customs and security without much trouble, and we made our way to the food court before we boarded our flight south. It was then Shibu passed me my ticket. I took a quick glance and then a much quicker double take. There on the ticket stub was the phrase "from Delhi to

Bhubaneswar". For a moment I couldn't speak, and then I blurted out, "We are going to Orissa?" My short-term mission's trip in India wasn't over, for we were off to visit my dear friend Joy Thomas!

52

Pushing a New Suzuki

As Shibu and I waited for our Orissa flight, we had time for lunch. Shibu had a pizza, and I had KFC. As I ate my chicken, I worked through my mind what I had just been told. Shibu's second surprise, our trip to see Joy Thomas, would involve two extra days in northern India. This didn't bother me because I had learned extra days in India are blessed days—thanks to Hurricane Sandy. See my book *The Uttermost Part*. Shibu wanted me to see the new sanctuary in Bhubaneswar. I had visited Orissa in 2012, but at that time the persecuted church of central Orissa was just getting settled in the capital. I was hoping to see my old friend Pastor John and maybe a few more of the Orissa boys, as well as spending a Sunday worshiping with the saints. As I sat in the Delhi International Airport, I pondered this extra, unexpected blessing.

Most of us have come to the realization there are some things we can know and there are some things we will never know this side of eternity. I am beginning to wonder when we get to eternity will the things we wondered about on earth be worth knowing about in heaven? I have come to the conclusion that a man has come to an understanding of these things when he knows which is which, to know or not to know! I have noticed that some of the unhappiest people are those that try to know what they can't know or ignore what they should know (Matthew 22:29). Even the Bible seems to highlight both sides of this issue ". . . it is given unto you to know . . ." (Matthew 13:11) and ". . . it is not for you to know . . ." (Acts 1:7) In two days, Shibu had surprised me twice in our original plans for the trip to the

Punjab, the side trip to see the Taj and now the side trip to see Joy. Shibu decided to hold onto his surprise until I needed to know, and I believe that is how the Good Lord works in our lives. Sometimes we want to know before the situation matures but a premature telling can bring misunderstanding and confusion. As with Shibu, I have learned to wait for God's revealing time. He does know best when an explanation is prudent, and He knows when to keep the information to Himself.

Our wait to go to Orissa was about two and a half hours. Around 4:00 on March 19, 2016, Shibu and I boarded Indigo Flight # 259 for Bhubaneswar. I was surprised to discover the flight time was under two hours. As I have mentioned before, I had always pictured India as a large country when in reality you can get to most places in India by plane in two hours or less, no matter which part of the country you are flying to. Delhi to Bhubaneswar was just 756 miles as the crow flies, and as with all India flights so far, it was a smooth, pleasant journey—my seventh flight in India! Having been to the Bhubaneswar Airport before, the transition wasn't difficult. We landed at dusk and there to greet us was Joy Thomas and his son Jason. One of the surprises one gets when only visiting someone every four years or so is the growth of the kids. I had known Jason since he was a little boy and now he was a young man, in his last year in high school. There was also something else waiting for us—another surprise?

As Joy led us to a parking lot, he told Shibu and me he had something to show us. Maybe a bit of history is in order first. I had followed the comings and goings of Joy Thomas and his family since 2006. Because of the severe persecution between 2007-2010, Joy had traveled to Orissa for years alone (1996-2006). He feared taking his family into the trouble and constant fighting. There were years this former railroad man had a price on his head from the militant Hindus of Orissa! Remember, Joy and his family are not from Orissa but Kerala. Over the years I visited Joy, his desire was to eventually move his family to Orissa, but he knew the timing had to be right. About a year before this visit, I had sent him money to make the move when he thought it would be right. He hated leaving his family in Kerala for months at a time while fulfilling his responsibilities as director of the Orissa Outreach Ministry of the Associated Missions of the IGBC. As the persecution died down, Joy felt the time was right. His family had only lived in Kerala so it was a big move, especially for his wife Gigi, their daughter Blesses, and their son Jason. The kids had to change schools and cultures and Gigi had to leave her family and friends, but the move happened and the family was now settled in the community of Khordha, about 17 miles outside of Bhubaneswar.

Also about the time of my last visit (2012), I began to realize just how difficult it was for Joy to get around visiting the various assemblies in the association. Now it was twenty assemblies in three different regions of Orissa. Upon returning to the States in 2012, I contacted my brother Michael. Michael had become a very successful businessman and had formed a foundation to help missionaries in foreign lands with purchases that were impossible without outside help. A case in point was the funds for a car for Joy's travels. Locally Joy would use a motorcycle, but, on his distant trips, he would have to take a train and have somebody pick him up. With his family moving to Orissa, he really needed a car. Through my brother's charitable gift, money was sent to the IGBC with instructions to buy Joy a car. Over the years I had asked about the car but I was told it was still in the works. As I had learned with other projects in India you must have patience. The problem with the car wasn't the money but getting the money from Kerala to Orissa. It seems if you send large sums of funds the government and the banks take a lot of it, so transactions have to be spread over many months if not years. The mission wanted to buy the car in Orissa, so it took time. Waiting for us in the parking lot of the Bhubaneswar Airport was a brand new Suzuki. The catch? Joy had just picked the car up that morning—three years to buy a car!

I thought it was providential that the day of my arrival, a day I didn't know would even happened, that my friend Joy would finally have the gift of a car from my brother, and I would be the first visitor to ride in my brother's donation! The four of us got into the car and headed for Joy's home. We first had to drive through a busy section of Bhubaneswar to get to the highway that led outside of town. Remember—no bypasses in India. I began to notice almost immediately that Joy was having a hard time driving the car. I was actually getting a bit nervous. It was then I was told that this was Joy's first car. Actually the first car he had ever driven much. Motorcycles and trains were Joy's means of transportation and driving a stick shift wasn't his thing. I thought we would never get out of town, and we barely did when Joy didn't see a street divider and drove up on it. No damage was done, but Shibu had had enough and took over the driving.

As we finally headed up a major highway (actually two lanes on each side like our superhighways), I became to notice something else quite troubling. The head lights seemed to be getting dim. I didn't say anything at first, but I could see that Shibu was having trouble seeing the road. I immediately understood the problem because I had a similar experience a few years back. Despite being a brand new car with barely twenty miles on it, the generator wasn't working, and the car was running on the battery. We only had until the battery failed before the car would die. How good is the Lord? We got off the main road in time, and the lane leading to Joy's house didn't contain any traffic. About a mile from our destination, the Suzuki died. Joy, Jason, and I literally had to push Joy's brand new car the rest of the way home. Another surprise and another first in India!

53

India/Pakistan Cricket Match

After pushing Joy's brand new car behind the cinderblock wall that separates one of the side streets of Khordha from Joy's front yard, we had a little fellowship time with him and his family before heading off to our home away from home for the next two nights. Because the car was dead, we had to make the mile journey on motorcycles through the dark lanes and alleyways to the hotel. I had vowed years before that I would never ride on a motorcycle with Joy Thomas ever again after a harrowing experience in Kerala. Joy was certainly a daredevil motorcyclist, not so much a car driver as we learned just a few hours before coming back from the airport. Shibu wanted to drive with Jason, and because there were two of us, I reluctantly got on behind Joy. Shibu and Jason were on the Thomas' motorcycle and Joy was driving their scooter. So technically I wasn't on a motorcycle with Joy, and I knew India scooters were not as fast as their motorcycles. It was pitch black (few street lights in India villages), so I couldn't see the danger, right? How much trouble could Joy get me in? We were only going to the other side of town.

If I didn't know better I would have thought that Joy had supercharged his scooter up to a professional racing machine. The way we zipped through the narrow streets and around the blind corners I was imagining meeting a brahma bull at every turn. We did have to travel downtown a bit and there were still a few vendors out and a few customers lingering despite the late hour. We barely missed a few pedestrians and a few other cycles. Shibu had left us in his dust, so we never saw him or Jason until we arrived at the

Bhagaban Villa Hotel on the Nayagarth Road. The mile-long trip seemed to take seconds, but to the Lord's glory we arrived safely and I made a second vow, but a vow I would have to break again before I left Orissa!

The sign might have read Villa, but by far it was the worst place we stayed on the trip. Because the other places were so fabulous this downgrade was more like the Indian hotels I had stayed in before. I had learned many trips before like the Apostle Paul wrote to the Church in Philippi, "Not that I speak in respect of want: for I have learned in whatsoever state (Kerala State or Orissa State) I am, therewith to be content." (Philippians 4:11) Even if Shibu and I did have to share a bed! We checked in and were ushered to a side door on the first floor of the building. The double doors into our massive room were locked with a padlock, which the attendant had a hard time opening. That was our first concern. The side of town we were on was a bit shady, but Shibu and I had been in worst places. Jason brought in our luggage, and we settled in. The next problem that arose was the water. Sure it was bottled water, but you could tell the bottles had been refilled. One of the dangers of India is the water, and I had been very careful throughout all my trips to never drink anything but bottled water. Eventually they brought us some bottles of water that didn't look like they had been tampered with. We settled in, and within a half an hour, Jason and Joy left for home. It was then Shibu turned on the TV.

I had heard about the big sports match occurring in India several times on our trip to the Punjab, but because of our busy schedule, we hadn't had time to watch the television. That is until our Saturday evening in Khordha. To say that cricket is big in India would be an understatement to the greatest degree, and a match between India and Pakistan is the biggest of them all. Imagine the World Series and the Super Bowl happening at the same time. So it wasn't long before Shibu was into the match, and I was trying to keep caught up with the action. I had, several times in my trips to India, been explained the game but for my western mind it has been a hard game to comprehend. Joshua, Shibu's son, is a big fan and I had watched a few games with him. I had even played cricket in the Simon's front yard with Jos and a few of his friends. Some say it is a kind of baseball, but don't tell any Indian that.

The Indians adopted cricket from the British, their national sport. As with the English, cricket has become part of the national fabric of the nation as both a sport and a national pride. Because of the already national rivalries between India and Pakistan (remember the competition on the border at Wagha I shared with you in an earlier chapter) when India and Pakistan play cricket, it is as if the fate of the entire country rests on the shoulders of the players. National respect and pride is on the line in every game, so, needless to say, the nations watch every ball. Speaking of the ball, it is about the size of our baseball, hard with a leather-cover. The bat has a flat blade, a long handle, and weighs in at about two and a half pounds. The game is played on a level, grassy field about 550 feet around, more like an oval or a circle. Two wickets (each made of three sticks twenty-eight inches high capped by two pieces of wood called bails that are laid in grooves across the top of the stumps of each wicket) stand twenty-two yards apart in the middle of the field. The area between the two wickets is called the pitch much like the pitcher's box in American baseball, just different and hard to explain.

The game is played by two teams of eleven men each. The toss of a coin will determine which team bats first (like football). At the end of each pitch stands an umpire, the sole judges on the rules and rulings during the game. As Shibu watched the game and I asked questions, the players, like the batsman, the bowler, and the wicketkeeper became clear to me, but not very interesting to me! As the evening passed, I caught myself napping more than watching. The time and distance we had traveled in our week in the North Country was beginning to take its toll. One by one each player on India's team had a chance to bat and unless the batsman got out he continued to bat and the score rose. Once the side was out only then could the other side bat, and, in the end, the team with the highest score won. As the evening progressed, I heard terms like "bowled-when the ball hits the wicket" and "the player is called out, or caught when a ball is hit and caught before it hits the ground". The terms were all explained to me by my gracious host, but little was registering because a deep tiredness was falling over me. I was able to stay awake until eleven but eventually exhaustion overpowered me, and I was gone. It was only in the morning that Shibu informed me that India won in the end—Go Team!

India is cricket-crazy and even a simple match in a local park brings hundreds of people out to watch. When their national team is playing somewhere around the world, (the great cricket countries are Australia, South Africa, Britain, Pakistan, and India) Indians will stay up all night to watch the match no matter where it is being played. If these matches are played in India a ticket to the game is hard to find. Winter is the main season for the professional teams with cities like Delhi, Kolkata, Mumbai, Chennai, Bangalore, and Kanpur being the great rival towns, but the noise of the fan blowing in the air-conditioner was more than enough to lull me to a deep sleep. I am afraid I cared little for this national sport and more for the rest that I craved. I knew the next day would be another hot day (actually recorded temperatures), and I knew I would need all the energy I could store up. Sorry India for disrespecting your team and your game by falling asleep in the middle of an important contest between India/Pakistan, but I was in your country to teach people how to play the game of life not a game of balls and bowlers and batsmen!

54

Sion Shramika Baptist Church

As I woke from a wonderfully, refreshing rest, I saw that Shibu was already up. It was then I learned that India had won the cricket match the night before. My first act was to take a shower in the small bathroom just off the backdoor of our room. The minute I opened the door the heat of the morning hit me. It was going to be another hot and humid day in Orissa. The bathroom was primitive so a bucket shower was in order. You fill a pail from the tap of cold water and dump it over your head, lather up, and clean up with more buckets of cold water over your head to rinse off. I had taken plenty of these showers in India, so it wasn't new. But, as usual, the water only cooled you and cleansed you until the hot, sticky air caused you to start sweating again. Getting back into our air-conditioned room helped, but I knew we would be soon out into the heat again.

Because we were spending the night again at the Bhagaban, we left all our things in the hotel as Joy picked us up around 9:30 AM for breakfast. I was dressed in my India Sunday best: white shirt, black pants, and sandals. The ride over to Joy's house was rejuvenating, and, for some reason, Joy went slowly. Because we had come in after dark, it was my first look at the small town (by India standards, but bigger than I originally thought) Joy and his family now called home. By the time we arrived at Joy's flat, the crowds were out. This was why we had to drive slower. The markets were crowded as were the streets, thousands of people going somewhere. There were even a few cars and the narrow streets were not wide enough for two, so someone had to pull over. Gigi had a typical Indian breakfast waiting including those famous half-fried eggs, toast, and plenty of fruit. I ate bananas. We talked and fellowshipped for about an hour. It was during this time I got one of my treasured souvenirs from my trip. It is nearly a year after this fifth trip to India that I am writing this chapter. On the back of the door in my study at the Emmanuel Baptist Church is a 2016 calendar I got from Joy. Indians like to announce events on calendars. Also on the back of my study door is a 2007 calendar given to me by the Nagaland Students of KBBC, a calendar I got when my daughter Marnie and I were there for graduation. Next to that calendar is a 2013 calendar from Kerala Baptist Bible College and Seminary promoting the summer mission's trip by two of the faculty and twelve students to Manipur in northeast India. The calendar I got at Joy's house was promoting the May 6-8, 2016 gathering of the Orissa church in Dangulu, the first convention in Orissa ever by the organization.

Around 10:30, a taxi (remember Joy's car was down) picked us up for the hour ride into the village of Shramika, another town in what is now the suburbs of Bhubaneswar. We were heading for the newest church plant in Orissa and only the second church sanctuary that had been built. It was brand new having only been dedicated a few months before. After my trip to Orissa in 2012, I had been praying for this construction, one of the reasons Shibu planned this side trip on our Punjab journey. He wanted me to see the progress of the new facility and meet the new pastor, Pastor Reuben Digal. The twenty-one miles took us an hour, but when we arrived, a crowd had already gathered. It was Palm Sunday and just as we drove up the street where the small sanctuary was located a procession of people carrying palm branches came down the street. I was surprised until I was told a large Roman Catholic Church was located nearby. One of the sad aspects of Catholicism in India is that it has taken on many of the characteristics of Hinduism in their focus rather than the rites and rituals of their faith. However, I soon turned my attention to the white building with the red cross on the front and the large banner that read: Sion Shramika Baptist Church-Orissa Mercy Mission-Independent Gospel Baptist Churches.

As I was ushered into the building, a series of Christmas songs was playing from a recording. Christmas songs I asked? These were not just your traditional Christian Christmas songs, but also a number of classic American Christmas Songs. The answer? They wanted the American to feel at home. Within a half an hour the building was filled. Every square inch of floor was covered. As usual I sat in one of a half dozen plastic chairs with everybody else on the floor. The crowd was also gathering in the small front yard of the sanctuary. We counted about 120. The heat was oppressive because the roof of the building was made of tin. They did a have a few fans, but they couldn't keep up. I think I drank a gallon of water to stay dehydrated through the two and a half hour service. There was plenty of congregational singing and a couple of specials. There were prayers and Bible reading and an offering. The ushers had a hard time getting around because the place was full. Besides the money given, I noticed, as I have always in Orissa, some people gave rice and fruit and other commodities. Then it was my turn.

I had decided to share a message with the believers of Sion Shramika called "What Time Is It?" based on Psalms 119:126: "It is time for thee, Lord, to work: for they have made void thy law." I developed the sermon around these points.

1. What time is it?—It is time for God's word to remain supreme—Psalm 119:126. I shared about us living in a day of a Biblical famine of hearing God's word (Amos 8:11) and the need to get back to the Scriptures.

2. What time is it?—It is time we seek the Savior again—Hosea 10:12. My thoughts were not so much on the world seeking (Isaiah 55:6), but the Church once again finding a renewed relationship with the Christ. (Revelation 3:16-18)

3. What time is it?—It is time for the church to self-judge—I Peter 4:17. We need to invoke the precepts of I Corinthians 11:31-32 again, for if we don't then the Good Lord will judge us. (II Corinthians 4:3-4)

4. What time is it?—It is time to wake up and not sleep—Romans 13:11-14. The Bible seems to be clear that one of the great errors of the Church in the last days will be sleeping at the wheel while on the job. (I Thessalonians 5:1-8)

5. What time is it?—It is time to be sober and serious for time is short—I Corinthians 7:29. It appears as if all the signs of the times point to the Coming of Christ, soon and very soon. (Titus 2:2, 2:4, 2:6)

What time is it? The clock is ticking, and we need to be ready for the Lord's return!

It was a wonderful if not hot time of fellowship with the saints of the Sion Shramika Baptist Church. My only disappointment was that Pastor John and his family were not there. I learned that John's son Moses, my driver in 2012, had been caught up in a motorcycle accident and was in the hospital. I did get a chance to see one of the other pastors of Orissa, a man I had first meet in 2006, but other than Joy he was the only one. Of course we had lunch, and once again I was catered to by Gigi who brought me French fries and fried chicken. It seems wherever I go in India I have a lady that spoils me with American food, if not American cooking. Afterward, I had to have my picture taken with everyone in the group including a group picture—another one of my cherished treasures from the trip. I especially enjoyed the time spent with the ladies' choir. Their morning song was wonderful, and they liked getting their picture taken with the preacher. Another amazing day visiting with the churches of India! That was #63!

55

Guru Caves of Udayagiri

We left the Sion Shramika Baptist Church just before 3:00 in the afternoon. As we climbed into the taxi that brought us, I recalled some of the interesting information I heard while eating with the flock. Talking over lunch, Jason told me that the hotel we were staying at (Bhagaban Villa) meant "God's House". I was glad I had a chance to visit a real house of God before going back to the Hindu house of god. Shibu told me that the men of the Sion church had built the sanctuary themselves in just eleven days running two different shifts and the sanctuary is open every morning at 5:00 AM for those that want to pray before they went to work. Try that in the States and see how many prayer warriors show up! Little did I know I was about to see just how dramatic the difference of worship there is in a Baptist Church in India and a Hindu shrine.

Four miles outside of Bhubaneswar and on our way back to Khordha, we stopped at one of the famous historic and religious sites of Hinduism in Orissa: the Udayagiri and Khandagiri Caves. I was still wishing for the Lingaraja Temple, the 11th century shrine I wanted to visit in 2012, but it seems that will have to wait for another trip. Again I was surprised with the stop, thinking we were in hiding again. It seems that Udayagiri is more of a tourist site, so an American might not stand out there. Joy and Shibu thought I might enjoy the stop, and I did. We parked in a lot just below the brow of two hills. This is what I learned about this unique spot. The twin hills (maybe three hundred feet) were honeycombed with manmade caves. Some are said to date back to the first century BC. The hill on the right,

Udayagiri (Sunrise Hill), has a rock stairway to the top. The hill on the left, Khandagiri (Broken Hill), has a paved path with just a gentle slope up to the caves. What makes the hills impressive is the fact they rise straight up from the very flat plains surrounding them. Built as a place for Jain monks—Jainism, one of the Hindu religious creeds resembling Buddhism was founded about 500 BC; its main teaching is reverence for wise and good men and respect for animals—to live and hide away from the world. I was surprised to find a few gurus still living there.

Our goal was to climb to the top of Udayagiri Hill and see the sights and sites. The temperature was well above 100 as we started the ascent. There were plenty of others around, and nobody seemed to pay any attention to the white man trying to get to the summit. Halfway up, we encountered our first beggar, a lightly clothed Indian with an outreached palm and a downward stare. I was told he was one of the monks who helped fund the temple at the top with his begging. As we reached the top, we came upon what they called the Rani Gumpha (Queen's Cave), the biggest of the eighteen caves on the side of the hill. A Hindu priest tried to talk me into ringing the bell, but I was more interested in the score of monkeys with their out stretched palms. I thought of the irony of the human and the ape and these words from the Epistle to the Romans, "And changed the glory of the uncorruptible God into an image made like to corruptible man, and to birds, and fourfooted breast, and creeping things." (Romans 1:23) Shibu wouldn't allow me to go in, another close call with a temple, again for another day. I could stare in and see lavishly sculpted friezes of monkeys and elephants and dancing girls. I turned the corner to climb the last few stone steps to the top when I saw him.

There in the mouth of a small cave was a half-naked man with long black hair. I had seen Gurus in pictures, but this was my first Guru face to face. What shocked me was his perfect English. He was sitting in the mouth of his cave asking for a handout. Unlike his buddy down the hill, he was vocal. He talked to me, asked where I was from, and was I an Englishman. Our conversation was short as Shibu encouraged me to move on up the hill. The Guru's cave was located about ten feet above the pathway I was on, so I got a chance to get a couple of good pictures of the Guru of Udayagiri before I passed him by for the summit. Once I reached the top of the hill I could see why Joy and Shibu wanted to stop, for the view and the vista were spectacular.

The first interesting site was the Dhaul Shant Stupa, the Buddhist shrine Joy and Shibu took me to in 2012. Despite the distance of probably twenty miles, I could make out the distinct hilltop on the other side of Bhubaneswar. The massive city lies between the two holy sites. I knew Bhubaneswar was big, but from on top of Udayagiri Hill its true size could be seen. It was also from on top of Udayagiri Hill we could get a great view of the Khandagiri Hill monastery across the narrow valley. Here the monks had carved out more chamber-like structures in the side of the hill. We could see clearly the fifteen caves of that complex. One of the unique features of the thirty-two caves of the two complexes is that they are all so short it is impossible to stand upright in them. This was, of course, done on purpose in keeping with the self-mortification and asceticism that Jain monks were expected to practice. Though I never saw any gurus on the Khandagiri side, I learned that many who practice Jainism do gather at the caves on an annual basis to meditate, especially in the month of January. The last thing I liked about the top of Udayagiri was the cooling breeze above the stifling air three hundred feet below. We stood there for a few minutes taking in the city of Bhubaneswar and the cooling breezes of a fading afternoon in Orissa.

My descent was slow and deliberate as Shibu called us to return to Khordha and supper. Why so much eating and little sightseeing? I would have stayed longer, but maybe the boys thought we had left the sipe (white man) out in the public eye too long. One by one I took the stone steps downward. There he was just where I left him, the man in a cave seeking spiritually by shutting himself off from the world, thinking he was more spiritual because he deprived himself of any creature comforts. I found his friend on the same step. As I passed him by, I was thinking what kind of life is this? What kind of testimony to one's faith can be seen in neglect and self-infliction? With each step, I praised the Everlasting One that He never expected His believers to live in such conditions. The site was impressive. The sights were breathtaking, but the purpose of both was depressing, down heartened, and dreary. At the bottom of the hill were the vendors. I saw them in Jerusalem just outside the most sacred sites of Christendom. I saw them outside the Dhaul Shant Stupa, the most sacred site of the Buddhist in Bhubaneswar. I saw them outside the Golden Temple, the most sacred site of the Sikhs. Most know the story of Jesus and the Woman at the Well (John 4), but have you ever considered in that story what the disciples were doing and what Jesus was doing? Jesus was soul-winning (John 4:10) while the disciples were shopping (John 4:8). In America, Sunday has been replaced as the day of service for a day of shopping. How many today quickly leave the sanctuary for the store after the service is over? There was a time I wouldn't shop on Sunday, and I, to this day rarely do, but I too have fallen into the reality of all world religions, the combining of soul-winning and shopping. The priests of Udayagiri tried to lure me into their rock temple, to ring their bell to worship their god, and, at the bottom, were the merchants selling their Udayagiri souvenirs to people like me. It was Sunday when I visited the Guru Caves of Udayagiri, but my purchase wasn't a trinket, but the truth that showed me the wonderful faith I believe in!

56

The Tale Continues
Lord, I Believe . . .

By late afternoon, we were back at Hotel Bhagaban Villa after an interesting stop at the guru caves of Udayagiri. Supper was at the Thomas' which included a taste of home. It seems Joy had told his upstairs neighbor (the Thomas' live in a duplex building with two homes on the ground floor and two more homes on the second floor) of our visit. One of the apartments on the second floor was occupied by a former English teacher, retired but still very active. When we arrived for supper, Ruth, whose last name I did not know, had two bottles of Coke in the old fashioned, iconic containers waiting for us. Joy didn't have a bottle opener, so he popped the caps with a screwdriver! The flavor was American even if the savor was Indian. We thanked the lady, after she returned from an afternoon of shopping, before we returned to the Bhagaban and a quiet evening of watching another cricket match: Afghanistan/South Africa. Once again I wasn't very interested so I turned back in my mind to the tale of my life I had been compiling since I started reminiscing periodically throughout this earth's farthest bounds trip:

"Someone has defined a creed as *"a half-way station between the Bible and the heart!"* Anyone that has traveled as far as I have on the Christian road of life sooner or later sets down and compiles what he or she really believes. In my over three-score pilgrimage, I have changed my beliefs on certain lesser things, but the weightier things I haven't altered since I first believed—since I first started for the Kingdom, since I first gave my heart to

Jesus Christ. Despite sensational ups and spectacular downs, I haven't fallen into the trap of glorying in past exaltations or past failures, living only in the mountaintop experience or valley exploit I have enjoyed or sorrowed over. I have been tempted at times, but building tabernacles on a summit isn't a part of my core beliefs, nor is pining over my many losses. Over the years, while others have fallen prey to the modern trends and the conformity of the times, I have stayed firm and stood unmoving on these basic statements. These phrases are still at the heart of my preaching and teaching, and it is my prayer that as you read them you too will crystallize your own belief structure. These articles of faith run together on these three important words: *Lord, I Believe:*

1. *That in trusting* what You did for me on Calvary You became my personal Saviour. Trusting speaks of dependence upon Jesus. "My" makes it personal. I have never known a time where I didn't have an intimate relationship with Jesus. I haven't been as faithful to that relationship as He has been to me, but He has always been a friend. "What a friend I have in Jesus . . ." Alexander Whyte said it best when he wrote, "Draw nigh to God and He will draw nigh to you. Act faith if you do not feel it . . . Christ is before you to take freely: accept Him, trust Him, believe what He says, assume that you are His and believe as if you were. Throw yourself in His direction even though you cannot reach Him. Even if you die doing this, He will take care of you. He does not say 'See,' He only says 'Look'; that is all you have to do, He will take care of the rest." Amen and Amen!

2. *That in yielding* to You all that I am and have You will use me for Your glory. Some like to use the word surrender, but I like the use of the word committal. Vance Havner once said, "We surrender to an enemy but we commit to a friend!" I didn't surrender to my wife the day we got married. I committed myself to her. Our relationship is now into the 50th year, 46 of them in marriage. Only then will we be meet for the master's use (II Timothy 2:21) and His glory (Matthew 5:16).

3. *That in receiving* the filling of the Holy Spirit, only then will I be able to glorify You. I found very early in my Christianity that though I received the fullness of the Spirit at my conversion (I Corinthians 12:13) that I often "quenched" (I Thessalonians 5:19) and "grieved" (Ephesians 4:30) the Holy Spirit resulting in my need to confess the sins and transgressions and iniquities that clogged the free flowing of the Spirit (Ephesians 5:18). We can only glorify our Saviour when His Spirit moves unobstructed through our life, our lifestyle, and our

living. But I have also been very careful not to make the Holy Spirit a figurehead in any of my activities because Jesus was very clear that the Spirit would never speak of itself (John 16:13). The Spirit will always bear witness of the Christ and so should we.

4. *That in looking* to You in all aspects of my life, I will fulfill Your ministry in me. (Hebrews 12:2) Whether it is in my calling, my health, or my life, I have believed from the beginning that I am immortal on earth until my life's work is over. Most Christians today only speak of immortality in a future sense—when we get to glory, our heavenly home and life—but God's protective hand is upon us until He calls us home. Job (Job 3) thought he would die; Peter (Acts 12) thought he would die in Herod's prison, but each had a work to do and God delivered them, and He will do the same for us. That is why the men and women of God have been bold as lions in reaching into the dark and dangerous places of the earth. That is why I feared not to go to Australia in 1972 or India in 2016. I believe that no harm will assail me, no enemy will assault me, and no cancer will kill me until or unless the good Lord allows it. I like what the great evangelist Sam Jones once said. *"God will feed a Christian if He has to put the angels on half rations!"* Yes, He cares that much.

5. *That in reaching* heaven I will find a citizenship (Ephesians 2:19) waiting and a mansion prepared (John 14:2). When I first believed in what Jesus did for me at Golgotha, I readily accepted eternal life as my prize (Romans 6:23). That belief I still hang on to despite the long exile here. I have never doubted heaven as a place. I shared for years that I had never been to Alaska, but I still believed in a place called Alaska. In the summer of 2104, I had the honor of traveling around Alaska with my son Scott and my wife. It was better than I imagined, and I think the same of Heaven when I get there (I Corinthians 2:9). Many Christians have it all mixed up today. We are citizens of heaven sojourning on earth, not a citizen on earth journeying to heaven! Most have lost their pilgrim characteristics, but I haven't. I care for little of this world in the area of stuff, possessions, or property. I am like the dark lady who once was overheard to say, *"I wears dis world like a loose garment!"* I am traveling light. I have but a loose grip on this world. I sing daily, "This world is not my home I'm just passing through; my treasures are laid up somewhere beyond the blue!" Like Vance Havner, "I am not looking for something to happen; I am looking for Someone to come!" When I went to public school in the 1950s and 1960s, I soon discovered that in some of my textbooks the

answers were in the back of the book. When I started studying the Bible, I discovered the same thing. I know how it all ends, and praise be to the Almighty! We will win in the end!"

It is wonderful to know that whether in India or in America I have found these beliefs a firm foundation, a solid stone, a glorious ground to stand upon, to rest upon, and to walk or run upon. I have tested these concepts for sixty years, and I haven't found any better!

57

Eight States in Ten Days

Shibu and I were up early on our tenth day on the road because the Bhagaban Villa Hotel had a 7:00 AM checkout time. I told you this was the worst place we had stayed. We paid our bill before we left which came to 1900 rupees or about $28 for Shibu and me to stay two nights, and that included the cricket matches! Not a bad price. Joy and Jason picked us up on their scooter and motorcycle for breakfast and a nearly four-hour wait before heading to the airport and a flight back to Kerala. I was getting used to the motorcycle. Joy cooked breakfast, which included those half-fried eggs. I ate three. The rest of the morning was a sweet time of fellowship with the Thomas family. Their daughter Blessen was heading off to college. Jason was finishing up his junior year in high school, and Gigi was doing what most Indian housewives do, keep the house in order. Joy talked mostly of the excitement building in the fellowship of the Orissa churches over the up and coming convention in May at Dangulu. They were expecting opposition to this first ever Christian gathering in the region, but they were unconcerned. I think Shibu was having more doubts, but Joy was unmoved. I have never met a man like Joy for boldness and brazenness in the face of physical persecution. It was a joy to be around a man like Joy!

Just before we left, I did take a few minutes to climb the staircase to the top of the roof to look around. I wanted to thank Ruth for the bottle of Coke again, but she was out. On the roof, I found an excellent view of Khordha; it was bigger than I thought. The day was developing into another scorcher, and I couldn't believe I thought it was going to be nice to get back to Kerala! The thing I remember best about my trip up on the roof was all the idol images and bowls of sacrifice scattered around the edge of the flat roof. It appears that those within the four-family complexes did a lot of worshipping on the roof. The images of Hindu gods and the bowls that contained offerings were burnt in the morning and in the evening. But, as I have always found, there seemingly was no hostility to Joy and his family, the only Christian family in the neighborhood. I, too, had yet to face an angry Hindu or Buddhist in my travels. All I have had direct contact with have been nothing short of kind and hospitable. The entire staircase and rooftop was also filled with beautiful plants, so the odor was divine adding to the pleasant surroundings. I enjoyed my little interlude before we headed off to the airport and our flight south.

The last thing I did in the courtyard of the complex was get a few pictures of Joy and his family with his new car. I wanted to show them to my brother. They had discovered during our visit the reason we had trouble on our first night in Orissa was because of a faulty alternator. It was a factory defect, so they were coming to replace it that afternoon. Our trip to the airport would have to be by taxi. Around 11:00 AM we were picked up and about an hour later we were being dropped off at the Bhubaneswar International Airport. Because non-passengers can't go into Indian airports, we had to say our goodbye to Joy on the sidewalk in front of the terminal. Once again I thought, "Was this my last visit with one of my best friends and fellow-companions in the Work of the Lord?" I have thought that each and every time we separate, but as with this last trip—an unexpected trip to Orissa—my hope is we will meet again this side of heaven. If not, my thoughts were the thoughts of Paul as he said goodbye to the Christians of Corinth. "Finally, brethren, farewell. Be perfect, be of good cheer, be of one mind, live in peace; and the God of love and peace shall be with you." (II Corinthians 13:11)

After passing through four levels of security by noontime, we still had a couple of hours to wait before our IndiGo flight from Bhubaneswar to Bangalore. This would be my eighth flight in India over the years and, like the other ones, this one was on time. The flight was smooth; the service was exceptional; and it was cheap, about $145! By 2:00 PM we were on our flight to Bangalore, now called Bengaluru, Karnataka and the Kempegowda International Airport, another one of the major hubs in the Indian air industry. We arrived safely around 3:30 with a nearly three-hour wait for our flight from Bangalore to Kochi. Shibu and I hadn't had lunch, so I got a smoked chicken sandwich, a bag of chips, and a bottle of water, which cost me 290 rupees ($4.32). I then picked up a small bottle of Coke (remember that taste of home?) for 20 rupees (29 cents)! It was while I was drinking that bottle of Coke that it hit me. I was now in my eighth state of India in ten days: Kerala, Tamil Nadu, Punjab, Haryana (remember our overnight train ride through the state?), Uttar Pradesh, Delhi (remember though Delhi is located in the State of Uttar Pradesh, like Washington DC (the district of Columbia), Delhi is its own district), Orissa, and now Bangalore, Karnataka. By 6:30, I was still walking around the massive airport complex realizing that my great India adventure was nearly over—a 3,740-mile trip in ten days. Every mile by plane, car, train, auto, cycle rickshaw, and that mile we walked was a thrill. As I write this chapter it is nearly 4 year later, and I would repeat that trip today!

We left Bangalore a little after 7:00 PM and were back in Kochi, Kerala by 8:00 PM. The first snag of our travels happened at Kochi Airport—no ride home. It seems there had been a mix up on the time of our arrival and Ronnie was late. My hope was to be back to the Simon's by 1:00 AM, which would make our travels a perfect eight-day journey, but the delay would seemingly throw the timing off, or would it? While we waited I looked around and saw another one of those Indian women that touched my heart. I have written of them before, their plight and position in a culture that gives little value to the fair sex. This woman had the Muslim veil on. I had seen a lot of them in my travels through the Middle East airports, but had rarely seen one in Kerala, but there she was hiding not doubt her beautiful face behind a black veil. No doubt heading somewhere with a husband or brother (women like that cannot travel alone), I was touched by the tragedy of her not knowing the truth of Galatians 3:28: "There is neither Jew nor Greek, there is neither bond or free, there is neither male nor female: for ye are one in Christ Jesus." I thought in this one woman all categories are covered for there is neither Arab nor Indian (which was she?), there is neither bond (and, Oh, what bondage she was under) or free, there is neither male or female (a second class citizen of her race at best in the oppressive religious faith she was in), but we could be, can be, one in Christ!

Ronnie eventually arrived near 9:00 AM. I was glad because, despite the time, the air was still very humid in Kochi, and to Ronnie's credit he got us home in two and a half hours, one of the fastest runs from Kochi to Edayappara I had ever made, and I have traveled that route many times before. On the way home, Shibu told me of a family trip to Rajasthan he and his family were going to make after my return to the States. It was then I realized what I could give the Simons for a gift for having taken such good care of me for nearly three weeks. Upon my return I set aside my final India funds to give Joshua and Abigail some extra funds for their trip and to pay for Julie and Shibu to stay a night in one of the famous palaces of Rajasthan. Before midnight I was once again settled into my prophet's chamber on the second floor of the Simon's house. Julie was waiting up for us and it was like coming home, a home I would be heading for the next day.

58

Last Day in Kerala

I was up by 8:00 AM and starting to pack for my long journey home. This has always been a sad day for me in India—my last day. Last time I got an extra forty-eight hours because of Hurricane Sandy, but no such storm would delay my departure to the States this time. I have treasured every day (#136) in India, even the part of a day I would have tomorrow (#137), but what would I do with my last full day in the sub-continent on this my fifth trip, a journey where we traveled further into earth's farthest bounds than ever before?

I started my last day in Kerala with a couple of Julie's wonderful bacon sandwiches for breakfast. Then like father—like son, I watched a cricket match with Joshua for about an hour. I checked the e-mail server, but it was still out so my family didn't know that I had survived my ten-day trip into eight India states safe and sound. It was then I was told I did have a ride into Kottayam for a short shopping spree to pick up a few items still on my to-get-list. Joshua also told me that there might still be a few elephants left over from the festival in Edayappara, but to my disappointment there weren't.

Also, to my surprise, Shibu picked me up around noon for what is now an annual-trip excursion into the big city of Kottayam for the Indian things my family and friends and myself have learned to expect when I return from India. Our first stop was at a book store to pick up an Indian recipe book that a Christian friend of mine wanted me to find for her. I bought "Ethnic Kerala Dishes" for 195 rupees ($2.91). While I was there, I also got four beautiful postcards of Kerala for my journal for 40 rupees ($1.48). We were off next to a clothing store where I picked up a shawl for my wife for 190 rupees ($2.83). My wife loves shawls and especially shawls from India. I have bought her one on every trip, and they are a treasure to her. She loves wearing the brightly colored shawls on cool Maine evenings! In our next store, I was looking for a scarf for my mother-in-law Opal, and I found her color (purple) and paid 305 rupees ($4.55), but in the process found another shawl for Coleen for 478 rupees ($7.13). She was going to get two! And guess what? As we traveled from store to store, we found a place selling magnum bars. Shibu and I had to have one for old time's sake. I bought an almond one, and it was just as good as the others we had shared on our mission's trip into Northern India.

Our last top and now a must stop was at the G Mart, India's version of Wal Mart, but not as large. Here I could get the rest of the items on my list and that list included the following: Tata Tea, Ahmad Tea, Eastern Dry Ginger, and five bags of Urban Salted Cashews. The tea and ginger were for my wife, and the cashews were for me. In my opinion, the best cashews I have ever eaten come from India. Yes, $34 dollars' worth of cashews, my only treat of the trip. In our travels in and out of Kottayam, I looked for a last elephant, but none was to be found. It was a pleasant four hours spent with my dear friend Shibu as we relived our adventures together. A last day in India isn't complete unless I spend it with Shibu, and upon our return to Edayappara, we still had one last meeting together at the weekly pastors/professors prayer meeting at Annamma's house.

At 7:30 I joined my Indian brethren in the living room at Shaju's for prayer and a final challenge. This was the eighteenth place I had preached in my three weeks in India. I decided I would share with the Kerala pastors and the KBBC professors that joined us a message I had recently put together during my stay in Kerala, a sermon I called "The Last Word" based on Numbers 23:10: "Who can count the dust of Jacob, and the number of the fourth part of Israel? Let me die the death of the righteous, and let my last end be like this!" I went on to share the last words of some of the great men of the Bible.

1. Jacob's Last Words of Worship—Hebrews 11:21.
2. Joseph's Last Words of Faith—Hebrews 11:22.
3. Moses' Last Words of Happiness—Deuteronomy 33.
4. David's Last Words of Challenge—I Kings 2:1.
5. Zechariah's Last Words of Death—II Chronicles 24:20-22.
6. Stephen's Last Words of Forgiveness—Acts 7:60.

7. John's last Words of Christ's Coming—Revelation 22:20-21.
8. Paul's Last Words of Departure—II Timothy 4:6-7.
9. John the Baptist's Last Words of Yielding—John 3:30.
10. Jesus' Last Words of Finishing—John 19:30.

We had a wonderful round of prayer as my last day in Kerala came to an end.

My final hours were spent napping in the Simon's prophet chamber. I would leave after midnight the next morning for the airport in Kochi. As I drifted in and out of sleep, (I have always been a terrible sleeper if I have an early rising hour. I have always been afraid that I will miss the time, so deep sleep comes hard on nights like this!) I learned a long time ago that the Good Lord created me as a singular person, not a plural person. I am a one-thought, one-deed, one kind-of-sleep man. Whether my last day in India, or my last hour of sleep, I think, meditate, devote myself to rest in the reality that God knows best. My desire was to stay in India for a month as I did in 2012, but my church family and, in particular the deacon board, thought a month away was too much, so we compromised on three weeks. We display the Lord's leading as much by what we refuse as by what we accept. I learned long ago the Lord is not as interested in mere quantity as he is in quality. We can often do more by doing less, and I learned this lesson again on this trip. It is no mark of godliness to be forever running about in a fury, our tongues hanging out in exhaustion, in some kind of "a glorified St. Vitus's dance". I have loved what Vance Havner once wrote. "These dear souls who argue that the devil never takes a vacation so why should we, should remember that we are not supposed to imitate the devil!" We should remember that while our Saviour was on earth He never hurried around; He seemed to be unhurried and would often say to His disciples: ". . . Come ye yourselves apart into a desert place, and rest awhile . . ." (Mark 6:31)

I am thankful for the last days in India, not because they were my last days, but because every one of them has been unhurried. In the nerve-wracking, maddening modern rush of America, India is still a very laid back place. They start when they start; they stop when they stop; they move at a gentler pace, and, despite a scheduled flight for the preacher, there was no hurry in getting him to the airport. I learned in my last day in India that the "Whoozits" at 10:00 or the "Whatsits" at 11:00 can wait and to wreck one's health on the altar of exhaustion is not God's way. His work will get done; He controls the clock, so to take time to rest before a long flight isn't a sin, for it would be a sin if you didn't rest. That is why I so appreciate the scheduling of Shibu. Did we travel far in ten days? Yes! Did we do a lot of things for the Lord in three weeks? Yes! But we also took time to rest, and rest we did. As I reached the last of my days in India, I wasn't tired at all; exhaustion was far from me, and I was rested for the 48-hour trip home. I am convinced this is why I have had perfect health (other than a broken tooth in my first trip) during my stay in Kerala and beyond. (Psalm 42:11 and Psalm 43:5)

Postlude
The Long, Long Road Home

I left the Simon's around 4:00 AM for my tenth trip between India and America. The Kottayam/Kochi road was clear of traffic, so our travel time was under three hours, a very good time. I said goodbye to Shibu, Joshua, and Shaji and entered the busy airport. It took me an hour to get through the levels of security, customs, and immigration. For the first time, I actually had to prove where I had stayed in Kerala. Despite the travel and the levels of security, I still had a two-hour wait before getting off the ground. By noontime on my day heading home, I was once again in the brand new Hamad International Airport in Doha, Qatar, my home for the next fourteen hours.

If you remember, I stayed in this airport fourteen hours on my way over. So what do you do when you have to spend over half a day in a foreign airport? Well, this is what I did. I first went to the only quiet room I have ever found in any airport, and I mean any. Actually I found a similar room in each wing of the gigantic terminal. During the first few hours I finished up my journal, the reason a year later I am able to write most of this book. I did a bit of reading. The only excitement took place at 2:00 PM when a 69-year-old man collapsed in the quiet room. Somebody called the paramedics, and within a few minutes, they were there checking him out. It appeared to be a fatigue issue, or that is what I could deduce from the conversation across the room. I got his age that he was European, and he was traveling alone. Eventually he was carted off on a stretcher and that was the last I saw of the elderly gentleman. I prayed he'd get home. For the rest of the afternoon I read, ate cashews, and napped. Around 6:00 PM I thought I would get supper. I had my mind on a cheeseburger, so I headed for the food court in the middle of the complex. There was a Burger King in the lobby, the only American-like restaurant I could find. I can say honestly that it was the worst cheeseburger I have ever eaten, the onion rings weren't much better, but the apple pie wasn't bad. I bought a five dollar bottle of water, the same bottle would have cost me five cents in India, and headed back to the quiet room, for I still had eight more hours to wait.

By 10:00 in the evening, I was just getting up from an hour and a half nap. I left the quiet room to find a television and catch up on the news. It was then I found out that President Obama had visited Cuba. Raised during the turbulent times with Cuba, the Cuban Missile Crisis I still remember, I couldn't understand Obama's visit. I watched a little of the Tampa Bay Rays playing a Cuban team winning 4-1, then I went in search of my Gate, C-4. I would have to wait two more hours before I could even board, which I did around 11:45 PM. I was the first passenger through the gate, a first for me. Since I left the Simon's house, a day had passed, and I was still only half way home.

After fourteen hours in Doha, I had a fourteen-hour flight (QR #727) to Philadelphia because, for some reason, I flew home by way of Tehran, Iran and Moscow, Russia. Sure enough, when we took off we flew due north. Just south of Moscow, we finally headed west over the southern Baltic States. I finally landed back in the good old USA around 9:00 AM on the 24th of March 2016. I was thirty-eight hours into my journey home, but now I had to wait another seven hours for my final flight to Maine. In that time, I was able to get through US customs and immigration in less than an hour. The lines were long, but the flow was steady. I was able to get a decent hamburger, and I found that my cell phone was working again and was able to call Coleen. She hadn't heard from me in two weeks and was a bit concerned, but when she found out that I was in the States she was much relieved. At 2:00 PM, I was waiting for my four o'clock flight out of Philadelphia when I meet a young man, and we struck up a conversation. I discovered he was a Christian, and he was on his way to Toronto, Canada for a job interview. What was really wonderful about his story was that he was an Arab/Christian from Nazareth, Israel. I had visited Nazareth in a 2010 trip and found the friendliest people of Israel to be the Arabs. This young man was Daniel Simaan. What drew me to him was the fact that he was reading his Bible. I have traveled all over the world in and out of forty-four different airports on one hundred twenty-three flights on twenty-two different journeys. My flight home would be my one hundred twenty-fourth, and I don't think I have ever seen anybody reading their Bible (I Timothy 4:13) on a flight or in an airport until I meet Daniel. I was impressed with the testimony of this young believer, and it was by far the blessing of this journey that wouldn't end for another five hours. I was reminded of this challenge from the pen of Paul when he wrote to the church at Thessalonica, "And we beseech you, brethren, to know them which labour among you..." (I Thessalonians 5:12) I doubt young Daniel Simaan and I will ever met against this side of glory, but it was an honor and privilege for me to get to know him in God's waiting room at the Philadelphia International Airport on my long, long way home!

By 4:15 I was on American Airlines Flight #3953 heading for Bangor, Maine and by 5:30 I was landing back on home soil. My dear wife was there to pick me up, but after a hug, she told me that I had one more call to make before I got home. The oldest member of our church, Madeline Carter, was dying in a nursing home just around the corner from the parsonage; it was on the way. One of my last calls before heading to India twenty-two days before was a pastoral call on Madeline. She was in her mid-90s and a lady I had ministered to for twenty-five years, including being there at the death of her beloved husband Mahlon. When I left she was doing pretty well, but by the time of my return, she was poorly and would only live a few more days. I had promised her that I wouldn't leave Emmanuel Baptist until I had her funeral which I did five days after my return from India. By the time I got home, my long, long road home was nearly forty-eight hours in length, but when you consider I spent nearly twenty-four hours in airports that was not bad at all. I tell everybody that the best sleep anyone ever gets is after such an epic road-trip.

Learning to travel is a lot like learning to drive a car. It is awkward at first, but persist in it long enough, and it becomes second nature, even the long, long trips. Such is the case for doing God's will. At first it seems scary and difficult, leaving home and homeland, but do it enough and you will find that "earth's farthest bounds" are within your reach. Along the way you will find and experience blessings that make the long hours, and even longer days, worth your time. The other aspect of a long, long road home is the opportunity to be still and know God (Psalm 46:10) and to think. We live in an age where thinking is almost taboo. Away from daily distraction, I found on these journeys to somewhere you could practice a precept of Paul's recorded in his epistle to the Philippians. "Finally, brethren, whatsoever things are true, whatsoever things are honest, whatsoever things are just, whatsoever things are pure, whatsoever things are lovely, whatsoever things are of good report; if there be any virtue, and if there be any praise, *think on these things*" (Philippians 4:8). One of the ways we grow in grace (II Peter 3:18) is in thought. Where better to think on spiritual things than on a long, long road home.

What you have read are my thoughts on this my fifth trip to "earth's farthest bounds". I hope these chapters have provoked some thought in you as well!

(Postscript: As I put this latest book project to bed I have just been invited back to India. It is still up to the Good Lord whether or not I take Shibu up on that invitation because of health issues with my wife and myself, but my desire is to go again and if I do be ready for another book!)

www.ingramcontent.com/pod-product-compliance
Lightning Source LLC
Chambersburg PA
CBHW070734160426
43192CB00009B/1434